Mary E. Swigonski, PhD, LCSW
Robin S. Mama, PhD
Kelly Ward, LCSW
Editors

From Hate Crimes
to Human Rights:
A Tribute
to Matthew Shepard

From Hate Crimes to Human Rights: A Tribute to Matthew Shepard has been co-published simultaneously as *Journal of Gay & Lesbian Social Services,* Volume 13, Numbers 1/2 2001.

Pre-publication
REVIEWS,
COMMENTARIES,
EVALUATIONS . . .

"**T**he book examines human rights and the struggles of marginalized peoples to find opportunity, peace, and wholeness. The readers will be pushed to examine their own biases and assumptions and challenged to engage the work of human rights for all people."

Terry L. Singer, PhD, Dean
Kent School of Social Work
University of Louisville
Louisville, KY

More pre-publication
REVIEWS, COMMENTARIES, EVALUATIONS . . .

"**B**rava! Mary Swigonski reminds us with incredible clarity why social workers and other social service professionals must become knowledgeable and culturally competent with GLBTQT[2] clients and colleagues.

This is a first rate, long-needed text that the scholar, the clinician, or the student will find both readable and useable in professional practice.

Seldom have I been tempted to read any journal in one sitting. I was completely engrossed in the solid organization, logic, and clarity of each article. I now find that I have a text that effectively explores the social context of GLBTQT[2] lives and presents a convincing justification for human service professionals to adopt actively social justice strategies and macro practice interventions."

George A. Appleby, MSW, PhD
Professor of Social Work
Pauline Lang Social Work Center
Southern Connecticut State University
New Haven, CT

Harrington Park Press
An Imprint of The Haworth Press, Inc.

From Hate Crimes
to Human Rights:
A Tribute
to Matthew Shepard

From Hate Crimes to Human Rights: A Tribute to Matthew Shepard has been co-published simultaneously as *Journal of Gay & Lesbian Social Services*, Volume 13, Numbers 1/2 2001.

The *Journal of Gay & Lesbian Social Services* Monographic "Separates"

Below is a list of "separates," which in serials librarianship means a special issue simultaneously published as a special journal issue or double-issue *and* as a "separate" hardbound monograph. (This is a format which we also call a "DocuSerial.")

"Separates" are published because specialized libraries or professionals may wish to purchase a specific thematic issue by itself in a format which can be separately cataloged and shelved, as opposed to purchasing the journal on an on-going basis. Faculty members may also more easily consider a "separate" for classroom adoption.

"Separates" are carefully classified separately with the major book jobbers so that the journal tie-in can be noted on new book order slips to avoid duplicate purchasing.

You may wish to visit Haworth's Website at . . .

http://www.HaworthPress.com

. . . to search our online catalog for complete tables of contents of these separates and related publications.

You may also call 1-800-HAWORTH (outside US/Canada: 607-722-5857), or Fax 1-800-895-0582 (outside US/Canada: 607-771-0012), or e-mail at:

getinfo@haworthpressinc.com

From Hate Crimes to Human Rights: A Tribute to Matthew Shepard, edited by Mary E. Swigonski, PhD, LCSW, Robin S. Mama, PhD, and Kelly Ward, LCSW (Vol. 13, No. 1/2, 2001). *An unsparing look at prejudice and hate crimes against LGBT individuals, in such diverse areas as international law, the child welfare system, minority cultures, and LGBT relationships.*

Working-Class Gay and Bisexual Men, edited by George Alan Appleby, MSW, PhD (Vol. 12, No. 3/4, 2001). Working-Class Gay and Bisexual Men *is a powerfully persuasive work of scholarship with broad-ranging implications. Social workers, policymakers, AIDS activists, and anyone else concerned with the lives of gay and bisexual men will find this informative study an essential tool for designing effective programs.*

Gay Men and Childhood Sexual Trauma: Integrating the Shattered Self, edited by James Cassese, MSW, CSW (Vol. 12, No. 1/2, 2000). *"An excellent, thought-provoking collection of essays. Therapists who work with gay men will be grateful to have such a comprehensive resource for dealing with sexual trauma." (Rik Isensee, LCSW, Author of* Reclaiming Your Life*)*

Midlife Lesbian Relationships: Friends, Lovers, Children, and Parents, edited by Marcy R. Adelman, PhD (Vol. 11, No. 2/3, 2000). *"A careful and sensitive look at the various relationships of [lesbians at midlife] inside and outside of the therapy office. A useful addition to a growing body of literature." (Ellyn Kaschak, PhD, Professor of Psychology, San José State University, California, and Editor of the feminist quarterly journal* Women & Therapy*)*

Social Services with Transgendered Youth, edited by Gerald P. Mallon, DSW (Vol. 10, No. 3/4, 1999). *"A well-articulated book that provides valuable information about a population that has been virtually ignored. . . ." (Carol T. Tully, PhD, Associate Professor, Tulane University, School of Social Work, New Orleans, Louisiana)*

Queer Families, Common Agendas: Gay People, Lesbians, and Family Values, edited by T. Richard Sullivan, PhD (Vol. 10, No. 1, 1999). *Examines the real life experience of those affected by current laws and policies regarding homosexual families.*

Lady Boys, Tom Boys, Rent Boys: Male and Female Homosexualities in Contemporary Thailand, edited by Peter A. Jackson, PhD, and Gerard Sullivan, PhD (Vol. 9, No. 2/3, 1999). *"Brings to life issues and problems of interpreting sexual and gender identities in contemporary Thailand." (Nerida M. Cook, PhD, Lecturer in Sociology, Department of Sociology and Social Work, University of Tasmania, Australia)*

Working with Gay Men and Lesbians in Private Psychotherapy Practice, edited by Christopher J. Alexander, PhD (Vol. 8, No. 4, 1998). *"Rich with information that will prove especially invaluable to therapists planning to or recently having begun to work with lesbian and gay clients in private practice." (Michael Shernoff, MSW, Private Practice, NYC; Adjunct Faculty, Hunter College Graduate School of Social Work)*

Violence and Social Injustice Against Lesbian, Gay and Bisexual People, edited by Lacey M. Sloan, PhD, and Nora S. Gustavsson, PhD (Vol. 8, No. 3, 1998). *"An important and timely book that exposes the multilevel nature of violence against gay, lesbian, bisexual, and transgender people." (Dorothy Van Soest, DSW, Associate Dean, School of Social Work, University of Texas at Austin)*

The HIV-Negative Gay Man: Developing Strategies for Survival and Emotional Well-Being, edited by Steven Ball, MSW, ACSW (Vol. 8, No. 1, 1998). *"Essential reading for anyone working with HIV-negative gay men." (Walt Odets, PhD, Author,* In the Shadow of the Epidemic: Being HIV-Negative in the Age of AIDS; *Clinical Psychologist, private practice, Berkeley, California)*

School Experiences of Gay and Lesbian Youth: The Invisible Minority, edited by Mary B. Harris, PhD (Vol. 7, No. 4, 1998). *"Our schools are well served when authors such as these have the courage to highlight problems that schools deny and to advocate for students whom schools make invisible." (Gerald Unks, Professor, School of Education, University of North Carolina at Chapel Hill; Editor,* The Gay Teen.*) Provides schools with helpful suggestions for becoming places that welcome gay and lesbian students and, therefore, better serve the needs of all students.*

Rural Gays and Lesbians: Building on the Strengths of Communities, edited by James Donald Smith, ACSW, LCSW, and Ronald J. Mancoske, BSCW, DSW (Vol. 7, No. 3, 1998). *"This informative and well-written book fills a major gap in the literature and should be widely read." (James Midgley, PhD, Harry and Riva Specht Professor of Public Social Services and Dean, School of Social Welfare, University of California at Berkeley)*

Gay Widowers: Life After the Death of a Partner, edited by Michael Shernoff, MSW, ACSW (Vol. 7, No. 2, 1997). *"This inspiring book is not only for those who have experienced the tragedy of losing a partner–it's for every gay man who loves another." (Michelangelo Signorile, author,* Life Outside*)*

Gay and Lesbian Professionals in the Closet: Who's In, Who's Out, and Why, edited by Teresa DeCrescenzo, MSW, LCSW (Vol. 6, No. 4, 1997). *"A gripping example of the way the closet cripples us and those we try to serve." (Virginia Uribe, PhD, Founder, Project 10 Outreach to Gay and Lesbian Youth, Los Angeles Unified School District)*

Two Spirit People: American Indian Lesbian Women and Gay Men, edited by Lester B. Brown, PhD (Vol. 6, No. 2, 1997). *"A must read for educators, social workers, and other providers of social and mental health services." (Wynne DuBray, Professor, Division of Social Work, California State University)*

Social Services for Senior Gay Men and Lesbians, edited by Jean K. Quam, PhD, MSW (Vol. 6, No. 1, 1997). *"Provides a valuable overview of social service issues and practice with elder gay men and lesbians." (Outword)*

Men of Color: A Context for Service to Homosexually Active Men, edited by John F. Longres, PhD (Vol. 5, No. 2/3, 1996). *"An excellent book for the 'helping professions.' " (Feminist Bookstore News)*

Health Care for Lesbians and Gay Men: Confronting Homophobia and Heterosexism, edited by K. Jean Peterson, DSW (Vol. 5, No. 1, 1996). *"Essential reading for those concerned with the quality of health care services." (Etcetera)*

Sexual Identity on the Job: Issues and Services, edited by Alan L. Ellis, PhD, and Ellen D. B. Riggle, PhD (Vol. 4, No. 4, 1996). *"Reveals a critical need for additional research to address the many questions left unanswered or answered unsatisfactorily by existing research." (Sex Roles: A Journal of Research) "A key resource for addressing sexual identity concerns and issues in your workplace." (Outlines)*

Human Services for Gay People: Clinical and Community Practice, edited by Michael Shernoff, MSW, ACSW (Vol. 4, No. 2, 1996). *"This very practical book on clinical and community practice issues belongs on the shelf of every social worker, counselor, or therapist working with lesbians and gay men." (Gary A. Lloyd, PhD, ACSW, BCD, Professor and Coordinator, Institute for Research and Training in HIV/AIDS Counseling, School of Social Work, Tulane University)*

Violence in Gay and Lesbian Domestic Partnerships, edited by Claire M. Renzetti, PhD, and Charles Harvey Miley, PhD (Vol. 4, No. 1, 1996). *"A comprehensive guidebook for service providers and community and church leaders." (Small Press Magazine)*

Gays and Lesbians in Asia and the Pacific: Social and Human Services, edited by Gerard Sullivan, PhD, and Laurence Wai-Teng Leong, PhD (Vol. 3, No. 3, 1995). *"Insights in this book can provide an understanding of these cultures and provide an opportunity to better understand your own." (The Lavender Lamp)*

Lesbians of Color: Social and Human Services, edited by Hilda Hidalgo, PhD, ACSW (Vol. 3, No. 2, 1995). *"An illuminating and helpful guide for readers who wish to increase their understanding of and sensitivity toward lesbians of color and the challenges they face." (Black Caucus of the ALA Newsletter)*

Lesbian Social Services: Research Issues, edited by Carol T. Tully, PhD, MSW (Vol. 3, No. 1, 1995). *"Dr. Tully challenges us to reexamine theoretical conclusions that relate to lesbians. . . A must read." (The Lavender Lamp)*

HIV Disease: Lesbians, Gays and the Social Services, edited by Gary A. Lloyd, PhD, ACSW, and Mary Ann Kuszelewicz, MSW, ACSW (Vol. 2, No. 3/4, 1995). *"A wonderful guide to working with people with AIDS. A terrific meld of political theory and hands-on advice, it is essential, inspiring reading for anyone fighting the pandemic or assisting those living with it." (Small Press)*

Addiction and Recovery in Gay and Lesbian Persons, edited by Robert J. Kus, PhD, RN (Vol. 2, No. 1, 1995). *"Readers are well-guided through the multifaceted, sometimes confusing, and frequently challenging world of the gay or lesbian drug user." (Drug and Alcohol Review)*

Helping Gay and Lesbian Youth: New Policies, New Programs, New Practice, edited by Teresa DeCrescenzo, MSW, LCSW (Vol. 1, No. 3/4, 1994). *"Insightful and up-to-date, this handbook covers several topics relating to gay and lesbian adolescents . . . It is must reading for social workers, educators, guidance counselors, and policymakers." (Journal of Social Work Education)*

Social Services for Gay and Lesbian Couples, edited by Lawrence A. Kurdek, PhD (Vol. 1, No. 2, 1994). *"Many of the unique issues confronted by gay and lesbian couples are addressed here." (Ambush Magazine)*

From Hate Crimes to Human Rights: A Tribute to Matthew Shepard

Mary E. Swigonski, PhD, LCSW
Robin S. Mama, PhD
Kelly Ward, LCSW
Editors

From Hate Crimes to Human Rights: A Tribute to Matthew Shepard has been co-published simultaneously as *Journal of Gay & Lesbian Social Services*, Volume 13, Numbers 1/2 2001.

Harrington Park Press
The Haworth Social Work Practice Press
Imprints of
The Haworth Press, Inc.
New York • London • Oxford

Published by

Harrington Park Press®, 10 Alice Street, Binghamton, NY 13904-1580 USA

Harrington Park Press® is an imprint of The Haworth Press, Inc., 10 Alice Street, Binghamton, NY 13904-1580 USA.

From Hate Crimes to Human Rights: A Tribute to Matthew Shepard has been co-published simultaneously as *Journal of Gay & Lesbian Social Services*, Volume 13, Numbers 1/2 2001.

The development, preparation, and publication of this work has been undertaken with great care. However, the publisher, employees, editors, and agents of The Haworth Press and all imprints of The Haworth Press, Inc., including The Haworth Medical Press® and Pharmaceutical Products Press®, are not responsible for any errors contained herein or for consequences that may ensue from use of materials or information contained in this work. Opinions expressed by the author(s) are not necessarily those of The Haworth Press, Inc.

Cover design by Anastasia Litwak

Library of Congress Cataloging-in-Publication Data

From hate crimes to human rights : a tribute to Matthew Shepard / Mary E. Swigonski, Robin S. Mama, Kelly Ward, editors.
  p. cm.
  "... co-published simultaneously as Journal of gay & lesbian social services, volume 13, numbers 1/2 2001."
  Includes bibliographical references and index.
  ISBN 1-56023-256-0 (alk. paper)–ISBN 1-56023-257-9 (alk. paper)
  1. Gay rights. 2. Gays–Crimes against. 3. Hate crimes. I. Swigonski, Mary E. II. Mama, Robin, S. III. Ward, Kelly. IV. Shepard, Matthew, D. 1998. V. Journal of gay & lesbian social services. v. 13, no. 1/2.
HQ76.5 .F76 2001
305.9′0664–dc21   2001024506

Indexing, Abstracting & Website/Internet Coverage

This section provides you with a list of major indexing & abstracting services. That is to say, each service began covering this periodical during the year noted in the right column. Most Websites which are listed below have indicated that they will either post, disseminate, compile, archive, cite or alert their own Website users with research-based content from this work. (This list is as current as the copyright date of this publication.)

Abstracting, Website/Indexing Coverage .... Year When Coverage Began

- *BUBL Information Service, an Internet-based Information Service for the UK higher education community <URL: http://bubl.ac.uk/>* **1995**

- *caredata CD: The social and community care database* **1994**

- *CNPIEC Reference Guide: Chinese National Directory of Foreign Periodicals* **1995**

- *Contemporary Women's Issues* **1998**

- *Criminal Justice Abstracts* **1997**

- *ERIC Clearinghouse on Urban Education (ERIC/CUE)*..... **1995**

- *Family Studies Database (online and CD/ROM) <www.nisc.com>* **1996**

- *Family Violence & Sexual Assault Bulletin* **1999**

- *FINDEX <www.publist.com>* **1999**

- *Gay & Lesbian Abstracts <www.nisc.com>* **1999**

(continued)

Special Bibliographic Notes related to special journal issues (separates) and indexing/abstracting:

- indexing/abstracting services in this list will also cover material in any "separate" that is co-published simultaneously with Haworth's special thematic journal issue or DocuSerial. Indexing/abstracting usually covers material at the article/chapter level.
- monographic co-editions are intended for either non-subscribers or libraries which intend to purchase a second copy for their circulating collections.
- monographic co-editions are reported to all jobbers/wholesalers/approval plans. The source journal is listed as the "series" to assist the prevention of duplicate purchasing in the same manner utilized for books-in-series.
- to facilitate user/access services all indexing/abstracting services are encouraged to utilize the co-indexing entry note indicated at the bottom of the first page of each article/chapter/contribution.
- this is intended to assist a library user of any reference tool (whether print, electronic, online, or CD-ROM) to locate the monographic version if the library has purchased this version but not a subscription to the source journal.
- individual articles/chapters in any Haworth publication are also available through the Haworth Document Delivery Service (HDDS).

From Hate Crimes to Human Rights: A Tribute to Matthew Shepard

CONTENTS

ABOUT THE EDITORS

Mary E. Swigonski, PhD, is Assistant Professor of Social Work at Monmouth University. A social work educator since 1981, she formerly served on the faculties of Upsala College and Rutgers University's Newark Campus. She teaches undergraduate and graduate courses in human behavior, social policy, research, and diversity. Her research interests include human behavior, diversity, lesbian and gay issues, and gender studies. As a member of the Council on Social Work Education, she serves on the Commission on Sexual Orientation and Gender Identity.

Robin S. Mama, PhD, is Associate Professor of Social Work at Monmouth University. She is currently the Program Director for the BSW Program at Monmouth and teaches social work practice, community development, and field practicum. Her published work has been in the areas of occupational health, violence in the workplace, and multicultural practice. Dr. Mama's research interests are in cultural competency and social development.

Kelly Ward, MSW, LCSW, CADC, is Assistant Professor of Social Work at Monmouth University and is ABD at Fordham University. Professor Ward teaches policy, human behavior, introduction to social work, and field practicum. She has presented nationally and published in the area of substance abuse practice. Her research interests include intergenerational substance abuse and other aspects of addiction.

About the Contributors

Jeane W. Anastas, MSW, PhD, is Professor and Associate Dean at the Ehrenkranz School of Social Work at New York University. A full-time social work educator since 1980, she formerly served on the faculties of Simmons College and Smith College School of Social Work. She is co-author with George A. Appleby of *Not Just a Passing Phase: Social Work with Lesbian, Gay and Bisexual People* (1998), author of *Design for Social Work and the Human Services* (2nd ed., 2000), both published by Columbia University Press, and serves on the Editorial Board of *Affilia: The Journal of Women and Social Work.*

Walt Boulden, PhD, has been a social work educator since 1990, with practice experience in domestic violence, sexual assault, mental health, children and families, LGBT issues, advocacy, and program development. He is past president of Wyoming's NASW and the United Gays and Lesbians of Wyoming. He currently teaches social work at Missouri Western State College and conducts local, state, regional, and national workshops on LGBT issues for law enforcement and mental health agencies. His 1999 doctoral dissertation "How can you be gay and live in Wyoming?" has been nominated for the Union Institute's Marvin B. Sussman Award.

Irene R. Bush, DSW, ACSW, is Associate Professor at Monmouth University in the Department of Social Work, where she teaches research and practice courses in the Families and Children in the Global Community concentration. Her research concerns prevention and early intervention issues, including permanency planning for children and prevention of substance misuse, child abuse, and hate crimes. Most recently, Dr. Bush has co-authored a study for the State of New Jersey on substance abuse issues related to welfare reform.

Stuart F. Chen-Hayes, PhD, NCC, is Assistant Professor and Acting Coordinator of the Graduate Counseling Program at Lehman College/

CUNY, Bronx, NY. Dr. Chen-Hayes has presented 120 professional counseling presentations and written numerous journal articles and book chapters on LBGT, multicultural, and social justice counseling. He is School Counseling Services coordinator for the Bronx Educational Alliance's middle-school GEAR-UP grant and coordinates the Lehman College Counseling Program's Education Trust Transforming School Counselor Education grant. His two-part video series on counseling LBGT youths, co-authored with Dr. Lynn Haley-Banez, was recently released by Microtraining Corporation.

Tom Diehm, MSW, is Senior Lecturer and Practicum Coordinator for the Alternative MSW Program of the University of Washington School of Social Work at the University of Washington, Tacoma. He has also taught at the University of Denver and University of Southern Colorado. His practice experience is in the fields of community mental health services and systems and in HIV prevention and education. His research focuses on human diversity issues, particularly ways in which educational institutions can nurture diversities.

Marceline (Marcie) Lazzari, PhD, MSW, is Director of the Alternative MSW Program at the University of Washington, Tacoma (UWT). She is also Interim Vice Chancellor for Academic Affairs for the UWT campus. She has numerous publications dealing with a range of diversity issues. Dr. Lazzari believes that the social work profession must broaden its understanding of diversity to include the innumerable combinations of human characteristics and choices that make each individual unique. While it is critical to understand oppression in relation to both individuals and groups, she believes we must cross diversity "barriers" and focus upon the serious issues facing this society, not the least of which is violence in its many forms.

Gerald P. Mallon, DSW, is Assistant Professor and Chair of the Human Behavior sequence at the Hunter College School of Social Work in New York City. He is the author of several books and numerous articles which focus on the experiences of gay and lesbian children, youths, and families.

Robin S. Mama, PhD, is Associate Professor of Social Work at Monmouth University. She is currently the Program Director for the BSW Program at Monmouth and teaches social work practice, community development, and field practicum. Her published work has been in the areas of occupational health, violence in the workplace, and multicultural practice. Dr. Mama's research interests are in cultural competency and social development.

Deana F. Morrow, PhD, LPC, LCSW, ACSW, is Assistant Professor of Social Work at the University of North Carolina at Charlotte where she teaches courses in clinical practice, human behavior, and gay/lesbian issues. Her primary area of research is in social work with gays/lesbians, and her publications have been on topics such as gay/lesbian identity development, coming out, gay/lesbian adolescents, older gays/lesbians, and gay/lesbian curriculum content in social work education. Dr. Morrow's clinical practice background is in mental health and health care, including both public and private sector services.

Dean Pierce, PhD, is Professor and Director of the University of Nevada, Reno, School of Social Work. An active member of the Council on Social Work Education, he serves on the Commission on Accreditation and was Co-chair of the Commission on Gay Men and Lesbian Women. He is also active with the Nevada Chapter of the National Association of Social Workers, having served as president, board member, and chair of the Western Coalition for the 1996 Delegate Assembly. Dr. Pierce serves on Nevada's Social Work Licensing Board. He is the author of *Social Work and Society* and *Policy for the Social Work Practitioner* and has presented dozens of refereed and invitational papers and workshops dealing with gay and lesbian issues.

Jane M. Simoni, PhD, is Assistant Professor at Yeshiva University in New York City. As an Aaron Diamond Postdoctoral Fellow at the Columbia University School of Social Work, Dr. Simoni conducted a longitudinal study of coping and psychological adaptation among 373 women living with HIV. Her main research focus is identifying how cultural strengths and social support mediate psychological well-being and resilience among stigmatized groups, such as gays and lesbians, ethnic minorities, and individuals living with HIV/AIDS.

Mary E. Swigonski, PhD, is Assistant Professor of Social Work at Monmouth University. A social work educator since 1981, she formerly served on the faculties of Upsala College and Rutgers University's Newark Campus. She teaches undergraduate and graduate courses in human behavior, social policy, research, and diversity. Her research interests include human behavior, diversity, lesbian and gay issues, and gender studies. As a member of the Council on Social Work Education, she serves on the Commission on Sexual Orientation and Gender Identity.

Carol T. Tully, PhD, is Professor and Associate Dean for the Kent School of Social Work at the University of Louisville. Dr. Tully has been in social work education since 1977 and has been publishing in the area of lesbian and gay issues since 1979. She has served as a case worker for the Richmond Department of Welfare, a training specialist for the Commonwealth of Virginia, an instructor for Virginia Commonwealth University, an assistant professor for West Virginia University and the University of Georgia, and an associate professor for Tulane. Beyond her lesbian and gay work, other areas of expertise include gerontology, curriculum development, accreditation issues, and the history of social welfare.

Karina L. Walters, PhD, is an enrolled member of the Choctaw Nation of Oklahoma. Currently, she is Assistant Professor at Columbia University School of Social Work, New York, where she teaches in the practice and research areas. Dr. Walters serves on the American Indian Community House Board of Directors in New York City and on the National Native American Indian HIV/AIDS Policy Advisory Board in San Francisco, CA. Dr. Walters provides clinical and research consultation to national and international American Indian agencies regarding program evaluations and needs assessments. Dr. Walters' research interests are American Indian, gay and lesbian, and women of color's mental health and health, particularly urban American Indian health and mental health–specifically, the identification of cultural factors that act as buffers between trauma and wellness outcomes (i.e., HIV risk behaviors, alcohol abuse, and mental health).

Patricia Washington is Assistant Professor of Women's Studies at San Diego State University. As a sociologist, she uses a gendered lens to examine social stratification, with an emphasis on social inequalities and efforts to eradicate those inequalities. She is specifically interested in how social location (race, class, gender, sexual orientation, etc.) impacts access to, and quality of, services provided by U.S. social institutions. Her current research focuses on hate and bias-motivated violence and the revictimization of lesbian and gay sexual assault survivors, especially on lesbians and gays of color.

Kelly Ward, MSW, LCSW, CADC, is Assistant Professor of Social Work at Monmouth University and is ABD at Fordham University. Professor Ward teaches policy, human behavior, introduction to social work, and field practicum. She has presented nationally and published in the areas of substance abuse practice. Her research interests include intergenerational substance abuse and other aspects of addiction.

Janice Wood Wetzel, PhD, is Professor at Adelphi University's School of Social Work in Garden City, New York, where she served as dean from 1989 to 1996. Dr. Wetzel is an international social work educator serving as a United Nations representative for the International Association of Schools of Social Work. Concerned with the at-risk status of oppressed populations whose human rights are denied, she has published widely advocating for the advancement of women in the United States and throughout the world.

ACKNOWLEDGMENT

One of the premises of these writings is that progress from hate crimes to human rights requires that we learn to respect, honor, and celebrate diversity. The authors of the manuscripts within this volume collectively embody an array of diversities, including a veritable rainbow of ethnicities, sexual orientations, and gender identities. Each of us is committed to working to end hate crime and to advocate for human rights. Toward those ends, the royalties from the sale of this book will go directly to a memorial fund that has been established at Monmouth University in Matthew Shepard's honor. The proceeds from that fund will be used to support students in their preparation for human rights advocacy.

Introduction

Mary E. Swigonski
Robin S. Mama
Kelly Ward

Where, after all, do universal human rights begin? In small places, close to home–so close and so small that they cannot be seen on any map of the world. Yet they *are* the world of the individual person: the neighborhood [s]he lives in; the school or college [s]he attends; the factory, farm or office where [s]he works. Such are the places where every man, woman, and child seeks equal justice, equal opportunity, equal dignity without discrimination. Unless these rights have meaning there, they have little meaning anywhere. Without concerted citizen action to uphold them close to home, we shall look in vain for progress in the larger world.

Thus we believe that the destiny of human rights is in the hands of all our citizens in all our communities. (Roosevelt, 1958, p. 1)

Both human rights and hate crimes begin in places close to home. Human rights are founded on the "recognition of the inherent dignity and of the equal and inalienable rights of all members of the human family . . . [and the belief that] disregard and contempt for human rights have resulted in barbarous acts which have outraged the conscience of mankind" (United Nations, 1948). Gay men, lesbians, bisexual, transgendered, and two-spirited (LGBT[2]) persons are deprived

[Haworth co-indexing entry note]: "Introduction." Swigonski, Mary E., Robin S. Mama, and Kelly Ward. Co-published simultaneously in *Journal of Gay & Lesbian Social Services* (Harrington Park Press, an imprint of The Haworth Press, Inc.) Vol. 13, No. 1/2, 2001, pp. 1-6; and: *From Hate Crimes to Human Rights: A Tribute to Matthew Shepard* (ed: Mary E. Swigonski, Robin S. Mama, and Kelly Ward) Harrington Park Press, an imprint of The Haworth Press, Inc., 2001, pp. 1-6. Single or multiple copies of this article are available for a fee from The Haworth Document Delivery Service [1-800-342-9678, 9:00 a.m. - 5:00 p.m. (EST). E-mail address: getinfo@haworthpressinc.com].

of their human rights through the perpetration of hate crimes in "small places close to home." This special volume examines an array of settings "close to home" where hate crimes, and the hate that underlie them, abrogate the human rights of LGBT[2] persons, and challenges the reader to take the work for the progress and protection of human rights into their hands.

The inspiration for this special volume is rooted in a particular hate crime: On Tuesday October 6, 1998, Matthew Shepard left a bar in Laramie, Wyoming with two young men, who kidnapped and beat him. They then bound him to a fence in a remote area outside of town, further beat him, and left him for dead hanging on the fence. More than twelve hours later, he was found, barely alive. On Wednesday evening, October 7, he was admitted to the hospital in critical condition. At 12:53 a.m. Monday October 12, 1998, Matthew Shepard died. Matthew's life was cut short by an act of hate. Everyone who knew Matthew recognized him as a warm, trusting, kind, caring, and gentle soul–the antithesis of hate. Matthew was my friend (MES). He was deeply committed to human rights and aspired to a career in diplomacy. This volume bears witness to Matthew's death in particular, and to the abrogation of human rights experienced by the community of lesbian, gay, bisexual, transgendered, and two-spirited (LGBT[2]) persons in general.

Anti-LGBT[2] crimes are characterized as the most violent bias crimes. LGBT[2] murder victims are more likely than heterosexual murder victims to "die brutal deaths characterized by dismemberment, multiple stabbings and severe bludgeoning. Their killers are less likely to be caught" (National Gay Lesbian Task Force, 2000). Sloan and Gustavsson (1998), in their edited volume *Violence and Social Injustice Against Lesbian, Gay and Bisexual People*, documented the multiple forms of violence perpetrated against LGBT[2] persons: sexual assault, robbery, vandalism, assault, intimidation, and harassment. This volume builds on and expands that work. This special collection examines the effects of hate on LGBT[2] lives and is a call to work for an end to the perpetration of hate crimes and to strengthen the protection of human rights.

Hate crimes are a violation of human rights. At their core, hate crimes violate Articles 1 and 3 of the United Nations' Universal Declaration of Human Rights:

Article 1: All human beings are born free and equal in dignity and rights. They are endowed with reason and conscience and should act towards one another in a spirit of brotherhood.

Article 3: Everyone has the right to life, liberty and security of person.

(United Nations, 1948)

Hate crimes are crimes perpetrated upon individuals because of the appearance of particular characteristics or because of their apparent membership in a particular group (Sloan, King, & Sheppard, 1998). Hate crimes function to restrict access to human rights. Particular human rights are denied to the immediate victim of the crime. Access to human rights is also restricted to those who demonstrate similar characteristics or are members of the same group; access is restricted by the threat and intimidation inherent in the nature of the crime. Hate crimes are perpetrated against individuals based on race, religion, sexual orientation, ethnicity, disability, gender, and other such characteristics and group memberships which act as marks of difference.

Only twenty-one states have hate crime laws that cover sexual orientation (NGLTF, 2000). Yet hate crimes based on sexual orientation are the third highest category of all hate crimes reported to the FBI, about 11% each year (race is the highest category, followed by religion, then sexual orientation, then ethnicity) (NCAVP, 1999). All hate crimes are underreported, but hate crimes against gay, lesbian, bisexual, and transgendered Americans are likely to be even further underreported. Many Americans are not open about their sexual orientation, and so many will not report the crime, even if it involves violence, for fear of being outed. The risk of losing jobs or of endangering family relationships is enough to compel silence (Anastas, 1998; Kopels, 1998). The fear of harassment by intolerant law enforcement officers is also a concern (Sloan, King, & Sheppard, 1998). The need for prevention and protection are particularly compelling for those who do not believe that they can rely on traditional means of redress, such as those within the LGBT[2] communities.

Hate, hate crimes, and human rights are intricately interrelated. Hate functions to mark individuals and groups as other, as less than human. Hate crimes abrogate human rights. The promotion of human rights protects against hate crimes. LGBT[2] persons are explicitly included only in hate crime laws, and not in all such laws. They are explicitly included in none of the human rights documents. The primary goal of this special volume is to provide the readers with increased knowledge and resources to understand the connection between hate and hate crimes and to support their actions to prevent hate crimes and to further the cause of human rights in general and for LGBT[2] persons in particular.

The special volume begins with a tribute to Matthew Shepard by Walter Boulden. It is a celebration of his life, hopes, and aspirations and an analysis and critique of the social conditions and context that ended his life all too abruptly.

The next three articles set the theoretical foundation for thinking about human rights, hate, and hate crimes. Janice Wood Wetzel introduces the issues surrounding the application of human rights to gay men, lesbians, bisexuals, transgendered, and two-spirited persons, asking: "weren't gays and lesbians human?" Mary E. Swigonski provides a critique of the misuse of Judeo-Christian scriptures to provide the moral justification for the exclusions of lesbian, gay, bisexual, transgendered, and two-spirited persons from the protections of human rights. Dean Pierce analyzes the role of language in rationalizing the perpetration of violence against queer people.

The next set of articles provide concrete examples of hate, hate crimes, and the violence that attends them as they abrogate human rights in the lives of particular groups of LGBT[2] individuals, or within particular life circumstances. Gerald P. Mallon examines the prevalence and effects of hate and violence in the lives of gay and lesbian youths in child welfare settings. Carol T. Tully discusses domestic violence as a betrayal of human rights. Jeane W. Anastas discusses the right to work and the right to equal treatment in the work place as human rights and analyzes the myths and realities of LGBT[2] in relation to those rights. Pat Washington examines the manifestation of hate as homophobia within communities of color and analyzes its support of violence and diminution of human rights. Karina L. Walters, Jane M. Simoni, and Pamela F. Horwath report the findings of their study of sexual orientation bias and service needs of gay, lesbian, bisexual, transgendered, and two-spirited American Indians. Deana F. Morrow discusses the impact of hate and violence for those who came of age in the pre-stonewall era, older gays and lesbians.

While each of the preceding articles addresses skills, strategies, or resources for addressing hate crimes and working for human rights, the final three articles take that issue as their primary focus. Thomas M. Diehm and Marceline M. Lazzari report the findings of a qualitative research project to explicate the university's role in promoting human rights through nurturing diversities. Stuart F. Chen-Hayes highlights the importance of providing culturally competent, anti-oppressive services with persons of all sexual orientations and genders and provides the Social Justice Advocacy Readiness Questionnaire as a vehicle for practitioner self-assessment. Irene R. Bush and Anthony Sainz discuss and apply five areas of competence for those who would work for difference, tolerance, and the prevention of hate crimes.

Together, these articles articulate the array of venues within which hate becomes manifest as hate crimes perpetrated against LGBT[2] persons. Hate crimes are committed in small places close to home, in the day-to-day world we inhabit together. Together, these articles also begin to articulate an array of strategies and tactics to create a culture of human rights, a culture that honors the dignity of all human beings, protecting their freedom from abuse, providing for their basic necessities, and supporting their communal solidarity. May our work carry from our lips to god's ear–from our hearts to your hands. "The destiny of human rights is in the hands of all our citizens in all our communities" (Roosevelt, 1958, p. 1).

REFERENCES

Anastas, J. (1998). Working against discrimination: Gay, lesbian and bisexual people on the job. In L. M. Sloan, & N. S. Gustavsson (Eds.). *Violence and social injustice against lesbian, gay and bisexual people* (pp. 83-98). Binghamton, NY: The Haworth Press, Inc.

Kopels, S. (1998). Wedded to the status quo: Same-sex marriage. In L. M. Sloan, & N. S. Gustavsson (Eds.). *Violence and social injustice against lesbian, gay and bisexual people* (pp. 69-82). Binghamton, NY: The Haworth Press, Inc.

National Coalition of Anti-Violence Programs. (1999). *Anti-lesbian, gay, bisexual and transgender violence in 1998.* [Annual report]. 240 West 35th St., Suite 200, New York, NY, 10001.

National Gay Lesbian Task Force. (2000). *Murder of African American man reflects twin diseases of racism, homophobia.* [Press release]. (http://www.ngltf.org/press/032400.html)

Roosevelt, E. (1958). *In your hands: A guide for community action for the tenth anniversary of the Universal Declaration of Human Rights.* [Speech]. (http://www.udhr.org/history/inyour.htm)

Sloan, L. M., & Gustavsson, N. S. (Eds.). (1998). *Violence and social injustice against lesbian, gay and bisexual people.* Binghamton, NY: The Haworth Press, Inc. (co-published simultaneously as *Journal of Gay & Lesbian Social Services*, 8(3), 1998).

Sloan, L. M., King, L., & Sheppard, S. (1998). Hate crimes motivated by sexual orientation: Police reporting and training. In L. M. Sloan, & N. S. Gustavsson (Eds.). *Violence and social injustice against lesbian, gay and bisexual people* (pp. 25-40). Binghamton, NY: The Haworth Press, Inc.

United Nations. (1948). *Universal Declaration of Human Rights.* (http://www.unhchr.ch/udhr/lang/eng.htm)

A Tribute to Matthew Shepard

Walt Boulden

On October 6, 1998, I received a phone call from a dear friend of mine. He was calling to tell me he was not going to be able to go to the movie with me that night. He was very apologetic because he knew it was my birthday, and, though this was not a birthday celebration, he was concerned about whether I would be disappointed. I just laughed and told him we would go to the movie later in the week. After all, we saw each other daily. That was the last time Matthew Shepard and I spoke.

Later that night, unknown to me, a chain of events unfolded that would cost Matt his life and turn the lives of those of us who loved him upside down and inside out. Matt went to a local bar for a drink following a meeting of the University of Wyoming's Lesbian, Gay, Bisexual, Transgendered Association. He had not been able to get any of his friends to go with him, so he had gone alone. While there, he met two men in their 20s who posed as gays and lured him outside. They kidnapped him at gun point, drove him to a remote area outside Laramie, tortured and pistol-whipped him while he begged for his life, tied him to a buck-rail fence, and left him hanging in the cold winds of this high plateau, located over 7,000 feet above sea level.

Some eighteen hours later, I received a phone call from Matt's

Walt Boulden, MSW, is Research Specialist for the University of Missouri-Kansas City Institute for Human Development.

Address correspondence to: Walt Boulden, 715 Cleveland Avenue, Kansas City, MO 64124.

[Haworth co-indexing entry note]: "A Tribute to Matthew Shepard." Boulden, Walt. Co-published simultaneously in *Journal of Gay & Lesbian Social Services* (Harrington Park Press, an imprint of The Haworth Press, Inc.) Vol. 13, No. 1/2, 2001, pp. 7-14; and: *From Hate Crimes to Human Rights: A Tribute to Matthew Shepard* (ed: Mary E. Swigonski, Robin S. Mama, and Kelly Ward) Harrington Park Press, an imprint of The Haworth Press, Inc., 2001, pp. 7-14. Single or multiple copies of this article are available for a fee from The Haworth Document Delivery Service [1-800-342-9678, 9:00 a.m. - 5:00 p.m. (EST). E-mail address: getinfo@haworthpressinc.com].

7

father, calling from Saudi Arabia. He told me that Matt was being transported by ambulance to a hospital in Ft. Collins and was in very serious condition–he had been beaten close to death. Through the blur of shock, I called some of his close friends and let them know what was going on. I got in the car and drove the 65 miles to the hospital–only to sit in a waiting room with other frustrated and shocked friends and family members, trying to console each other when no amount of consolation could possibly help make sense of what was going on. We were living our worst nightmare. Matt was not going to make it, and it was becoming very clear that he was brutally beaten and left to die because he had let the wrong people know he was gay.

The next hours and days felt like a blur, yet are also forever seared into my memory. Nothing could have prepared me for the horror, the grief, or the onslaught of the media as the community and world awoke to the reality that Matt had been so brutally attacked. At 12:35 a.m., Monday October 12, he died, and things became even more surreal.

As I contacted friends who had known Matt, I was able to get a message to Dr. Mary Swigonski, who had met Matt at a Baccalaureate Program Directors conference in Nashville. Like everyone else who ever met Matt, he had made an impression on her, and she always asked about him when we corresponded. In the following weeks, as all of us searched for a way to give some meaning to the senseless brutality of Matt's murder, Mary suggested dedicating this publication to Matt and focusing it on Hate Crimes and Human Rights. At that time, she asked if I would write a tribute to Matt. Thus, even after six months, I sit at my computer and try to see past the horror and grief and find a way to share with people who did not know him who Matt was.

With the shock and exhaustion wearing thin, the memories of Matt still have to fight their way past the horrible image of his broken and battered body lying in the hospital bed of that intensive care unit. But Matt has made it back into my consciousness, past the horror, the shock, and the exhaustion. His smile dances before my eyes as I write.

All those who were graced with the gift of knowing Matt know the smile I am talking about. Matt never smiled with just his mouth. His whole face and body would light up. His eyes would dance and his vibrancy and energy radiated from his whole being. It never mattered where we were, when I would meet Matt, he would bounce up to me, throw his arms around me in a hug only Matt could give, and immediately start into some conversation that would quickly suck me in. And we were lost in whatever topic was on his mind when we bumped into each other. His insight, his humor, and concern, all poured out, regardless of whether we were talking about world affairs, a class, a friend, or clothes and fashion. Throughout the conversation, Matt would pause, assume a very introspective posture, and take a draw from his cigarette, always careful to blow the smoke away from anyone sitting near. And I'd have to smile. It was at this moment that I'd see all the care that Matt put into his appearance, the way his hair looked, the way his clothes reflected his mood, the way he was sitting. I might point that out, and we would laugh and talk about presentation and fashion and wanting people to have a favorable first impression.

When I say Matt would bounce up to me, the image is crystal clear. Again, anyone who knew Matt knows what his "bounce" was like. We would talk and laugh about the way he walked. I'd remind him that he once told me he used to practice the way he walked; we'd laugh. He told me his African American friends would tell him he walks "like a brother." Again, we'd laugh. Matt was very proud of that compliment. I'd tell him he was so skinny because he used up too much energy with his "bounce."

There is another particular memory of a time with Matt which comforts me when I am especially feeling the loss of my friend. When Matt was only about 15, we would often go walking in the mountains above Casper. This must have been sometime in the fall, because Matt was really excited about showing me where some wild strawberries were growing. Now, I had lived in Casper all my life and had never heard of any wild strawberries on Casper Mountain, so, naturally, I was giving him a hard time, and accusing him of leading me on a "snipe" hunt.

I have to stop here and explain something. Wyoming is a state where the average yearly precipitation is about 10.5 inches. And most of that comes in heavy winter snows. Wyoming is also a state where you count the growing season in days, not weeks or months. I've personally seen it snow in June, July, and in August. If the late spring frost doesn't kill everything in the garden, and it survives the summer drought, the early fall frost will get it. So, the idea of strawberries growing wild at 8,000 feet seemed a little far-fetched to me. But Matt was determined to show me that it was possible and, at the same time, share one of his favorite childhood memories.

As we drove up the mountain, Matt told me of the area that we were going to see, a favorite place of his, because he used to go there and camp with his family. We drove into the small, empty camp area, parked the car, and Matt could hardly wait to lead me out among the trees, where we got down on our hands and knees. Matt said, "You have to look really close, because they are really little." Then he showed me a tiny little leaf; saying he thought that it was the kind of plant we were looking for. So there we were, crawling around on our hands and knees, with our noses almost on the ground, pawing through the underbrush–when Matt jumped up and shouted, "I found one!" and came running over to me. He had me put out my hand and carefully placed this little tiny berry about this big () in the middle of my palm. I will never forget how excited he was. Of course he said, "Taste it! Eat it!" I couldn't *not* eat it. So I picked this tiny little thing up and put it in my mouth. And low and behold, it really was a strawberry. By now, he was jumping up and down and laughing and saying, "See? I told you so. I knew it!" In the midst of his laughter, he said, "Now you have to find one!"

So back onto our hands and knees we went. My nose was about 3 inches off the ground as I examined these tiny little plants, trying to find a strawberry. Pretty soon I heard, "I found another one!" and "I found another one!" and "Here's one!" By now, Matt's laughter and joy was beginning to turn into concern, because he really wanted me to find one–so I would know how great it felt. He came over, took me by the hand, led me over to another area and said, "Try in here." Back on my knees, I could find the plant, just no strawberries.

This was when I told Matt that I am color-blind when it comes to some reds and greens and that I had been trying to find these tiny berries by looking for their shape in the middle of all those little leaves. Matt squatted down right next to me and said, "Why don't you try a little over to the left, that area looks good." So, I start running my hands through these tiny leaves, because I couldn't see any berries. Matt said, "Try a little bit back to your right." I felt around and still could not see or feel any of the berries. Finally, Matt reached down, took my hand, and laid it right on top of a berry in front of me, and said, "Try right there." I don't know how long he had been watching that berry, and me fumbling all around it, before he decided to help me out. But, he wanted so badly for me to share that experience of finding a wild strawberry on my own. He would never have reached over, picked it, and handed it to me, because that would have spoiled it. I had to find it, myself.

I often think of all the teasing and hard times Matt could have given me when he found out that I am color-blind. But that wasn't Matt. He didn't do that to other people. He just wanted to share his love of life. Besides, he knew all too well what it felt like to be on the other side of that kind of teasing. Matt was just a good kid.

There are other images that also present themselves when I think of Matt. Like him showing up at my door in Laramie and asking: "Am I bothering you?" His eyes were not dancing, and he was not offering his energetic hug. His eyes had the look of a little boy who had just seen a scary movie. He'd come in and asked if he could "just hang." He'd have his backpack and schoolbooks with him. He would either sit and watch TV for a little while or take his books out and start doing homework. After some time, he'd start talking about hearing someone call out "faggot" or hearing someone talk about "queers." We'd talk about how this touched Matt at the core of his heart, how scared he was, and how he just needed to feel safe again. Then he'd just hang around, regrouping and trying to harden himself. Something that never came easy for Matt, because he was not the type of person to "be hard."

After some time, the Matt with the dancing eyes would start coming back, and he'd be off to class or to meet a friend for coffee. Matt would be okay again for a while. But Matt lived much of his life in fear, though most who saw him might not have guessed that was the case.

I knew Matt for almost seven years. I met him when he was still in his mid-teens. I had seen Matt perform in a stage presentation of "Our Town" a couple years prior to actually meeting him. I always thought it was strange that I remembered him and his performance so clearly. I am the kind of person who usually cannot remember the name of my favorite actor or singer. Yet Matt had shown such presence on stage that I had looked his name up in the program, and it had stuck. When I was introduced to him later, I recognized his name and where I had seen him before. When I asked him about the performance, Matt beamed with pleasure that I would have remembered him, and our friendship was sealed forever.

Matt loved the theatre and performed in several productions put on by Casper College and by the local community theatre group in Casper. He was hypersensitive to his surroundings and to his appearance. Matt wanted people to know him and like him at a level far deeper than superficial "small-talk," but believed people judge each other with first impressions. In many ways, I think that, for much of Matt's life, he felt he was "on stage" and giving a performance even as he walked through everyday life.

It was a sight to behold to watch Matt walk across the room at a gay dance club and to see every head in the building turn to follow his steps. He had a presence that would not be denied and always attracted numerous gay men to approach him or "hit on him." Yet after that initial entrance, when I would go looking for Matt, I would find him sitting in some corner with a new friend talking about politics or world affairs.

Matt grew up in a small town of 40,000 people. He lived on the same block, played with the same children, and went home to the same house for the first fifteen years of his life. Matt loved routine and stability. When he talked about going to church, he talked about the comfort of the tradition and the ceremony. Matt anchored himself to family and community. He often talked about being a member of the community of the world and was very concerned with environmental issues and world affairs

When his family moved overseas, and Matt was faced with moving from the comfort and stability of Casper, he was both frightened and thrilled. He was just starting the process of "coming out" to himself, and we had often talked about how scary that was for him because he knew how intolerant the people of Wyoming are of people who are too feminine or of people who acknowledge that they are gay. So, in some ways, he saw being able to venture into the international arena as a way of maybe finding a more tolerant atmosphere for him to live in. He was also thrilled by the prospect of being able to travel and see parts of the world that he had never thought he would be able to see. This was very exciting to a young man so interested in people and world affairs. At the same time, he was very frightened by the idea of living away from the only place he had ever known as home. He was also very concerned about being separated from his best friend–his mother–and having to live in a boarding school in Switzerland while she was going to be living in Saudi Arabia.

Living in Europe and the Middle East had a profound effect on

Matt. As a young man just discovering what it meant to be gay, it was not an easy time. Matt found himself more solidly back in the closet while living overseas than he had been living in the states. His boarding school was very conservative, and he was all alone, without supports to help him wade through all the conflicting emotions and thoughts that so often accompany the early stages of "coming out" to one's self. Yet, Matt was in love with the beauty, the tradition, the history, the atmosphere, and the mystique of Europe and the Middle East. As he drank in and was seduced by all the wonders of the area, he truly felt more and more like a citizen of the world.

Like many of us who have to face a world hostile to us, whether because we love those we "should not" love or because we have the wrong skin tone or because we have the wrong ethnic background, Matt struggled with depression born of fear and rejection. Matt was often exposed to, and afraid of, the cruelty of the world. He was very aware of the horrific conditions that so many of the people of the world were living in. He had seen those conditions and met the people living in them. He also experienced firsthand the harassment and violence which came from a world where oppression is the rule, not the exception.

Yet, these experiences also galvanized Matt's desire to become not only involved in world affairs and world politics, but also to focus his heart and soul on the human rights of all people. Matt loved people and meeting people. Even after returning to the states, Matt was very capable of spending his last dime to pay for a meal for a homeless person and then of sitting over that meal with him or her for a couple hours talking about life and the struggles to survive.

Matt was a wonderful young man. He was only 21 years old. He had his whole life ahead of him, and his future held the potential for greatness. He was pursuing a college degree that he felt would open doors for him to enter into the Foreign Service. That is where he aspired to begin his fight to secure human rights for all humans, worldwide. Matt's future, all his potential, and all his aspirations were cut short, leaving us all to wonder what "could have been."

Matt was a unique young man, and at the same time he was very typical. He was his parent's son. He was his brother's brother. He was his grandparent's grandson. He was the boy next door, the kid in class sitting next to you. He was the blonde-haired, blue-eyed little boy who used to run down the street with his buddies laughing and playing ball. He laughed, he cried, he felt deeply, he worried about all people, including those he loved and those he had never met. He followed local and world affairs; he wanted to love, to be loved, and to fit in.

Matt was very special to those of us who knew and loved him. But Matt was no more unique nor special than James Byrd, Billy Jack Gaither, Nichols West, Elizabeth Kelle Davidson, Eric Moore, Roxanne Ellis, Michelle Abdill, or any of the other numerous men and women who have been brutally murdered by those who hate everyone who does not fit their mold. Matt was no more unique than the other 33 gay men and lesbians who were also killed in 1998 because of their sexual orientation.[1] Each of these men and women had loved ones, friends, and parents who knew them as unique and special. Each of them laughed and cried and wanted to love and be loved. Each of them just wanted to be allowed to live a life without fear and oppression.

My Dearest Matt:

You touched the hearts and souls of the world with a spirit and presence that could not be extinguished even by your brutal murder. You will always live in the memories of those of us lucky enough to have known you. And whether you wanted it or not, you will also live forever as a reminder to all who fight for human rights that our work is far from done and that the price of inaction and complacency is too high. While your fight is over, ours must continue with renewed focus and determination. Rest in peace. You have earned it.

Walt

NOTE

1. National Coalition of Anti-Violence Programs. (1999). *Anti-lesbian, gay, bisexual and transgender violence in 1998*. [Annual report]. 240 West 35th St., Suite 200, New York, NY, 10001.

Human Rights in the 20th Century: Weren't Gays and Lesbians Human?

Janice Wood Wetzel

SUMMARY. This article seeks to answer the question raised in its title. To that end, the evolution of the United Nations *Universal Declaration of Human Rights* is discussed in the context of lesbian and gay rights, internationally and in the United States. The political and psychosocial dynamics of homophobic hatred are addressed, including the correlation of human rights abuses to heterosexism and the denigration of the feminine. The article discusses institutionalized gay oppression that serves to deny human rights, demonizing gay and lesbian people to such a degree that hate crimes become feasible. Finally, the importance of the globalization of non-governmental organizations on behalf of LGBT human rights advocacy is stressed. *[Article copies available for a fee from The Haworth Document Delivery Service: 1-800-342-9678. E-mail address: <getinfo@haworthpressinc.com> Website: <http://www.HaworthPress. com> © 2001 by The Haworth Press, Inc. All rights reserved.]*

Janice Wood Wetzel, PhD, is affiliated with Adelphi University.

Address correspondence to: Janice Wood Wetzel, Adelphi University, School of Social Work, South Avenue, Garden City, NY 11530 (E-mail: wetzel@adelphi.edu).

For the purposes of this article, the term "lesbians and gays" includes bisexuals and transgendered people, the constituents of the international LGBT movement.

[Haworth co-indexing entry note]: "Human Rights in the 20th Century: Weren't Gays and Lesbians Human?" Wetzel, Janice Wood. Co-published simultaneously in *Journal of Gay & Lesbian Social Services* (Harrington Park Press, an imprint of The Haworth Press, Inc.) Vol. 13, No. 1/2, 2001, pp. 15-31; and: *From Hate Crimes to Human Rights: A Tribute to Matthew Shepard* (ed: Mary E. Swigonski, Robin S. Mama, and Kelly Ward) Harrington Park Press, an imprint of The Haworth Press, Inc., 2001, pp. 15-31. Single or multiple copies of this article are available for a fee from The Haworth Document Delivery Service [1-800-342-9678, 9:00 a.m. - 5:00 p.m. (EST). E-mail address: getinfo@haworthpressinc.com].

KEYWORDS. Universal Declaration of Human Rights, international human rights, United States and human rights, gays and lesbians, LGBT, hate crimes, heterosexism, institutionalized oppression

The title of this article raises a troubling question. The answer, like the question itself, is embedded within the fundamental principles of human rights as they are contained in the United Nations' *Universal Declaration of Human Rights*. It is the standard reference for all UN human rights efforts throughout the world, including the United States.

THE EVOLUTION OF HUMAN RIGHTS

The United Nations' *Universal Declaration of Human Rights*, introduced to the world in 1948 by Eleanor Roosevelt, evolved over time into a body of agreements that etched into posterity the original aspirations of the founders. Article 2 states that everyone is entitled to all of the rights and freedoms set forth in the document "without distinction of any kind, such as race, colour, sex, language, religion, political or other opinion, national or social origin, property, birth or other status." Human rights are defined as including the health and well-being of all human beings. The essential resources to meet such a standard are detailed as food, clothing, housing, medical care, and necessary social services. It also calls for the right to security in the event of unemployment, sickness, disability, widowhood, old age, or other lack of livelihood in circumstances beyond one's control (Article 25, p. 1). By the end of the 20th century, the *Universal Declaration of Human Rights* had become an international civil and political canon of economic, social, and cultural rights.

The human rights system is built upon the premise that governments are obligated to create the conditions under which human rights laws can be fulfilled, thus providing each individual with freedom from human rights violations (either by the government itself or by others). These international agreements underscore the requirement that human rights are expressed concretely in the real lives of the people.

At its inception, the UN was concerned first of all with civil and political rights that are designed to ensure freedom from any curtailment of individual liberty. Later, social justice, freedom from want, and participation in economic, social, and cultural aspects of life were recognized as essential to the realization of human rights (*United Nations Universal Declaration of Human Rights*, 1948; Wetzel, 1993 & 1996; Wronka, 1998).

More was needed if the UN was to have the legal force to implement the collective ideals of its member nations. Two international covenants were developed to meet the challenge. The first was the *International Covenant on Civil and Political Rights*, and the second, the *International Covenant on Economic, Social and Political Rights* (see Tessitore & Woolfson, 1997-1998). The covenants were designed to guarantee a social and international legal order essential to the realization of human rights.

The UN took ten years before it ratified these covenants in 1966, and even then the task remained elusive. Without focusing on specific populations-at-risk, except in the most blatant cases, it was difficult to discern what the barriers and catalysts to the recognition of human rights were. The struggle continues within the UN to this day even though about 60 population-specific UN human rights treaties have been ratified, providing an even stronger legal mandate to fulfill human needs. Gay and lesbian rights are not among them.

HUMAN RIGHTS
AND THE UNITED STATES GOVERNMENT

The United States has long had an aversion to the concept of human rights, as compared with civil and political rights, as they are played out in the international arena. Unlike domestic civil and political rights that can be modified based upon internal, cultural, and religious values, human rights are universally applied, transcending customs that discriminate to the detriment of a particular class of individuals and groups. The fact is that the *Universal Declaration of Human Rights* is distinctive in that it gave the world, for the first time in history, the right to ask questions of countries about what were previously considered to be their internal affairs. In effect, it was no longer acceptable for one nation to say to another, "What we do in our country is our own business." Nonetheless, a decade before the turn of the 20th century, the document was considered to be customary international law and even non-member nations, however reluctantly, recognized the fact that the world would not turn its back on social and humanitarian concerns within its borders (Wetzel, 2000; in press).

Such outside influence did not sit well with conservative presidents and members of Congress in the United States. From the beginning, they were hostile to a number of the basic tenets of human rights principles. As time progressed, when the *International Covenant on Civil and Political Rights* was signed and ratified by Congress, the *International Covenant on Economic, Social, and Cultural Rights* was not, nor has it ever been (Alston, 1990; Hannum & Fischer, 1993; Wronka, 1998). Conservative right wing and isolationist groups argued during deliberations that human rights promised "socialism by treaty" and the destruction of the "American Way" (Evans, 1998b, p. 9). For the same reasons (fear of international intrusiveness and aversion to human rights principles thought to be antithetical to conservative American values), neither the *Convention on the Elimination of All Forms of Discrimination Against Women* (United Nations, 1985) nor the *Convention Against Torture, and Other Cruel, Inhuman and Degrading Treatment or Punishment* (United Nations, 1987) were ratified as of the year 2000. Even the *Convention on the Rights of the Child* (United Nations, 1989) was not. Indeed, it was never even signed, ostensibly on the grounds that such international influence would encroach on "family values" in the United States. If the rights of children are thought to be antithetical to family values, resistance to the rights of gays and lesbians shouldn't come as a surprise. Interestingly, however, the *Convention on the Elimination of All Forms of Racial Discrimination* was endorsed by the U.S. at the height of the civil rights movement in 1965. Timing, it would appear, is all.

INTERNATIONAL HISTORY
OF GAY AND LESBIAN RIGHTS

Following a series of police raids and unrelenting harassment, riots erupted in 1969 at a gay bar called the Stonewall Inn in New York City's Greenwich Village. The event is usually credited as the beginning of the gay rights movement. While gay males, lesbians, bisexuals, and transgendered people were in attendance, the present day international LGBT human rights movement has diverse origins and influences. It "owes a major debt to the women's movement which opened up issues of sexuality and sexual identity as legitimate areas of collective struggle" (Amnesty International, 1999, p. 15).

Amnesty International-United Kingdom's (1997) global studies of human rights and abuses reveal that United Nations' member states that supported human rights documents have "provided an important framework for combating violations against ethnic minorities and women, yet there was not recognition in the international community that gays and lesbians require–and deserve–similar protections" (p. 8). Their research brought them to the conclusion that gay men and lesbians around the world remain at-risk. Although case studies demonstrate that a woman in prison may be singled out for rape because she is a lesbian, although a man may suffer police violence because he is known to be a homosexual or believed to carry the AIDS virus, human rights violations on the grounds of sexual identity are not yet expressly forbidden by any international law (p. 8).

Even when Amnesty International voiced its concern about sexual minorities in its proposals at the World Conference on Human Rights in Vienna in 1993, a gathering that provided a pivotal turning point in human rights work, according to Wronka (1998), their concerns were not included in the *Vienna Declaration and Programme of Action* (Amnesty International, 1997; United Nations, 1993).

On the positive side, the United Kingdom's branch of Amnesty International reports that when the new Republic of South Africa, a formerly homophobic country under apartheid, ratified its constitution, it became the first nation to incorporate sexual orientation in its anti-discrimination doctrines. Having experienced unending abuses, the framers and the people agreed that they wanted their new country to be a nation of rights.

The International Gay and Lesbian Human Rights Commission (1999a; 1999b) cites the case of *Toonen v. Australia* in 1994 as a landmark in international gay and lesbian rights legislation. The UN Human Rights Committee ruled at that time that the sodomy law of the Australian State of Tasmania violated the country's obligations under Articles 2 (re nondiscrimination) and 17 (re the right to privacy) of the *International Covenant on Civil and Political Rights* (United Nations, 1966). The references to sex in Article 2 were deemed by the Committee to include sexual orientation.

The European Convention for the Protection of Human Rights and Fundamental Freedoms has proved to be helpful in supporting a series of decisions that advance gay and lesbian rights. Ireland, for example, struck down all Irish laws as constitutionally invalid that were in violation of the *European Convention*. As for the U.S., ten states, as of 1997, explicitly prohibit discrimination on the basis of sexual orientation. But sixteen others have sodomy laws on the books that criminalize private consensual sex between adults, five of them explicitly in reference to same-sex partners.

Given that there is increasing public awareness of gay and lesbian rights issues and some indication of progress in the courts, the question asked by Amnesty is *"why is it that general human rights protections so often fail to shield gay men and lesbians from serious abuses?"* (Amnesty International–United Kingdom, 1997, p. 9). The reasons are numerous, and are always reflective of further oppression. Amnesty points out that abuses proliferate and a climate of secrecy is created by governments that "promote, fail to challenge, or attempt to disguise persecution of gays and lesbians" (p. 11). They also own up to the fact that human rights organizations like themselves and the international media have been slow to take up the gay and lesbian cause. Understandably, homosexuals who have been victims of repression often don't report the violence against them for fear of reprisal by the perpetrators and the public. Further, discriminatory treatment is often masked behind bogus legal pretexts, and many organizations deny having any homosexuals in residence, so great is the taboo. Still others stridently defend their right to punish that which they view as a criminal offense (p. 11) . . . and so it goes, ad infinitum.

In sum, gay men and lesbians are found to be anonymous victims of oppression, as well as victims of overt, blatant human rights abuses. Amnesty International, therefore, has concluded that part of its mission to defend the human rights of all people must include identifying, exposing, and combating human rights abuses that specifically target individuals because of their sexual orientation. They consider sexual orientation to be a fundamental dimension of human identity and as such should be a basic human right.

By 1997, Romania, Cyprus, Bosnia, Macedonia, and Croatia were the only European countries that still criminalized homosexual acts, generally, but by no means only, targeting gay men. In response to advocacy attempts from a number of countries and human rights organizations to overturn Romania's Article 200 of the Penal Code prohibiting homosexual relations between consenting adults that cause a public scandal (and how could it not under such conditions), the Romanian government retaliated by extending the scope of the legislation to include private homosexual relationships, plus five years of imprisonment for exercising their right to freedom of assembly and expression.

There are twelve countries today that call for the execution of people convicted of committing homosexual acts. Throughout the world, from Zimbabwe and Afghanistan to Turkey and Greece, from Iran and China to Mexico and the United States of America, gay men and lesbians are arrested, beaten, tortured, and killed for being who they are. Whether or not there are laws to protect them, all too often they are left without recourse. The attitudes of people make the difference. Anne, a human rights campaigner from Texas, brought the facts to life when she spoke movingly in the Amnesty International-Netherlands film, *Breaking the Silence*, in 1994:

> The laws forbidding homosexual acts often act as a kind of mandate for violations . . . They have killed gays and lesbians in Texas because they believe (them) to be less than human. I believe it's very important that people understand why the murders happen and that such murder is a result of hatred. It is committed by young teenage men. Those men were not born haters. They were taught to hate by a society that continues to pass laws against lesbians and gay men, that continues to demonize lesbians and gays, that preaches hatred from the pulpit. (Amnesty International-United Kingdom, 1997, p. 41)

ARE GAYS AND LESBIANS HUMAN?
IT'S NOT AN ACADEMIC QUESTION

By dehumanizing and marginalizing gays, lesbians, bisexuals, and transgendered people, "leaders know that they are fostering a climate in which the public will not be concerned" about their human rights. They become, in effect, "less than human." Even killing provokes little or no public outrage in many cases (Amnesty International, 1999, p. 9):

> After all, if they are less than human, why should they enjoy full human rights? When those in power brand members of certain groups as "less than human" solely because their identity separates

"them" from "us," they pave the way for gross human rights abuses against such groups. (Amnesty International, 1999, p. 9)

Evans (1998) provided a comprehensive, critical reappraisal of human rights on the occasion of the United Nation's 50th anniversary of the *Universal Declaration of Human Rights.* His introductory article on *Power, Hegemony and Human Rights* points out the disjuncture between the theory and practice of human rights, citing an abundance of "literature about utopian visions and legal solutions, but little to say about the social and political context in which violations take place" (Evans, 1998b, p. 1). Peterson and Parisi's contribution entitled *"Are Women Human? It's Not an Academic Question"* provides an historical analysis and conceptual framework that examines the time worn oppression of women (1998, pp. 132-160). Their perspective is useful in helping us to understand the social and political context that, by extension, results in unrelenting gay and lesbian oppression as well.

THE PSYCHOSOCIAL DYNAMICS
OF HOMOPHOBIC HATRED

Peterson and Parisi's analysis hearkens back to ancient Greece where masculinity, the normalization of heterosexuality, and "stateness" became not only symbolic constructions but historically interdependent processes. By so doing, ancient Greece engraved in stone the rejection of all but heterosexual forms of identity and subjectivity, family forms, and group reproduction (with centralized authority and hierarchical divisions of labor). Women's subordination to male-defined interests, denial of self-determination, decision-making, and repudiation of bonding among women in their own interest became normalized as well. From that time on, all sexual orientations and gender identifications other than heterosexual male and masculine privilege have been denied and repressed, while male-defined interests over females and femininity are made manifest (Peterson & Parisi, 1998).

"Hence, and this is key," the authors conclude, "gender hierarchies naturalize not only intra- but also inter-group asymmetries" (p. 139). That is to say, not only are females denigrated, but anyone or anything associated with the feminine is thus objectified as an appropriate target of domination and deemed unacceptable, not fully human. It is certainly true of women and so-called minorities. And by extension, it is certainly true of gay males and lesbians.

It is not by chance that calling males by a feminine name is the consummate insult. Little boys are socialized from their earliest days not to be a "sissy," while the deriding epithets directed at older boys and men are likely to be of a more sexually explicit order, generally vulgar, and always degrading. Men's fear of tapping into their feminine nature becomes so deeply embedded in their psyches that they must protect themselves from being so-labeled at all costs. That cost is more than apparent in homophobic hate crimes directed at males.

The threat of lesbianism to heterosexual men can be experienced by women as feelings of rejection by males, and is often expressed by men as the unacceptability of women who are not dependent on a male. But greater clarity is brought to the issue as experienced by traditional heterosexual women who consciously or unconsciously are male-defined. The audacity of lesbians' rejection of the rule of femininity (centering on male-defined interests) and jeopardizing the position of male dominance is anathema to traditional women who have internalized the rules of society and their own oppression.

Andrew Sullivan, a self-proclaimed gay man held in ill repute by other gays, was featured on September 26, 1999, in the *Sunday Magazine* section of the *New York Times*. He no doubt compounded his unpopularity with the gay community in addition to any number of other oppressed groups with his outrageous article unabashedly stating that we can't and shouldn't win the fight against hate. His argument is based on his observation that those who have been victims of hatred often grow to hate the perpetrators, may become victimizers themselves, and even identify with their accusers' low estimation of them. In Sullivan's mind, these facts reflect on the initial victims and lead him to conclude that hate crimes are not just crimes against oppressed populations, but are so ubiquitous that nothing can be done.

Despite all of the information Sullivan has accumulated, he reveals unknowingly a consummate ignorance of the psychological and social dynamics of oppression. His unfamiliarity with the subject would just be embarrassing were it not so harmful. For that reason, his faulty concepts must be challenged. He appears to be unfamiliar with the very subject of his treatise when he contends ever so importantly that "we speak of institutional racism . . . as if an institution can feel anything" (p. 55). At the risk of being patronizing, I am compelled to point out that institutionalized racism, like other kinds of institutional discrimination, is the practice of discrimination through normal daily operations. It is thought by many to be even more significant than that committed by bigoted individuals. The term refers to the denial of opportunities and rights to individuals and groups that is woven into the fabric of the culture so subtly that it goes unnoticed. We become so socialized to normative structures, customs, and attitudes that perpetuate discrimination and oppression that we do not recognize them as discriminatory.

Rules, policies, and practices of organizations that are regarded as "simply doing business" are typical of such oppression. Inferior schooling, poorer health care, inadequate counseling, encumbering responsibility for the care of relatives, hiring and promotion practices, and bias in lending and leasing are all part of the picture. Other examples relevant to their situation are: denial of the right to marry and adopt, absence of serious representation of gays in the media, inhumane "don't ask, don't tell" military policies, and other gag rules that require them to keep their identities a secret in everyday life. Such institutionally sanctioned denigration is a powerful determinant of life possibilities for gays and lesbians.

Sullivan concludes, in his righteous fashion, that "hate is only foiled when the hated are immune to the bigot's power" (p. 113). A noble idea that has a faint aroma of victim blaming. He is right to a degree, of course, though he apparently doesn't appreciate why. Gays and lesbians, like every other human being, behave like everyone else. It is commonplace for oppressed people to internalize their own oppression (as Sullivan himself appears to have done), believing deep in their psyches that there may be truth to the hateful slurs visited upon them (Freire, 1970).

Nor is Sullivan apparently familiar with the theories of social psychologists like Thibaut and Kelley (1986) who years ago illumined our understanding of power and dependence, so relevant to the subject of hatred. Power, they posit, is control over others derived from others' dependence. (Sullivan is on safe ground so far.) But dependence is defined as due to the inequities of the social environment (here we find one of Sullivan's dark holes). Does he really believe that Matthew Shepard could have been immune to the bigots that murdered him so sadistically? The writer seems to ignore the fact that when homophobia is institutionalized, bigots can hurt gays and lesbians . . . not just psychologically and socially, but economically and physically. Power and hatred are not to be dismissed so summarily.

Sullivan, to his credit, gives space to the ideas of Young-Bruehl (1998) whose book, *The Anatomy of Prejudices*, details her typology of three distinct kinds of hatred which she perceives as character types. They are not necessarily observed in any one person in a single discrete form: (1) *obsessive haters* (who fantasize that the very existence of minorities threaten them, so must be eliminated); (2) *hysterical haters* (prejudices that are used unconsciously to appoint a group to act out forbidden sexual and sexually aggressive repressed desires); and (3) *narcissistic haters* (rooted most commonly in men's inability even to imagine what it is to be a woman, a failing rarely challenged by men's control of our most powerful public institutions).

> Women are not so much hated by most men as simply ignored in nonsexual contexts, or never conceived as true equals. The implicit condescension is mixed, in many cases, with repressed and sublimated erotic desire. (Sullivan, 1999, pp. 55-56; Young-Bruehl, 1998)

Given the correlation hypothesized between hatred of gays and denigration of the feminine, one might conjecture a resemblance to narcissistic haters who oppress gays and lesbians, not to mention the obsessive and hysterical variety.

HUMAN RIGHTS AND HETEROSEXISM

Despite the fact that Article 2 of the *Declaration of Human Rights* states that "Everyone is entitled to all the rights and freedoms set forth in this *Declaration*, without distinction of any kind," it is clear that such rights have been selectively intended and applied (United Nations, 1948; Peterson & Parisi, 1998, p. 147). For example, the high-flown sentiments of inclusiveness set out in the *Universal Declaration of Human Rights:*

> do not affirm the right of women to freedom from masculine dominance and the structural violence it constitutes against women *and others stigmatized by association with the feminine* [italics mine]. . . . The consequences are that women [*and others*

stigmatized by association with the feminine] are systematically denied due process under international human rights law. . . . (Peterson & Parisi, 1998, p. 147)

Amnesty International's documentation in recent years of the abuse of homosexuals clearly acknowledges their shocking at-risk status. Peterson and Parisi (1998) contend that governmental heterosexism and the heterosexual family that embodies the public-private division, both of which are privileged in human rights documents, render all other sexual/affective relations deviant. "By normalizing heterosexism, non-heterosexuality of any kind is stigmatized as abnormal, thus fueling persecution for all those who don't conform" (p. 146). Despite the fact that governments have set the stage for oppression of homosexuals, they refuse to take responsibility for their protection. On this basis, the authors make the case that governments actually promote homophobic oppression through heterosexism, an institutionalized oppression that must be countered in the interest of human rights:

> If we do not simultaneously work to dissemble heterosexist oppression, we resign ourselves to perpetuating, not eliminating, direct and indirect violence against all who are "othered" as feminine. (p. 154)

Gerstmann (1999) would probably agree with their conclusion. Focusing on the subject of the U.S. Constitution and the failure of class-based equal protection under the law, particularly in relation to gays and lesbians, the title of his book, *The Constitutional Underclass*, says it all. The author explains that the Supreme Court divides people into legal classes that receive uneven levels of protection. By switching between the terms, "suspect class" and "suspect classification," the Court can require some groups to show that they meet the criteria for political powerlessness while allowing other groups who are far more politically powerful to benefit from strong constitutional protection.

When gays and lesbians try to move up the equal protection hierarchy, the courts tell them that they do not meet the criteria for protection because they are not politically powerless (that is, a suspect class that should be protected by the courts). Yet, when whites seek protection against race-based affirmative action programs, courts do not require that they prove that they are politically powerless, which they obviously are not. Similarly, gender is assessed as a quasi-suspect classification (thus only partially protected), protecting men who are in fact more politically powerful than women, from discrimination. This arbitrary practice has never been explicitly recognized by the Court, much less justified. It should come as no surprise that gays and lesbians are among those who receive the least protection, hence the subject of Gerstmann's title, *The Constitutional Underclass.* When they try to meet the qualifications for "equal protection of the laws," they do not qualify under any conceivable definition of the term. Instead, they are told that their status is voluntary, while other groups categorized as voluntary are protected.

Gerstmann does not contend that gays and lesbians should receive greater protection against discrimination than heterosexuals. Rather, he argues that no group should receive more protection than another. His point is that (a) rights should not be based upon criteria such as political powerlessness, and (b) criteria, terminology and methodology should be consistent for all groups. It is not too much to expect in a democratic republic ostensibly ruled by law. The Supreme Court in recent history appears to be in agreement.

On May 20, 1996, gay rights forces won a major victory when the Supreme Court ruled in their favor that Colorado's constitutional amendment that forbade laws protecting homosexuals from discrimination was unconstitutional, violating their right to equal protection. The ruling did not decide the legality of homosexual conduct, but affirmed the right of gays to seek protection from discrimination in employment, housing, and public accommodations. The future holds promise.

THE NEW POLITICS OF HUMAN RIGHTS

The idea of human rights has been globalized and institutionalized during the last half of the 20th century. Still, it would be foolish to think that progress is a foregone conclusion. Many governments, including the United States, continue to resist the inherently political nature of human rights, resenting the threat to their sovereignty:

> The "new politics" of human rights is therefore far from benign but increasingly becoming a domain of conflict and struggle between competing value systems and cultures brought into in-

tense interaction by the processes of globalization. (McGrew, 1998, p. 201)

At the same time, a global politics of contestation and empowerment has been mobilized by NGOs (non-governmental organizations) throughout the world. There are over 200 NGOs associated with human rights issues in the U.S., with equivalent numbers in the UK and across Europe. Similar organizations are mushrooming in the developing world. Not only are the numbers escalating, but so too is their level of activity (McGrew, 1998).

Social movements, particularly those associated with NGOs within and beyond the human rights realm, now play an increasingly significant role, domestically and globally, with attendant increasing resistance on the part of governments. NGO power arises from their ability to mobilize public and political opinion around specific "life issues" that promote rights for humanity as compared with specific sectional or promotional interests (McGrew, 1998). Gay and lesbian rights, only recently coming to the fore, meet this criteria. Addressing the fact that it is difficult to measure objectively the realization of human rights, Brett (1995) concludes optimistically that the growing resistance of governments to human rights NGOs might be seen as a measure of their success.

In order to assess the future success of gay and lesbian human rights, it makes sense to stay apprized of advances on the women's human rights front because they are often precursors to the possibility of gay and lesbian rights. Although women were included in the *Universal Declaration of Human Rights*, their rights have remained invisible, subject to the whims of culture, religion, and custom. It wasn't until 1993 that women's rights were cited specifically as human rights at The World Conference on Human Rights in Vienna. Violence against women was universally acknowledged for the first time in history as a women's human rights issue. These actions were enhanced when they were agreed to by consensus at the 4th World Conference on Women in Beijing in 1995. "Women's rights as human rights" was the final article on the *Beijing Programme of Action* (United Nations, 1995) on the last day of the conference. It was the result of a compromise vote following the rejection of a proposal on lesbian rights, the idea being that women's rights should encompass lesbian rights in any case. Given the resistance to passage and the dwindling time that was available, the delegates tabled lesbian rights as a specific issue until a future date. There is a "Beijing + 5" international women's meeting scheduled for the year 2000. Advocates of lesbian rights all over the world are working to place the issue on the agenda.

On another front, on September 28, 1999, it was reported that the European Court of Human Rights ruled unanimously that Great Britain's longstanding ban on homosexuals in the military violated Article 8 of the European Convention on Human Rights which states that "everyone has the right to respect for his private and family life, his home and his correspondence." At that time, Britain had no constitution or bill of rights similar to that of the United States, so, along with 40 other European countries, it signed the *European Convention on Human Rights* which obliges it to abide by the court's rulings, even to the extent of changing its laws if necessary. The European Court is a court of last resort, equivalent to our Supreme Court, but composed of judges from seven different nations, one of whom is British. Their 7-0 judgment should provide cogent arguments for those advocating an inclusive military presence in the United States. Realistically speaking, however, it also provides an unmistakable example of feared international intrusiveness to those who are already opposed to gay and lesbian rights, the *Universal Declaration of Human Rights*, and other human rights agreements (Lyall, 1999).

"Anti-gay 'hate crimes' are increasingly occupying the attention of the human rights community," according to Amnesty International-United Kingdom (1999). Campaigning for lesbian, gay, bisexual, and transgendered rights under the rubric of human rights is a powerful means of affirming the universality of human rights, the concept that no one can be deprived of their birthright, despite the proclivities of culture, religion, and tradition.

Amnesty International (1999) advises: (1) that all approaches must be "LGBT-sensitive"; (2) in so doing, one must be particularly sensitive to cultural differences in the use of language because self-definitions and perceptions of sexuality vary between and within cultures; (3) a gender-specific perspective must be maintained in all research and action strategies (the UN calls this "gender-mainstreaming"). The experience of boys and girls, and men and women in all cultures is very different, including in the LGBT world; (4) respect for the wishes and needs of victims of human rights abuses is paramount when deciding on action techniques; and finally, (5) Amnesty International advises that one must be strategic. While attending to cases and issues as they arise, always consider them within the context of long-term objectives.

Because human rights in any country are intrinsically related to global human rights, the most pressing issue challenging those who advocate for gays, lesbians, bisexuals, and transgendered people is how to marshal the forces of globalization. Only by doing so can the advancement of human rights and social justice be ensured in the next millennium (McGrew, 1998). Let no one have to ask one hundred years from now: "Weren't gays and lesbians human in the 21st century?"

REFERENCES

Alston, P. (1990). U.S. ratification of the covenant on economic, social and cultural rights: The need for an entirely new strategy. *American Journal of International Law, (84)* 365-393.

Amnesty International-United Kingdom. (1999). *The louder we will sing: Campaigning for lesbian and gay human rights.* [handbook]. London: Amnesty International-United Kingdom.

Amnesty International-United Kingdom. (1997). *Breaking the silence: Human rights violations based on sexual orientation.* London: Amnesty International-United Kingdom.

Brett, R. (1995). The role and limits of human rights NGOs at the United Nations. [Special Issue] *Political Studies, 43,* 96-111.

Evans, T. (Ed.). (1998). *Human rights fifty years on: A reappraisal.* Manchester and New York: Manchester University Press.

Evans, T. (1998b). Introduction: Power, hegemony and the universalization of human rights. In T. Evans (Ed.), *Human rights fifty years on: A reappraisal* (pp. 1-23). Manchester and New York: Manchester University Press.

Freire, P. (1970). *The pedagogy of the oppressed.* New York: Seabury Press.

Gerstmann, E. (1999). *The constitutional underclass: Gays, lesbians, and the failure of class-based equal protection.* Chicago: Chicago University Press.

Hannum, H., & Fischer, D. (1993). *Guide to international human rights practice.* Philadelphia: University of Pennsylvania Press.

International Gay and Lesbian Human Rights Commission. (1999a). *Sexual orientation and the human rights mechanisms of the United Nations: Examples and approaches* [monograph]. Prepared by IGLHRC with the assistance of the International Lesbian and Gay Association, San Francisco, CA.

International Gay and Lesbian Human Rights Commission. (1999b). *A global overview: Criminalization and decriminalization of homosexual acts.* [information sheet]. San Francisco, CA.

Lyall, S. (1999). European court tells British to let gay soldiers serve. *New York Times*, September 28, p. A8.

McGrew, A. G. (1998). Human rights: Coming to terms with globalization. In T. Evans (Ed.), *Human rights fifty years on: A reappraisal* (Chapter 8, pp. 189-210). Manchester and New York: Manchester University Press.

Peterson, V. S., & Parisi, L. (1998). Are women human? It's not an academic question. In T. Evans (Ed.), *Human rights fifty years on: A reappraisal* (Chapter 6, pp. 132-160). Manchester and New York: Manchester University Press.

Sullivan, A. (1999). What's so bad about hate? *New York Times Magazine*, September 26, Section 6, pp. 50-113.

Tessitore, J., & Woolfson, S. (Eds.). (1997). *A global agenda: Issues before the 52nd general assembly of the United Nations*. New York: Rowman and Littlefield Publishers, Inc.

Thibaut, J. W., & Kelley, Ha. H. (1986). Power and dependence. *The social psychology of groups*, Volume 7 [reprint]. (pp. 100-125). New York: John Wiley & Sons.

United Nations. (1948). *Universal declaration of human rights*.

United Nations. (1966). *International covenant on civil and political rights*.

United Nations. (1985). *Convention on the elimination of all forms of discrimination against women* (CEDAW).

United Nations. (1987). *Convention against torture, and other cruel, inhuman and degrading treatment or punishment*.

United Nations. (1989). *Convention on the rights of the child*.

United Nations. (1993). *Vienna declaration and programme of action*, World Conference on Human Rights.

United Nations. (1995). *Beijing programme of action*, Fourth World Conference on Women.

Wetzel, J. W. (1993). *The world of women: In pursuit of human rights*. London: McMillan Press, Ltd. and New York: New York University Press.

Wetzel, J. W. (1996). On the road to Beijing: The evolution of the international women's movement. *Affilia: Journal of Women and Social Work, 11*(2, Summer), 221-232.

Wetzel, J. W. (2000). Women and mental health: Global perspectives. *International Social Work, 43*(2), 205-215.

Wetzel, J. W. (submitted for publication). Human rights in action: Progressive challenges for social work.

Wronka, J. (1998). *Human rights and social policy in the 21st century*. New York: University Press of America, revised edition.

Young-Bruehl, E. (1998). *The anatomy of prejudices*. Cambridge, MA: Harvard University Press.

Human Rights, Hate Crimes, and Hebrew-Christian Scripture

Mary E. Swigonski

SUMMARY. This article seeks to contribute to a culture of human rights by challenging the use of Hebrew and Christian scriptures to characterize LGBT[2] persons as moral transgressors and to justify or rationalize hate crimes against them. Scriptural passages used to support claims of immorality of LGBT[2] persons–texts of terror–are examined. Then scriptural passages that are affirming of LGBT[2] relationships–texts of empowerment–are considered. The author discusses implications for social work of advancing a culture of human rights. *[Article copies available for a fee from The Haworth Document Delivery Service: 1-800-342-9678. E-mail address: <getinfo@haworthpressinc.com> Website: <http://www.HaworthPress.com> © 2001 by The Haworth Press, Inc. All rights reserved.]*

KEYWORDS. Human rights, hate crimes, gay, lesbian, Hebrew-Christian scriptures

"All human beings are born free and equal in dignity and rights" (United Nations, 1948). Human rights begin with the assertion that all

Mary E. Swigonski, PhD, LCSW, is affiliated with Monmouth University.

The Scripture quotations contained herein are from the New Revised Standard Version Bible, copyright 1989 by the Division of Christian Education of the National council of Churches of Christ in the U.S.A. and are used by permission. All rights reserved.

[Haworth co-indexing entry note]: "Human Rights, Hate Crimes, and Hebrew-Christian Scripture." Swigonski, Mary E. Co-published simultaneously in *Journal of Gay & Lesbian Social Services* (Harrington Park Press, an imprint of The Haworth Press, Inc.) Vol. 13, No. 1/2, 2001, pp. 33-45; and: *From Hate Crimes to Human Rights: A Tribute to Matthew Shepard* (ed: Mary E. Swigonski, Robin S. Mama, and Kelly Ward) Harrington Park Press, an imprint of The Haworth Press, Inc., 2001, pp. 33-45. Single or multiple copies of this article are available for a fee from The Haworth Document Delivery Service [1-800-342-9678, 9:00 a.m. - 5:00 p.m. (EST). E-mail address: getinfo@haworthpressinc.com].

human beings have inherent dignity and worth (Perry, 1998; Wronka, 1995, 1998). The dignity and worth of all human beings may be inherent, but the meaning and implications of that dignity and worth are socially defined. Declarations of human rights, and their interpretations, are social constructs, reflecting the moral conscience of a civilization at a given moment in time (Martin, 1947 in Wronka, 1998, p. 24; Witkin, 1998). Morals define the norms of behavior that are accepted, they define how individuals and groups should behave in order to be considered respectable and worthy within a community and culture (Countryman, 1988). Through social definitions of morality, some human beings are rendered as having less dignity and worth than others.

Hebrew and Christian scriptures are a source of moral rules that have been woven throughout contemporary western industrial cultures. Particular passages from those scriptures have been used to justify claims that the expression of love between lesbians, gay men, bisexuals, transgendered, and two-spirited persons (LGBT[2]) is immoral and outside culturally accepted behavior. Those scriptures have been used to render LGBT[2] lives as having less dignity and worth than other human lives. Hebrew and Christian scriptures have been used to characterize LGBT[2] persons as moral transgressors, as individuals who stand outside the cloak of protection of human rights, and to justify or rationalize hate crimes against them.

This article challenges the veracity of that use of scriptures. The purpose of this article is not to challenge anyone's faith or beliefs. Rather the goal is to contribute to a culture of human rights, to reconceptualize the moral valuation of human relationships to embrace greater acceptance and celebration of diversity. First, the scriptural passages used to support claims of immorality of LGBT[2] persons–texts of terror–are examined. Then scriptural passages that are affirming of LGBT[2] relationships–texts of empowerment–are considered. In conclusion, the implications for social work of advancing a culture of human rights are discussed.

TEXTS OF TERROR

For all of the moral censure and condemnation associated with scriptures, only six passages are construed as condemning homosexuality. Robert Goss (1993) calls these passages collectively the "texts of terror" because popular interpretations of them are terrifying to the lives of LGBT[2] persons. They are used as the justification for name-calling, for acts of psychological, spiritual, and physical violence, and for hate crimes. Those texts are *Genesis 19*; *Leviticus 18:22* and *20:13*; *Romans 1:26-27, 1 Corinthians 6:9*, and *1 Timothy 1:10*.[1] Genesis 19, the story of Sodom, is discussed most extensively because it is often quoted as an explicit condemnation of homosexuality.

Genesis 19:1-29 Sodom
(Narrative Passages Said to Illustrate Wrongness of Homosexuality)

Choon-Leong Seow (1996) summarizes this passage in the following way: Angels are sent from heaven to verify the reputation of Sodom and Gomorrah for sinfulness. The narrative characterizes the cities as wicked and sinful, but does not detail the exact nature of those sins. Lot meets the visitors and invites them to stay with him, as is required by the laws of hospitality of the time. That night, the trouble starts. The men of the city surround Lot's household and demand that the strangers be brought out so that they "may know them" (*Genesis 19:5*). Lot begs the mob not to harm his guests and offers his two daughters in place of the strangers. The mob persists. The angels strike the individuals within the mob blind, and Lot and his family escape town (except of course for his wife who is turned into a pillar of salt).

There is consensus among many respected biblical scholars that the point of this story is not to condemn homosexual acts. Boswell (1980) notes that there are at least twenty-seven references to Sodom throughout the Hebrew Scriptures and none of those references indicate that the sin of Sodom is homosexuality. The sins of greed, injustice, inhospitality, insensitivity to the need and pain of others, and general wickedness are all catalogued as sins of Sodom; but, homosexuality is not (Boswell, 1980; Countryman, 1988; Hasbany, 1989; Helminiak, 1994; Jung & Smith, 1993; Seow, 1996; Spong, 1991). Yet, popular perceptions of it as a condemnation of homosexuality persist.

The story of Sodom and Gomorrah had no connection to homosexuality at all until the 1 CE, when the Jewish philosopher and scrip-

---

1. Scripture quotations contained herein are from the New Revised Standard Version Bible, copyright 1989 by the Division of Christian Education of the National Council of Churches of Christ in the U.S.A., and are used by permission. All rights reserved. Citations next to the quoted text indicate the particular book, chapter, and passage of the text.

tural commentator Philo of Alexandria wrote his commentary on it (Bailey, 1955, pp. 21-25). Philo was concerned with elaborating the precise nature of the sins of Sodom and Gomorrah. His elaboration was based on his imagination of what those sins might have been. The images he constructed were so vivid that the early Christian Church fathers adopted them, and they have been passed on to this day.

The townsmen's threat of rape of the angels ought not to stand as justification for the condemnation and prohibition of consensual, loving relationships. It is unjust and bad logic to equate violence, aggression, and sexual assault with consensual sex practices. The association of the word Sodomy with homosexuality infuses into our language and culture false accusations based on fanciful and fallacious extrapolations of the meaning of a text offered by one author (Philo of Alexandria) two thousand years ago.

We will next briefly consider each of the other texts of terror in turn.

Leviticus 18:22; 20:13 (The Holiness Code)
(Legal Texts of Explicit Prohibition)

"You shall not lie with a man as with a woman; that is an abomination" (*Leviticus 18:22*). "If a man lies with a male as with a woman, both of them have committed an abomination; they shall be put to death; their blood is upon them" (*Leviticus 20:13*). These are the only texts in the Bible where male same-sex intercourse is explicitly forbidden. Both prohibitions are written within a series of injunctions intended to distinguish the Jews from the pagans among whom they were living (Boswell, 1980, p. 100; Helminiak, 1994, pp. 43-54; Horner, 1978, pp. 71-85; Seow, 1996, p. 18). These passages are concerned with protecting the purity of the Jewish community. Countryman (1988) describes purity as placing the fully human in the center of the social system, and dirt (what is perceived as not belonging in association with the people because it is unfamiliar, irregular, unhealthy, or otherwise objectionable) is cast outside. The ideas of purity and holiness contained in the Levitical code are culturally conditioned (Boswell, 1980; Helminiak, 1994; Horner, 1978; Jung & Smith, 1993; Seow, 1996). The Hebrew word "toevah," which is translated as abomination, is not indicative of something particularly horrid, but rather indicates ritual uncleanness–as in eating unclean food, or engaging in intercourse during unclean times (Boswell, 1980, p. 100; Countryman, 1988, p. 30). The weight given to many of the Levitical prohibitions has already been reinterpreted within the context of contemporary cultural practices.

Romans 1:18-32
(Lists of Inappropriate and Wrongful Behavior)

In this passage Paul is writing about the immorality of the pagan Gentiles: "For this reason God gave them up to degrading passions: Their women exchanged natural intercourse for unnatural, and in the same way also the men, giving up natural intercourse with women, were consumed with passion for one another. Men committed shameless acts with men and received in their own persons the due penalty for their error" (*Romans 1:26-27*). Seow (1996, p. 24) reminds us that Paul is describing the ritual practices of pagan morality and that he is describing a culturally conditioned point of view. Boswell (1980, p. 109) argues that this passage is not a discussion of "gay persons but only homosexual acts committed by heterosexual persons" acts not consistent with their "nature." Horner (1978, p. 104) suggests that the passage is intended to teach about the consequences of promiscuity–of any sexual variation. The point is that the passage is not necessarily, or even probably, a condemnation of LGBT[2] relationships and expressions of love, but rather a condemnation of irresponsible (unnatural) sexual acts.

1 Corinthians 6:9-11

"Do you not know that wrongdoers will not inherit the kingdom of god? Do not be deceived! Fornicators, idolaters, adulterers, male prostitutes, sodomites (malakoi, arsenokoitai), thieves, the greedy, drunkards, revilers, robbers–none of these will inherit the kingdom of God" (*1 Corinthians 6:9-11*). This is a list of those wrong doers (and wrong doings) that will be excluded from heaven (Seow, 1996, p. 24). Malakoi, translated as sodomite, more likely refers to men who are morally weak, whose behavior is less than respectable overall (Boswell, 1980, pp. 106-107; Helminiak, 1994, p. 85; Jung & Smith, 1993, p. 75). Arsenokoitai, the word translated as pederasts, is literally untranslatable (Waetjen, 1996, p. 109). Seow (1996) surmises that Paul may have coined the word himself, combining the words aresn (male) and koitos (bed). It appears that in his use Paul is referring to an action that any man might choose to perform, whatever orientation, a perversion that could be taken to be self-evidently abnormal and diseased (Martin, 1996, p. 118). This appears to be more appropriately analogous to non-consensual sexual behavior, or perhaps sexual harassment, than to long-term committed relationships.

1 Timothy 1:8-11

This is another list with a word translated as sodomite: ". . . the law is laid down not for the innocent but for the lawless and disobedient, for the godless and sinful, for the unholy and profane, for those who kill their father or mother, for murderers, fornicators, sodomites [arsenokoitai], slave traders, liars, perjurers, and whatever else is contrary to the sound teachings that conform to the glorious gospel . . ." (*1 Timothy 1:9–11*). The text is a general call to avoid misleading the community in moral matters. It commends caution and careful discernment, not premature judgements (Jung & Smith, 1993, p. 77). It is a call to refrain from abusive sexual acts (Helminiak, 1994, p. 85).

Considered individually or together, these passages say nothing about long term LGBT[2] relationships based on love, caring, commitment, and fidelity. While they have been used to argue that homosexuality is bad, in fact, they say relatively little about homosexual behaviors. They do address the proper relationships among neighbors and between individuals and strangers. They do condemn violence and certain forms of sexual behavior: behaviors that are characterized as carrying excessive violence and lacking in commitment to love and fidelity.

Because many aggressive anti-homosexual factions so vociferously cite the texts of terror as a justification for their condemnations of LGBT[2] relationships as immoral, early work focused on refuting those claims. Scholarship is only now emerging that goes beyond a defensive posture. The next section highlights key points from that body of scholarship.

TEXTS OF EMPOWERMENT

The same-sex, loving relationships in Hebrew and Christian Scriptures do not look exactly like lesbian, gay, bisexual, and transgendered relationships look today. But patterns of heterosexual relationships as described in those scriptures do not look the same as lived today either. Virginia Mollenkott (1992) identified more than 18 different forms of families mentioned or implied in Hebrew or Christian scriptures. Patterns of relationship, both heterosexual and LGBT[2], have changed over the past two thousand years. The pattern of relationships that any of us call family do not look or act the same as they did in times of these scriptures.

I refer to the passages that can be read as affirming of lesbian, gay, bisexual, and transgendered relationships, as "texts of empowerment." John Boswell (1980) and Tom Horner (1978) were among the first scholars to draw attention to the relationships between David and Jonathan, and Ruth and Naomi. Nancy Wilson (1995) cites over forty such passages. Some of the more extensive passages include *I Samuel 18-20*, *II Samuel 1:26* (David and Jonathan); the *Book of Ruth* (Ruth and Naomi's relationship); *Acts 8:26-40* (Philip baptizes an Ethiopian Eunuch); *Matthew 8:5-13*, and *Luke 7:1-10* (cure of a centurion's male companion).

Space limitations preclude a detailed analysis of each of these, so I have chosen to focus on the story of Ruth and Naomi. There are very few women included in the Hebrew and Christian scriptures, so, when they are included, the story they tell is of particular importance.

The Book of Ruth

Horner (1978) and West (1997) offer similar summaries of this narrative. The story begins with Naomi, her husband, and sons leaving Palestine, and moving to Moab to escape the famine. The husband dies. Naomi's sons marry Moabite women. Ten years pass, and the sons die. Naomi is widowed, with no sons, no heirs to care for her. As childless widows, Naomi and her daughters-in-law, Orpah and Ruth, are on the margins of their society (West, 1997, p. 53). Naomi decides to return to Bethlehem, her hometown, and encourages Orpah and Ruth to leave her and to try to find new husbands. Orpah bids her goodbye. Ruth turns to Naomi and says:

> Do not press me to leave you or to turn back from following you! Wherever you go, I will go; and wherever you lodge, I will lodge; your people will be my people, and your God, my God.

> Where you die, I will die, and there will I be buried. May the Lord do thus and so to me, and more as well, if even death parts me from you! *(Ruth 1:16-17)*

There are two important things to note about this passage. First, the Hebrew word that describes Ruth's connection to Naomi is the same word used in *Genesis 2:24* to describe the relationship of a man and woman in marriage (West, 1997, p. 53). Second, this is an expression of love between two women. Heterosexual culture has tacitly recognized the passion and commitment embodied in this quotation by co-opting it for use in marriage ceremonies. It is time to recognize the original nature of that relationship.

The story doesn't end there. Naomi and Ruth return to Bethlehem and look up Boaz, a distant relative (a middle aged unmarried man). In ancient Israel there was a law that required the brother of a dead man to marry his widow and have a child by her to carry on the male lineage of the clan *(Deuteronomy 25:5-10* quoted in West, 1997, p. 56). The application of that law to the circumstances of Naomi, Ruth, and Boaz is somewhat ambiguous, but Naomi used it to send Ruth to see Boaz at night, and eventually Ruth bears Boaz's son.

How did the town's people react to all of this? They proclaimed, "Blessed be the Lord . . . for your daughter-in-law who loves you, who is more to you than seven sons . . ." *(Ruth 4:15)*. The townswomen name the child Obed, saying "A son has been born to Naomi" *(Ruth 4:17)*. These proclamations can be taken as an acknowledgment of Naomi's spousal relationship to Ruth (West, 1997, p. 59). Naomi and Ruth continue to live together under the patronage of Boaz. Even if the relationship between Ruth and Naomi is not sexual (which cannot be known for certain), there is certainly a powerful affectional preference between these two women.

Nancy Wilson (1995) shares a last word left by an old maid who died in Boston during the Victorian era. This woman and a friend shared an apartment together "for economic reasons." They were pitied much of their lives. On her tombstone, she had inscribed, "I haven't *missed* as much as you think!" From this quote, I suggest the following lesson: If it looks like love, speaks like love, acts like love, it probably is love, and it probably acts like love in *all* of its manifestations. We should proclaim and celebrate that love instead of rationalizing it away.

Some key themes in the other texts of empowerment are discussed below.

I Samuel 18-20, II Samuel 1:26

"When David had finished speaking to Saul, the soul of Jonathan was bound to the soul of David, and Jonathan loved him as his own soul" (*1 Samuel 18:1*). "Jonathan made David swear again by his love for him for he loved him as he loved his own life" (*1 Samuel 20:17*). And at their parting, ". . . they kissed each other, and wept with each other" (*1 Samuel 20:41*). The relationship between David and Jonathan is quite passionate. But might they not have been simply friends? Horner (1978, p. 28) replies to that question: "when two men come from a society that for two hundred years lived in the shadow of a culture which accepted homosexuality; when one of them–who is the social superior of the two–makes a public display of his love; when the two of them make a lifetime pact openly; when they meet secretly and kiss each other and shed copious tears at parting; when one of them proclaims that his love for the other surpassed his love for women– and all of this is present in the David-Jonathan liaison–then we have every reason to believe that a homosexual relationship existed."

Matthew 8:5-13, Luke 7:1-10

"Lord, my servant is lying at home paralyzed, in terrible distress" (*Matthew 8:5*). In *Matthew 8:5-13* and *Luke 7:1-10* the same story is told about the centurion who approaches Jesus so that his "servant" might be cured. It would be odd for a centurion, a high military official, to be so caring about a slave. Approaching a Jewish miracle worker for a cure meant that the centurion was risking profound ridicule (Horner, 1978). Horner notes that in Matthew's version of the story, the earlier account, directed to a Greek-speaking Jewish audience, the word for servant is "pais"–"boy," or "servant," and also "lover." Luke, writing in a much more Greek milieu, changes the word "pais" to the more neutral "doulos" ("servant" or "slave"), aware of its homosexual implications to any reader with a Greek background. The actions of Jesus in the story affirm the request and the relationship between the centurion and his "servant"/lover.

Acts 8:26-40

In this passage an angel of the Lord directs Philip to baptize an Ethiopian Eunuch (a group specifically excluded from membership in the people of Israel for sexual reasons by *Deuteronomy 23:1*). This entire passage is about the inclusion in the Church of the excluded. Not only is a racially/ethnically excluded group embraced, but that person is also a sexually excluded individual (Wilson, 1995).

What are the implications of these reflections on the meaning of these scriptural passages? Paul Spector (1997) argues that human rights education should be anchored in local cultures through appeals to local scriptures, constitutional foundations, and laws. Hebrew and Christian scriptures have been used to exclude LGBT[2] persons from the constitutional and legal protections of human rights. The texts of empowerment stand in contrast to the texts of terror offering an explicit affirmation of LGBT[2] relationships, and an anchor for their inclusion in human rights. Social workers have a responsibility to develop their knowledge about these scriptures and their meanings, and a role in challenging the abrogation of the dignity of LGBT[2] persons and in supporting the promotion and protection of their human rights.

CONCLUSIONS

The argument of this article is that a careful reading of Hebrew and Christian scriptures permits and supports the conclusion that LGBT[2] relationships hold the same moral possibilities as do heterosexual relationships. The texts of terror condemn acts of violence and violations of prescriptions of ritual purity, but not LGBT[2] relationships grounded in fidelity. The acts that are condemned have nothing to do with personal identity or relationships based on love. The texts of empowerment describe *and affirm* loving, faithful relationships that today would be described as lesbian, gay, bisexual, transgendered, or two-spirited.

As much as I would like the weight of the discussions in this article to convert readers to believing that Hebrew and Christian scriptures are embracing of sexual diversity, I recognize that one short piece of writing cannot accomplish that. As a lesbian, I am also wary of imposing conversion on those who are not seeking personal change. It is my hope that this article will encourage further study and reflection on the range of possible meanings of both the texts of terror and the texts of empowerment, and encourage one to carefully consider their implications. Consider that in the 1600s groups quoted the story of Ham in Genesis to justify defining Africans as subhuman without souls and to legitimate enslaving them (Wilson, 1995). Earlier in this century, groups quoted passages throughout the Hebrew and Christian scriptures to justify defining women as inferior human beings who appropriately belonged to men as their property (Mollenkott, 1992). History demonstrates that the meanings ascribed to scriptural passages change over time.

It is time to move beyond the use of Hebrew and Christian scriptures to define LGBT[2] folks as immoral, which acts to deny the veracity of their human rights. It is time to emphasize the texts of empowerment that stand as an explicit affirmation of LGBT[2] relationships, and an anchor for their inclusion in human rights, to build a culture of human rights that includes LGBT[2] persons. A culture of human rights would espouse values and embody social institutions (family, education, government, religion, economy, and social welfare) that promote and protect individual and communal human rights, that celebrate common human values as they are manifest through the diversity of human cultures, and that provides venues for empowerment and redress of grievances. Shulamith Koenig (1997, pp. xv-xvi) offers three principles to further the development of a culture of human rights:

1. Human rights constitute the common heritage of all humankind;
2. Human rights should frame human discourse and dialogue;
3. Human rights are needed to protect people from harm and to help them protect themselves.

Human Rights as a Common Heritage

The particulars of human rights are socially defined, but the principle of human rights is universally affirmed. The principle of human dignity is articulated in each of the major world religions (Wronka, 1995). It is the common heritage of LGBT[2] persons as well.

Human Rights as the Frame of Human Discourse and Dialogue

Employing human rights as the framework within which hate crimes and violence are addressed shifts the focus of the discussion from inappropriate critiques of the morality of particular acts to respect for human dignity, the dignity of all, including LGBT[2] persons.

Human Rights Protect People From Harm

Human rights are inherently about relationships (Meintjes, 1997) and about the distribution and use of power within relationships between individuals, groups, society, and the state. Human rights are, in the end, what we accord each other in the context of our cultures and political contexts (Spector, 1997). Human rights articulate an internationally affirmed paradigm of values and principles for advocacy in challenging anti-LGBT[2] rhetoric and hate crimes.

The precepts and values of human rights expressed in the United Nation's *Universal Declaration* are central to social work's professional identity (Witkin 1998). Freedom from the abuse of power, provision of basic necessities, and solidarity are inseparable from social work theory, values, ethics, and practice (Witkin; 1998, Wronka, 1995). Social workers have a significant role in ensuring that this common heritage is equitably accessible to all human beings, including LGBT[2] persons. It is time for social workers to actively join with groups such as the Human Rights Campaign, the National Gay and Lesbian Task Force, Amnesty International's OutFront, the International Gay and Lesbian Human Rights Commission, American Civil Liberties Union's Lesbian and Gay Rights Project, and others as they confront the perpetrators and sources of hate crimes and work to advance the cause of human rights.

REFERENCES

Bailey, D. S. (1955). *Homosexuality and Western Christian tradition.* New York: Longmans, Green & Company.

Boswell, J. (1980). *Christianity, social tolerance, and homosexuality: Gay people in Western Europe from the beginning of the Christian era to the Fourteenth Century.* Chicago: University of Chicago Press.

Countryman, L. W. (1988). *Dirt, greed and sex: Sexual ethics in the New Testament and their implications for today.* Philadelphia: Fortress Press.

Goss, R. (1993). *Jesus acted up: A gay and lesbian manifesto.* San Francisco: Harper San Francisco.

Halsall, P. (1998). Lesbian, gay, and bisexual Catholic handbook. (http://www.bway. net/~halsall/lgbh.html)

Hasbany, R. (Ed.). (1989). *Homosexuality and religion.* Binghamton, NY: Harrington Park Press.

Helminiak, D. (1994). *What the Bible really says about homosexuality.* San Francisco: Alamo Square Press.

Horner, T. (1978). *Jonathan loved David: Homosexuality in Biblical times.* Philadelphia, PA: Westminister Press.

Jung, P. B., & Smith, R. F. (1993). *Heterosexism: An ethical challenge.* Albany, NY: State University of New York Press.

Koenig, S. (1997). Foreword. In G. J. Andreopoulos & R. R. Claude (Eds.), *Human rights education for the twenty-first century* (pp. xii-xvii). Philadelphia: University of Pennsylvania Press.

Martin, D. B. (1996). Aresnokoites and Malakos: Meanings and Consequences. In R. L. Brawley (Ed.), *Biblical ethics and homosexuality: Listening to scripture* (pp. 117-136). Louisville, KY: Westminster John Knox Press.

Meintjes, G. (1997). Human rights education as empowerment: Reflections on Pedagogy. In G. J. Andreopoulos & R. R. Claude (Eds.), *Human rights education for the twenty-first century* (pp. 64-79). Philadelphia: University of Pennsylvania Press.

Mollenkott, V. (1992). *Sensuous spirituality.* New York: Crossroads Press.

National Council of the Churches of Christ in the U.S.A., Division of Christian Education. (1989). *New revised standard version Bible.* New York: Oxford University Press.

Perry, M. (1998). *The idea of human rights: Four inquiries.* New York: Oxford University Press.

Seow, C. L. (1996). Textual Orientation. In R. Brawley (Ed.), *Biblical ethics & homosexuality: Listening to scripture* (pp. 17-34). Louisville, KY: Westminster John Knox Press.

Spector, P. (1997). Training of trainers. In G. J. Andreopoulos & R. R. Claude (Eds.), *Human rights education for the twenty-first century* (pp. 176-193). Philadelphia: University of Pennsylvania Press.

Spong, J. S. (1991). *Rescuing the Bible for fundamentalism: A bishop rethinks the meaning of Scripture.* San Francisco: Harper San Francisco.

United Nations. (1948). *Universal declaration of human rights.*

Waetjen, H. (1996). Same-sex sexual relations in antiquity and sexuality and sexual identity in contemporary American society. In R. Brawley (Ed.), *Biblical ethics & homosexuality* (pp. 103-116). Louisville, KY: Westminster John Knox Press.

West, M. (1997). The Book of Ruth: An example of procreative strategies for queers. In R. E. Goss & A. A. S. Strongheart (Eds.), *Our families, our values: Snapshots of queer kinship* (pp. 51-60). New York: Harrington Park Press.

Wilson, N. L. (1997). Queer culture and sexuality as a virtue of hospitality. In R. E. Goss & A. A. S. Strongheart (Eds.), *Our families, our values: Snapshots of queer kinship* (pp. 21-33). New York: Harrington Park Press.

Witkin, S. L. (1998). Human rights and social work. *Social Work 43*(3), 197-202.

Wronka, J. (1995). Human rights. In R. L. Edwards (Ed.), *Encyclopedia of Social Work, 19th Edition* (pp. 1405-1418). Washington, DC: NASW Press.

Wronka, J. (1998). *Human rights and social policy in the 21st century.* New York: University Press of America.

Language, Violence, and Queer People: Social and Cultural Change Strategies

Dean Pierce

SUMMARY. The lives of queer people are too frequently filled with violence–physical attacks, social discrimination, and hate-filled verbal assaults. Language serves multiple purposes in the violence that is directed at queers. While the words themselves become instruments of psychological harm, they, in turn, are used to rationalize or justify acts of physical violence and social discrimination (Pierce, 1990). To analyze the issues regarding queer people, social discourse, and violence, this essay addresses: communication rules about queers and a formula for change in the discourse; the history of changing labels and meaning; enforcers of the dominant discourse and its rules of communication; and the role social workers should play in challenging and shaping the discourse. *[Article copies available for a fee from The Haworth Document Delivery Service: 1-800-342-9678. E-mail address: <getinfo@haworthpressinc. com> Website: <http://www.HaworthPress.com> © 2001 by The Haworth Press, Inc. All rights reserved.]*

KEYWORDS. Social discourse, violence, communication rules, queer people

INTRODUCTION: VIOLENCE AND FREE SPEECH

The lives of queer people are too frequently filled with violence–physical attacks, social discrimination, and hate-filled verbal assaults.

Dean Pierce, PhD, is affiliated with the School of Social Work, University of Nevada Reno.

[Haworth co-indexing entry note]: "Language, Violence, and Queer People: Social and Cultural Change Strategies." Pierce, Dean. Co-published simultaneously in *Journal of Gay & Lesbian Social Services* (Harrington Park Press, an imprint of The Haworth Press, Inc.) Vol. 13, No. 1/2, 2001, pp. 47-61; and: *From Hate Crimes to Human Rights: A Tribute to Matthew Shepard* (ed: Mary E. Swigonski, Robin S. Mama, and Kelly Ward) Harrington Park Press, an imprint of The Haworth Press, Inc., 2001, pp. 47-61. Single or multiple copies of this article are available for a fee from The Haworth Document Delivery Service [1-800-342-9678, 9:00 a.m. - 5:00 p.m. (EST). E-mail address: getinfo@haworthpressinc.com].

Queer-bashing can be conceptualized as a range or continuum of violent and abusive behaviors. These behaviors range from the verbal abuse of name calling (or psychological labeling), through acts of social and legal discrimination, to physical violence and murder. Language serves multiple purposes in the violence that is directed at queers. While the words themselves become instruments of psychological harm, they, in turn, are used to rationalize or justify acts of physical violence and social discrimination (Pierce, 1990).

This conception of queer-bashing poses questions regarding the American value of political free speech and the role of language in the violence that is directed at queers. Supposedly, each person has the right to speak freely, even if such speech might lead to harm to others. Our political system, however, limits speech if it poses a clear and present danger to others, or if it creates a climate of or causes sexual harassment. There is no consensus on action regarding hate speech or harassment aimed at queer people (Siegel, 1991). Although some states have passed statutes about hate-based crime, the issue of hate filled language has not been settled. Yet, for queers, certain words and the meanings they contain are clearly destructive of life, in its spiritual, psychological, and physical forms.

Implicit in the question about free speech is that some speakers have not been listened to, some people and their words have been silenced. For all of us in a so-called free society, the right to speak, the right to use almost any words we choose, the right to share knowledge about ourselves is held to be fundamental to our interactions as a free people. However, in this country, queer voices and healthy, positive commentary about queers are excluded from the conception of free speech.

An exploration of social discourse is critical to understanding why such commentary is absent. The words and meaning used in social discourse about a group of people reflects the worth and meaning a culture assigns to it. Social discourse about a group is maintained by rules of communication. These rules determine how to define group behavior, which words to use in polite conversation, and what topics, if any, can be publicly addressed. These rules, of course, are learned through socialization, including parenting and education, and are enforced by legal and religious institutions and by traditional scholarship and social service programs. Foucault refers to these related processes as a dominant discourse (Foote & Frank, 1999).

The dominant discourse, however, does not necessarily go unchallenged and should not be viewed as static and unchanging. For example, Ann Hartmann (1992) writes:

> Another example of the hegemony of global, unitary knowledge has been the invisibility of women and of people of color in the social sciences. . . . Other examples include the definition of homosexuality as a disease with resulting elaborate and even destructive protocols for cure.
> The political nature of knowledge is well illustrated by the fact that each of these privileged truths has been challenged, not primarily by alternate theories from the sciences but by sociopolitical movements that lead to what Foucault (1980) called the insurrection of subjugated knowledge. The women's movement encouraged women to break silence and tell their stories. . . . The civil rights movement and the rich flowering of African American literature has begun to make visible the African American experience (Collins, 1990). . . . Gay and lesbian pride, which was sparked by the Stonewall resistance, potentiated the insurrection of yet another subjugated knowledge and the official depathologizing of homosexuality. (p. 483)

Challenges to the dominant discourse indicate cultural change and, in a sense, point to a different way to conceptualize freedom of speech in social discourse. In other words, free speech is not possible when the rules of communication in the dominant discourse create a conversational monopoly based in censorship and silencing to control communication about a group.

To analyze these issues regarding queer people, social discourse, and violence, this essay addresses the following:

- communication rules about queers and a formula for change in the discourse;
- the history of changing labels and meaning;
- enforcers of the dominant discourse and its rules of communication; and
- the role social workers should play in challenging and shaping the discourse.

SOCIAL DISCOURSE AND COMMUNICATION RULES

Two interrelated issues face those who wish to communicate freely regarding lesbian, gay, bisexual, and transgender persons. One is how to transform or rehabilitate words that inaccurately and negatively label homosexuality. The other is how to expand the social discourse by modifying the current restrictive communication rules about homosexuality that stifle true freedom of speech.

First, how can we transform the meaning of the word homosexual so that it is positive to queer people, or how do we refurbish the word queer so that heterosexuals are not distressed by its impoliteness? To achieve the goal of using honest, comfortable words that show respect for lesbian and gay persons, the meaning and process of communicating about homosexuality has to be reconstructed. The process of transforming or restructuring language is a phenomenon Foucault refers to as reverse discourse, a move that reverses cultural meanings and uses these changes as an organizing principle for the achievement of positive attitudes (Myrick, 1996).

The second issue relates to the rules of communication we use in our social discourse about homosexuality. Theses rules, used either alone or in combination, distort and limit our conversation about queers, thereby, preventing free speech. There are eight rules or principles which guide conversations about queers:

1. Being polite (comfort vs. discomfort);
2. The rule of symbolic opposites;
3. Controversy over exactly "what" is being labeled;
4. The widely held view that homosexuality is unspeakable and untouchable;
5. Language similarity regardless of political persuasion or ideological stance;
6. The notion of Social Construction of Reality;
7. Denial that homosexuality makes a difference; and
8. Homosexuality as the "same-sex" adjective.

An examination of these rules also demonstrates how they can lead to a reverse discourse.

Being Polite: Comfort vs. Discomfort

One way speakers attempt to give a positive twist to comments about homosexuality is to use words that are generally thought of as polite. For example, most consider the word homosexual to be a more polite choice than the word queer. The use of the word queer makes many people uncomfortable, because to them it clearly reveals a deep disrespect for lesbian and gay people. The word homosexual is thought to be more acceptable. To some queers, however, the implicit pathological overtones of the term homosexual creates discomfort. At issue, of course, is that the language used to label queer persons both creates and explicitly exposes the attitudes held about them. Language that is considered to be polite only covers up negative attitudes and inhibits an open, honest discourse about queers.

Symbolic Opposites

One way heterosexuals have of speaking about homosexuals is to use what is called the rule of symbolic opposites. The majority group attempts to maintain power and self-coherence by creating a negative other (Myrick, 1996). The distinction between heterosexual and homosexual persons is not based on any true difference, but on hierarchical opposites. The term heterosexual becomes the primary term and represses the term homosexual. The homosexual person is produced in and through language to constitute the heterosexual's negative. Homosexuality then is a symbolic construction used to brand it as the enemy of heterosexuality or family (Flannigan-Saint-Aubin, 1992). This rule is a primary source of an unbalanced, mostly negative social discourse about queers.

Exactly "What" Is Being Labeled

Usually same-sex desire is seen as an activity or behavior only, not necessarily as an attribute that defines a person. People who experience same-sex desire, or who engage in same-sex encounters, are labeled homosexual, based exclusively on their sexual behavior. Competing for recognition is a definition that invokes a conception of personhood. Whereas the deviance definition invokes an act, the personhood definition leads to subjective and positive evaluations of individuals (Flannigan-Saint-Aubin, 1992; Halley, 1993; Myrick, 1996) and to a fuller social discourse.

Unspeakable and Untouchable

One of the longest-standing stereotypes about homosexuality is that same-sex relationships are both morally and literally unspeakable.

Such belief systems served as a means of silencing homosexuality and stifling any positive public speech about same-sex desire. This stereotype, however, permitted and encouraged negative speech about same-sex attraction. According to Cady (1992), the earliest written statement of this stigma comes from Peter Cantor who denounced same-sex desire as unspeakable and later from Lord Douglas's poetic reference to "the love that dare not speak its name" (p. 90).

The concept of same-sex sexuality as something untouchable has a similarly long history and is often expressed through the language of pollution and disease. For instance, in the mid-eleventh century Peter Damian stated that homosexuality "surpasses all (other vices) in uncleanness; it pollutes the flesh." Gregory IX called homosexuals "more unclean than animals." Ellis and Symonds stress that homosexuality "was a loathsome and nameless vice, only to be touched with a pair of tongs, rapidly and with precautions" (Cady, 1992, p. 91).

The pressure to keep homosexuality unspeakable and untouchable continues in the dominant discourse. By labeling homosexuality as unspeakable and untouchable, society has successfully silenced speech about queer persons and maintained the negative attitude, stereotypes, and language about same-sex love and desire (Johansson & Percy, 1994; Siegel, 1991).

Political Persuasion and Ideological Stance

Although many assume that liberal or progressive political ideologies expand the discourse and soften or modify negative attitudes and labels applied to lesbian and gay persons, evidence does not support this assumption. For example, Johansson and Percy (1994) found not one sentence on the subject of homosexuality that is even slightly positive in the writings of Marx, Engels, Lenin, Trotsky, Stalin, and Mao Tse-tung.

Social Construction and Subjugated Knowledge

Foucault argues that communication about sexuality which presents itself as objective, educative, and/or informational is in actuality a discourse in which one side of a politically-charged issue is stated as a value-free truth. He developed this point by examining nineteenth-century medical discourse, which labeled non-procreative sexuality, especially homosexuality, as deviant (Flannigan-Saint-Aubin, 1992; Myrick, 1996). From his work comes the notion of subjugated knowledge, in which alternative ideas about marginalized people are suppressed by traditional scholarship.

Denial That Being Queer Makes a Difference

Common to the discourse about homosexuality are efforts to dismiss it as making no significant difference in the lives of people. It is often stated that people are basically the same except for their sexual orientation, which plays no major role in understanding or relating to them. This attitude, obviously, devalues homosexuality and reduces the attention paid to it in social discourse.

Homosexuality as an Adjective

If homosexual means same-sex, then homosexual could be used as an adjective to denote a range of same-sex behaviors, social structures, and individuals. For example, male dorms (or barracks) are homosexual as are many social organizations, such as professional football and the Roman Catholic Church. Donovan (1992) notes that in its generic sense the word homosexuality includes numerous activities and social transactions between persons of the same gender. According to his line of thinking, the all-male board of directors, the businessman's club, the girl's school, the religious order, or church women's circles are all homosexual in this primary sense of the word.

We limit free speech on the issue of homosexuality through these rules of communication. It is not a guarantee of free speech when these principles protect and encourage those who denigrate homosexuality and restrict those who would speak positively about queers. In other words, thoughtless adherence to the political conception of free speech, without challenging the dominant discourse, has subsidized hate speech and related violence aimed at queers.

Using some of the eight principles discussed above, an equation for understanding the current cultural transformation (the dialectic of a reverse discourse) in relation to language about queers would be:

- Using 6 (social construct) and 5 (politics)
- To expand 3 (what is labeled) and eliminate 4 (unspeakable)

- Which, of course, challenges 1 (politeness) and
- 7 (denial), resulting in a cultural/linguistic transformation.

HISTORY OF QUEER LABELS:
A CHANGING SOCIAL DISCOURSE

The terms and definitions used in the discourse about queers have changed over time. Although negative attitudes may be more constant, recently terms have emerged that express conceptions of homosexuality as behavior, activity, personhood, or as a group of people. For men, the labels have included: sodomite, bugger, pederast, homosexual, sexual invert, faggot, gay, homophile, queer, and sexual minority. For women, the labels have ranged from: romantic friend, Boston marriage, female sexual invert, lesbian, gommorrhean, dyke, queer, and sexual minority. (See Table 1 for a list of some labels and the communication rule they represent.) Today, the struggle over labels reflects cultural tensions and change. It is important to keep in mind that the hegemony of the older discourse (and its labels) is being challenged.

The term sodomy, which first appears in Latin about 1175, was used in medieval theology and law to stigmatize homosexual activity. Sodomy is derived from *sodomite*, the word used in Genesis for an inhabitant of Sodom. It came to signify anyone who practiced the vice for which God allegedly destroyed the city. Philo Judaeus dubbed it "the crime against the laws of nature" (Johansson & Percy, 1994, p. 10), and it acquired a wider meaning in Christian usage. Sodomy in the broadest sense can signify any of various forms of nonreproductive sexual activity. In the late Middle Ages the notion prevailed that the sister city of Gomorrah had been a hotbed of lesbianism, so that, as late as the time of Marcel Proust, *gomorrhean* could mean lesbian.

A term preserved for men by British legal usage (dating from a 1533 statute of Henry VIII, which was the first English law against sodomy) was *bugger*, from Latin Bulgarus, originally a designation for religious heretics traced to the Bogomils of Bulgaria. Contrary to popular belief, any reference to *faggot* is found no earlier than in a 1914 dictionary of American slang. Semantically it has no tie to the faggots used in the middle ages to burn sodomites. The English Act of 1533 made hanging the penalty for buggery. Eighteenth-century writers adopted the term *pederast* to identify gay men. In Ancient Greek, pederast meant boy-lover or was paraphrased as a devotee of Socratic love. At about the

TABLE 1. History of Language

MALE			FEMALE		
DATE	WORD	RULE	DATE	WORD	RULE
1175	Sodomite	(3) what labeled: behavior and individual sin	Middle Ages	Gomorrhean	(3) what labeled; behavior and individual sin
1533	Bugger	(3) what labeled: behavior (4) Unspeak-able and Untouch-able	Eighteenth Century	Romantic Friends (Non-sexual)	(1) Polite Usage
Eighteenth Century	Pederast (Boy Love)	(3) what labeled: behavior and individual sin	Nineteenth Century	Boston Marriage (Non-sexual)	(1) Polite Usage
Mid-Nineteenth Century	Homosexual (Group illness or deviance)	(2) Symbolic Opposite of hetero-Sexuality and Family (3) From Individual Behavior to group illness (1) Later Usage	Mid-Nineteenth Century	Female Homosexual (Group illness or deviance)	(2) Symbolic Opposite (3) From Individual Sin to Group Illness (1) Later
Mid-Nineteenth Century	Sexual Invert	(2) Symbolic Opposite	Mid-Nineteenth Century	Female Sexual Invert	(3) Symbolic Opposite
Early Twentieth Century	Faggot	(3) & (4)	1870-1890	Lesbian	Now (5) up to 1775 = Wine
1930s-1950s	Homophile	(4) Symbolic Opposite			
1960s	Gay	(5)	1930s	Dyke	(5) Political Stance
Current	Queer	From 3 & 4 to 5		Queer	From 3 & 4 to 5

same time, women who experienced love for other women were re-ferred to as *romantic friends*. A century later such relationships were referred to as *Boston marriages* (Johansson & Percy, 1994).

In the mid-nineteenth century, the term *homosexual* was coined to designate persons oriented solely toward others of the same sex. The new concept negated the older view of the sodomite who committed a sin but was the same in mind or body as other human beings. A similar concept used during the same period was *sexual invert*. The concept when applied to women was *female homosexual*. Prior to the second half of the nineteen century, unalterable traits such as sexual orientation were not usually ascribed to any group (Johansson & Percy, 1994).

However, in the nineteenth century, as sexuality became a subject of discourse, homosexuality and heterosexuality were named by medical professionals, and identities came to be constructed on that basis. The medical establishment and sexologists, such as Kraft-Ebing and Freud, labeled same-sex desire as deviant. By the beginning of the twentieth century, same-sex desire and behavior were stigmatized and pathologized. As a result, lesbian and gay persons became subjects of psychological cures (Minton, 1992; Myrick, 1996) and were subjected to indefinite confinement in asylums, receiving electroshock, prefrontal lobotomies, castration, and other forms of treatment. The American Psychiatric Association, in 1973, and the American Psychological Association, in 1974, finally removed homosexuality from their official diagnoses (Johansson & Percy, 1994).

It was not until the end of the nineteenth century (between 1870 and 1890) that the term *lesbian* was applied to women. According to the Oxford English Dictionary, up until about 1775, the most frequent use of lesbian referred to a wine from the Greek isle of Lesbos (Simpson, 1989). Myrick (1996) notes that medical discourse which presented same-sex desire as homosexual identity, provided the definition that would lead groups of lesbian and gay persons to band together in urban communities, neighborhoods, and networks. Words such as *faggot* (c. 1915) or *dyke* (1930s) came into use in these homosexual communities.

From the 1930s through the 1950s, *homophile* was the term used by activists. Many in the homophile movement supported the prevailing belief that homosexuality was psychologically abnormal. They interpreted the condition of homosexuals as an unfortunate consequence of social discrimination and sought social assimilation (Seidman, 1993). Activists eventually scorned the term homosexual and came to use the term *gay*. Gay is a Middle English borrowing from Anglo-Norman French, which meant "fond of sexual pleasures and available for erotic liaisons," and in British English prostitutes were called "gay girls" (Johansson & Percy, 1994, p. 15). The contemporary American political context has narrowed the meaning of gay to someone who consciously identifies with a community fighting for its rights. *Community* replaced *minority*.

A new word, *queer*, has emerged to replace gay and refers to both males and females. Queer was first used by a group that broke off from the AIDS Coalition To Unleash Power (ACT UP) in March 1990 and styled itself Queer Nation. Use of this word has been met with mixed reactions, largely due to its past negative connotations, and its current politically radical ones (Donovan, 1992).

The competing words and definitions used today reflect tension and change as our culture grapples with the place of homosexuality in it. Conservative legal and medical professionals cling to homosexual and speak of a sexual minority. Many popular writers use gay and lesbian and refer to a community. Some activists strongly resist queer because they dislike the other meanings and associations it has, such as odd, eccentric, counterfeit. Young radicals increasingly prefer queer and nation. Homosexual connotes a plea for toleration and legal reform, gay a term of liberation demanding respect, and queer an expression of defiance and community.

CULTURAL CHANGE AND THE VOICES OF RESISTANCE

In spite of the silencing mechanisms of our cultural institutions, the debate about the meaning and worth of homosexuality has moved from the focus on perverted activity, to personhood, and on to political, community, and human rights. Currently, these competing definitions and conceptions reflect cultural change, with resistance centered in the language and activities of the religious and political opponents of homosexuality.

It is the practice of many groups (religious, national, or tribal) when faced with changing attitudes and language about non-normative behavior to shun and silence those who, in their view, violate these deeply held norms. Shunning and silencing is carried out by the group in power to limit and/or destroy the growth and spread of those who fail to observe traditional, valued behaviors. When a baby is shunned by parents, the so-called failure to thrive syndrome emerges. When a group is shunned, they literally cease to exist to those who reject them. For queers, the dominant discourse and the closet, both for individuals and for institutions, is the cultural process used to shun lesbians and gays.

In American culture this shunning and silencing has escalated to the public condemnation of homosexuality by the political activists of the religious right. America's conservative political element has consolidated old myths about homosexuals and refers to these as comprising the so-called homosexual agenda. They use erroneous information and traditional language in the social discourse to nurture the myths that add up to defining a group that is not oppressed or discriminated against and which is wealthy, psychologically abnormal, numerically insignificant, well organized, and politically powerful (see Table 2).

They use these myths to create fear among potential allies and work to maintain the cultural silence about and mistrust of queer people. They adhere to the old rules of communication and use traditional denigrating language in social discourse. They struggle to contain or limit the use of new, positive knowledge and words.

SOCIAL WORK AND QUEER DISCOURSE

Social work can act on its commitment to social justice by challenging the dominant discourse about queers and contributing to a quick-

TABLE 2. The Language of Resistance

MYTHS	REASONING	TRUTH
1. Special rights vs. civil rights	Limited definition of minorities	Minority equals oppression
2. High income level	Demonstrate privileged economic class	The income of lesbians equals that of other women
3. Lesbian/Gay super organization; "homosexual agenda"	Demonstrate access to political process and power	Variety of organizations, funding problems
4. Queers equal 1% of the population	Insignificant group for purposes of civil rights	Estimates range from 5% to 20%
5. Choice not birth	Abnormal choices regarding psychosocial development	Normal growth and development
6. Conversion is possible	A choice, not a natural group	Homosexuality is biologically determined
7. Will destroy businesses	Create fear among potential allies	Homosexuals operate and participate effectively in business
8. Affect education through recruiting	Create fear among potential allies	Homosexuals are valued parts of education

ening of cultural change in the form of a reverse discourse. At least three avenues are available to the profession, including:

1. Confronting those who enforce the rules of communication in the dominant discourse;
2. Ending the scholarly subjugation of knowledge; and
3. Breaking professional silence about queers.

Confronting Those Who Enforce the Dominant Discourse

As noted, a reverse discourse, or language transformation must occur in order to bring about a complete and balanced social discourse. To achieve such an open and comprehensive discourse requires strengthening the changes in language and culture that have already begun. It also requires challenging the actions of certain organized religions and their political allies who wish to maintain the dominant discourse. If social work can speak the language of empowerment about queers and counter slanderous assertions, then the distortions and failure to thrive syndrome that have been forced on homosexuals will be eradicated.

Ending the Scholarly Subjugation of Knowledge

Stanley L. Witken (1999) observes:

> The congruence of social work and social constructionism places the profession in a position to exercise leadership in the translation of constructionist thought into research and practice. Instead of emulating conventional forms of practice and enquiry, constructionism provides a vehicle for extending our unique professional identity and societal agenda. Who are better prepared than social workers . . . to amplify and legitimate subjugated knowledge; to challenge "oppressive constructions of gender, prejudice, sexuality, childhood, colonialism, race and racism, madness, (and) disability" . . .
>
> Ultimately, our vision of a just society and the kinds of relationships that such a society should support will guide our work. For social workers and social constructionists, this vision requires that we encourage, facilitate, and legitimate diverse knowledge traditions and forms of expression. There is no intrinsic

> reason, apart from the interests of particular groups, to privilege one form of . . . [communication] . . . or to limit knowledge claims to certain criteria. . . . We social workers believe that it is important for those who are silenced–for whatever reason–to have a voice. (p. 7)

His sentiments should also be applied to queers. Social work must join others to free subjugated knowledge and end the stranglehold on and distortion about queer lives that mark current scholarship. Young doctoral students eager to study queerdom should not be intimidated by warnings about dire consequences for their careers if they pursue such research. Mainstream social work journals must drop their practice of not publishing queer material. Social work educators and practitioners should add queer publications to their reading.

Breaking the Silence

The antidote to shunning and slander, of course, is embracing, including, and celebrating the presence of queers and positive knowledge about them in all aspects of professional social work. An example of how to do so is found in the words of the Reverend Jessie Jackson. He states:

> I have often been asked why I, as a non-gay person, have been insistent that the rainbow coalition have a lavender stripe. . . There are two reasons. First, I affirm them as members of the human family because it is morally right. Second, my sense of community and communication is inspired by my grandmother's quilt. Each patch was beautiful in its own right . . . Yet, alone, they were scraps. Sewn together, they formed a wondrous . . . quilt. (Jackson, 1991)

Simply start talking and asking about queers. Collect positive stories about queers and tell those to others. Read and speak about queer literature. Sponsor and attend speak-outs and conferences about queers.

Taken together, actions in these three arenas would go far to end the monopoly and censorship that have long defined and justified the marginalization of queer people. Moreover, they would contribute to the achievement of the profession's commitment to social justice.

REFERENCES

Cady, C. (1992). Teaching homosexual literature as a "subversive" act. In H.L. Minton (Ed.), *Gay and lesbian studies* (pp. 89-107). New York: The Haworth Press, Inc.

Collins, P.H. (1990). *Black feminist thought: Knowledge, consciousness, and the politics of empowerment.* New York: Unwin Hyman.

Donovan, J.M. (1992). Homosexual, gay, and lesbian: Defining the words and sampling the populations. In H.L. Minton (Ed.), *Gay and lesbian studies* (pp. 27-47). New York: The Haworth Press, Inc.

Flannigan-Saint-Aubin, A. (1992). The mark of sexual preference in the interpretation of texts: Preface to a homosexual reading. In H.L. Minton (Ed.), *Gay and lesbian studies* (pp. 65-88). New York: The Haworth Press, Inc.

Foote, C.E., & Frank, A.W. (1999). Foucault and therapy: The disciplining of grief. In A.S. Chambon, A. Irving, & L. Epstein (Ed.), *Reading Foucault for social work* (pp. 175-203). New York: Columbia University Press.

Foucault, M. (1980). *Power/knowledge: Selected interviews and other writings.* New York: Pantheon Press.

Halley, J.E. (1993). The construction of heterosexuality. In M. Warner (Ed.), *Fear of a queer planet: Queer politics and social theory* (pp. 82-102). Minneapolis/London: University of Minnesota Press.

Hartmann, A. (1992). In search of subjugated knowledge. *Social Work, 37,* 483-484.

Jackson, J. (1991). What do gay rights have to do with civil rights? *The Advocate, 570,* 90.

Johansson W., & Percy, W.A. (1994). *Outing: Shattering the conspiracy of silence.* New York/London: Harrington Park Press.

Minton, H.L. (1992). The emergence of gay and lesbian studies. In H.L. Minton (Ed.), *Gay and lesbian studies* (pp. 1-6). New York: The Haworth Press, Inc.

Myrick, R. (1996). *AIDS, communication, and empowerment: Gay male identity and the politics of public health messages.* New York/London: Harrington Park Press.

Pierce, D. (1990). Who speaks for lesbian/gay adolescents: Voices to be silenced, voices to be heard. *Women and Language, 13,* 35-39.

Seidman, S. (1993). Identity and politics in a "postmodern" gay culture: Some historical and conceptual notes. In M. Warner (Ed.), *Fear of a queer planet: Queer politics and social theory* (pp. 105-142). Minneapolis/London: University of Minnesota Press.

Siegel, P. (1991). Lesbian and gay rights as a free speech issue: A review of relevant caseload. In M.A. Wolf & A.P. Kielwasser (Eds.), *Gay people, sex, and the media* (pp. 203-259). New York/London: Harrington Park Press.

Simpson, J.A., & Weiner, E.S.C. (Eds.). (1989). *The Oxford English dictionary* (2nd ed.). New York: Oxford University Press.

Witken, S.L. (1999). Constructing our future. *Social Work, 44,* 5-8.

REALITIES OF HATE CRIMES

Sticks and Stones Can Break Your Bones: Verbal Harassment and Physical Violence in the Lives of Gay and Lesbian Youths in Child Welfare Settings

Gerald P. Mallon

SUMMARY. Utilizing the narratives of 54 youths and 88 child welfare professionals, this article explores the experiences and lives of gay and lesbian youths in child welfare agencies in three cities–New York, Los Angeles, and Toronto–who have been subject to verbal harassment and physical violence within those systems. The author additionally explores the multiple layers of verbal harassment and violence in both the youths' families and in the foster care system, offering recommendations to social work practitioners interested in creating gay and lesbian affirming environments. *[Article copies available for a fee from The Haworth Document Delivery Service: 1-800-342-9678. E-mail address: <getinfo@haworthpressinc. com> Website: <http://www.HaworthPress.com> © 2001 by The Haworth Press, Inc. All rights reserved.]*

Gerald P. Mallon, DSW, is Assistant Professor at the Hunter College School of Social Work in New York.

[Haworth co-indexing entry note]: "Sticks and Stones Can Break Your Bones: Verbal Harassment and Physical Violence in the Lives of Gay and Lesbian Youths in Child Welfare Settings." Mallon, Gerald P. Co-published simultaneously in *Journal of Gay & Lesbian Social Services* (Harrington Park Press, an imprint of The Haworth Press, Inc.) Vol. 13, No. 1/2, 2001, pp. 63-81; and: *From Hate Crimes to Human Rights: A Tribute to Matthew Shepard* (ed: Mary E. Swigonski, Robin S. Mama, and Kelly Ward) Harrington Park Press, an imprint of The Haworth Press, Inc., 2001, pp. 63-81. Single or multiple copies of this article are available for a fee from The Haworth Document Delivery Service [1-800-342-9678, 9:00 a.m. - 5:00 p.m. (EST). E-mail address: getinfo@haworthpressinc.com].

KEYWORDS. Violence, verbal harassment, gay and lesbian youths, child welfare settings

One need not look to rural Wyoming for examples of brutality towards gay and lesbian youths. Those young persons, and particularly the youths whom I have studied (Mallon, 1998), adolescents in child welfare settings, have always been at very high risk for verbal harassment and physical violence. Constantly negotiating life in an environment where the threat of violence is an ever-present reality, the gay and lesbian young people I interviewed reported never feeling completely secure or confident about their existence. Their sense of safety in child welfare settings (group homes, foster homes, and large congregate care centers) was tenuous and fragile.

This article explores the experiences and lives of gay and lesbian youths in child welfare agencies in three cities–New York, Los Angeles, and Toronto–that have been subjected to verbal harassment and physical violence within those systems. The author additionally explores the multiple layers of verbal harassment and violence in both the youths' families and in the foster care system, offering recommendations to social work practitioners interested in creating gay and lesbian affirming environments.

Many young people enter the foster care system because it offers sanctuary from abusive family relationships and violence that occurs in their homes. Rindfleisch (1993, p. 265) writes, "Once in placement, children and youths are presumed to be in an environment superior to that from which they were removed. So they are not thought to need protection beyond that provided by state licensing activities." For too many youngsters, the brutality they experienced prior to coming into a child welfare placement did not stop once they entered the system.

Lesbian and gay young people are targeted for attack specifically because of their sexual orientation (Comstock, 1991; Garnets et al., 1992; Herek, 1990; Herek & Berrill, 1992). North American culture, pervaded by a heterocentric ideological system that denies, denigrates, and stigmatizes gays and lesbians, simultaneously makes lesbians and gay men invisible and legitimizes hostility, discrimination, and even violence against them. Gay men and lesbians must assess issues of safety in their lives on an everyday basis. When gay or lesbian people engage in behaviors allowed for heterosexuals (such as same-gendered individuals walking down a street holding hands or kissing a same-gendered partner), they make public what Western society has prescribed as private. They are accused of flaunting their sexuality and are, thereby, perceived as deserving of or even asking for retribution, harassment, or assault.

The children in my study reported that verbal harassment was often inaugurated at home within their own family systems. Many of these young people reported that relatives and others in their community helped to increase the momentum of this violence by joining in the harassment. The extent to which gay and lesbian young people experienced verbal harassment and physical violence in foster care placements, by their peers and by staff charged with caring for them, was astounding to me. The stigma attached to being gay or lesbian often prevented them from reporting their victimization (Goffman, 1963). Many young people reported that when the abuse was acknowledged, the victims themselves were blamed. Consequently, at times, more than half of the informants in this study choose the apparent safety of the streets over the foster care system.

Tirades from family members, peers, and, in some cases, staff members that began with taunts such as "you fucking faggot," "bulldyke," "homo," and "queer" in some cases escalated into punches, beatings, burnings, and rape. Gay and lesbian young people deemed as disposable individuals, deserving of being jostled into line or kept in the closet, frequently found environments which were so poor, where the fit was so bad, that many felt as though they literally had to flee for their lives. Some of those who migrated to a safer environment found the safety and fit that they were searching for. Others found even less favorable complementarity (Meyer, 1996).

FEAR FOR ONE'S PERSONAL SAFETY LED TO HIDING

Seventy-eight percent of young people and 88% of Child Welfare professionals interviewed for this study reported that it was not safe for gay and lesbian adolescents in group homes or congregate care settings to self-identify as gay or lesbian. One professional from New York interviewed for this study linked the issue of safety with the phenomenon of hiding:

> In most agencies, it's just not safe for a gay or lesbian young person to be identified. If the other kids know that they are gay or

lesbian . . . they harass them, or worse. Sometimes when the staff find out they either treat the young person differently or close their eyes to some of the situations, which occur after-hours. It's just not safe for them to be out and because they are not out, then the staff believe that they don't exist.

Young people in New York, Los Angeles, and Toronto, where the study was conducted, concurred that they perceived a sense of real fear on the part of gay and lesbian young people. Several noted that, although some of their peers were open about their sexual orientation in social settings away from their group homes, they were closeted in their group home. Steven, a 17-year-old from New York, commented:

> People are afraid to tell people that they are gay. I mean I used to hang out in the Village with boys from my group home, but we never talked about being gay. The staff didn't know that we were gay. You made sure some of them didn't know because then they would make your life miserable. I tell you, sometimes the staff people were worse than the kids were.

In Los Angeles, Angelo made similar comments about his peers with respect to their fears:

> I knew people in my foster home and group home who were gay but they went out of their way to make it look like they were not gay. They were hiding it. They were afraid of getting beat up or discriminated against. There was a guy in my group home–he had a girl but we dated secretly.

VERBAL HARASSMENT AT HOME

Many gay and lesbian young people perceive that they are different even as young children. This difference separates them from their own families. In response to their perceived difference, families, who pre-scribe conformity amongst their members, frequently engage in verbal harassment as a means to keep them in line (D'Augelli & Hershberger, 1993; Pharr, 1988; Savin-Williams, 1994). Gayle, a 19-year-old young woman from New York, was warned to remain closeted:

> I told my grandmother that I was gonna come out of the closet and she said–Girl, you better get right back in!

Young people recalled, with vivid and often painful exactness, the experience of verbal antilocutions made against them by their immediate family members. Sharte recalled his mother's bitterness toward his behavior, which he perceived as normal:

> I was eight when I entered foster care. It was the relationship between me and my mother that was the primary reason for me coming into fostering care. We never talked about me being gay or anything, but there were certain things that my mother would say to me, that let me know, she knew. She would say things like: stop being a little girl, you know. Things like, you little sissy, I'm not raising a little girl, I'm not raising no punk.

The experience seemed to be standard for young men as well as for young women. Maura told a comparable story of parental rejection:

> My mother couldn't deal with the fact that I was a dyke, that's why I came into placement. She kept saying–why can't you act like a girl, I mean, she was always trying to get me to wear dresses and stuff, I mean, I just didn't feel comfortable. Every time I wore a dress I felt like a guy in drag. I just wished she could have let me be myself.

Although the majority of gay and lesbian young people interviewed for this study did not enter placement because they were thrown out of their homes, the threat that their disclosure might prompt such a reaction from their families was always a fear that kept many "in line" and in the closet. Coming out or being found out by family members in most cases precipitated a crisis (Fraser et al., 1991).

THE "GARBAGE" METAPHOR

The metaphor of the "throw away child" was common within the narratives of several young people who used "garbage" metaphors to describe their treatment by their families. Recalling the experience of feeling "dumped on," Tracey, a New York young person, said:

> My relationship with my family was not the greatest. I guess the best way to describe my relationship with my family was, they

were the dump truck and I was where they dumped all of their garbage. No one ever paid any attention to me, unless they were mad and then they would scream at me and dump on me. It wasn't that great.

Raul, a Puerto Rican young man, recalled the verbal abusiveness of his mother when he came out to her:

I have known that I am gay all of my life, but when I came out to my mother, she was not able to accept that fact, she went wild, screaming *maricon, pendejo*, all of these really terrible curses, I was her only son and all. She threw all of my clothes out in a big plastic garbage bag and threw me out. I had nowhere to live.

VERBAL HARASSMENT
FROM FOSTER AND ADOPTIVE PARENTS

Verbal harassment was so commonplace in group hómes, foster homes, and congregate care settings that most young people almost forgot to mention it. All but one of the young people interviewed noted that they had been the victims of verbal harassment because of their sexual orientation. Foster parents and even adopted parents were not immune from engaging in verbal harassment.

A Child Welfare professional from New York acknowledged that some foster parents asked to have some young people removed from their homes because they perceived them to be gay or lesbian. And Remee, a young person from Los Angeles, corroborated this acknowledgment with her own real life experience; she recalled:

There was only one foster home that I was in that it was bad. They found out I was gay cause I was talking on the phone to my girlfriend. The foster mother heard our conversation and immediately told my roommate to move out of our room. She said she thought I might get into a mood and want to have sex with her. I mean we had been roommates for two years. I wasn't attracted to her. But to make matters worse, then she called the agency to ask to have me removed because she said she didn't have a license to have gay people in her home.

VERBAL HARASSMENT FROM PEERS

Being different from your peers is hard when you are an adolescent; adolescents do not always tolerate difference. Overwhelmingly (93%), gay and lesbian adolescents interviewed experienced a great deal of verbal harassment from peers in their group homes, congregate care settings, or foster homes. James, an African-American young person from Los Angeles, conceptualized his ability to adapt to constant verbal abuse by describing it as a "protective shield":

> Kids noticed that I was not like other kids, they thought I was weird, then came all of those negative words: Faggot, homosexual, you know this and that. In every group home I have been in there has been harassment, but I learned to put up a shield and ignore it. But inside I remember it.

Child Welfare staff members corroborated these accounts of peers' verbal abusiveness, as illustrated by this statement:

> That's why in this particular program that they don't admit being gay, because this particular population would definitely be rough on them. When we bring it up, they laugh at the subject and make little cracks and things like that and you can tell the kids in the room who are kind of dealing with the subject, but they are so denigrated by the other kids that they would never come forth.

Another Child Welfare professional suggested that the jokes helped to deteriorate the young person's sense of self-esteem; he commented:

> There's jokes, sometimes there are intolerable jokes, both practical jokes and verbal jokes. It's really rough for gay kids. The other kids really torture them. It really gets to them. I have had kids who come back to their rooms after a weekend home visit and have anti-gay graffiti written on their walls, condoms filled with dishwashing liquid put on their doorknob, you know, just plain harassment.

THE "WELCOMING" PROCESS

Most young people reported that the verbal harassment and anti-locutions were worse when they first arrived, as Wilem recalled:

> Up at Mount Laurel, there was a lot of verbal harassment, espe-
> cially at first when I first came, then it dropped off, that was until
> they were angry with me, then it would all start up again–you
> fuckin' homo, suck my dick, you know, stuff like that.

Some young people reported that their peers alluded to their fear of
diseases as a factor in the process of verbal harassment. The myth that
HIV illness and AIDS is a gay disease remains a powerful falsehood
as this comment suggests:

> Well they were like, what they would call me is faggot, or you
> homo, or you suck this or you suck that. The straight kids were
> always saying things like–just keep your faggot shit on that side
> of the room, don't be bringing none of your faggot diseases or
> faggot shit in here.

Jared's experience, which suggested that his peers referred to religion
as a justification for their harassment, was a comment that was frequently heard from the young people interviewed for this study:

> I had to deal with a lot of verbal abuse–you faggot or kids telling
> me you should be ashamed of yourself or the religious fanatics
> saying that you are an abomination against the Lord. The break-
> ing point came when I started working, I mean I was out all day
> working and then I had to come back and listen to this shit–that's
> when I said forget it and I left.

THE CUMULATIVE EFFECTS OF VERBAL HARASSMENT

Continual verbal harassment erodes one's sense of self-worth, self-esteem, and internal sense of fit (Miranda, 1996; Wadley, 1996a, 1996b).
Constant badgering, name-calling, and snide remarks are injurious to
one's mental health. The old adage "sticks and stones can break my
bones, but names will never harm me" is not true. Names can and do
hurt. Although several young people reported how the constant harassment wore them down, this narrative from Angelo's interview best
illustrates this point:

> One weekend when I went on a home visit my roommate found a
> copy of *The Advocate* [a gay news magazine] and he passed it all

around to the other guys and they all wrote their comments on it like: Come to my room and bend over and I'll give it to you. That's when I decided to leave. They had me to the point where I was crying inside, but I wouldn't let them see it. It scared me more than it bothered me. But they never let up. In such a short time they made me feel so bad, it got to me. I was only there for two or three months.

Mike's comments spoke about the hurt that many youths experienced as they sought to find a good fit within an environment that was polluted by verbal harassment:

I get really tired of the harassment, I mean if somebody calls you something it really hurts a lot, even if it's true and even if you're proud of yourself, it really hurts a lot, you don't want to be reminded time and time again, you just want to live your life, you just want to do what you want to do, you don't want people nagging you all the time or asking you a whole bunch of questions, I mean it really gets on your nerves.

PHYSICAL VIOLENCE

Fear of Escalation from Verbal to Physical Abuse

In many cases, the gay and lesbian young people reported that they were fearful of the likelihood that verbal threats would turn into physical violence. When verbal harassment turned to physical violence, many young people left these environments in search of another where the threat of violence was not as impending. Gerald, a Trinidadian youngster from a New York agency, recalled that he left placement when the verbal harassment which he had been experiencing in his group home turned to hate graffiti on his bedroom walls:

Kids were always calling me fag and other hurtful things. Once I went to the city on a home visit and when I came back I found written on my wall the words, "Kill Fags." It was around the time that a friend of mine was killed and I thought, if they killed her and they have already been harassing me, maybe I'm next, so I left.

Gay and lesbian adolescents in out-of-home care Child Welfare settings are placed at special risk for violence not by any inherent factor related to their sexual orientation, but because of the biases, discriminatory behaviors, and inequalities of power in the agencies around them. More than one half (52%) of the young people interviewed indicated that they were victims of physical violence directly related to their gay or lesbian orientation.

Violence which occurred within Child Welfare agencies was in some cases perpetrated by other young people, in other cases by staff members. For many, physical abuse was seen as the last straw before they "absconded" to the streets. These young people's experiences resonated with the experiences (Fitzgerald, 1996; Holdway & Ray, 1992; Janus, Archambault, & Brown, 1995; Meston, 1988; Webber, 1991; Zide & Cherry, 1992) of other young people who exited out-of-home care. For the young people in this study, physical violence was the decisive factor that constituted a poor fit. At this point, many young people voluntarily fled their placements. Many felt that their lives depended upon leaving placement. The stories of these 27 young people are filled with pain. Their narratives chronicle the most heinous accounts of a poor environmental fit. They are stories about rape, violence, and fear.

Physical Violence by Family Members

For some young people, the violence which they experienced began with their own families. Families frequently react with violence toward the news that their child is gay or lesbian (Hetrick & Martin, 1987; Hunter, 1990; Hunter & Schaecher, 1987). A Child Welfare advocate for children in New York suggested that many families whom he saw in Family Court also participated in the process of physical abuse:

> We just keep seeing kids getting beat up and thrown out of their houses, kids getting beat up by their fathers for being gay or young lesbians getting sexually abused by male relatives trying to change them so they won't be gay. Or lesbians getting pregnant so they prove they are women. I mean gays and lesbians are different from other minority groups, if a kid is getting beat up because they are gay, who do they go to for services? They usually can't go home and tell why they are getting beat up.

Despite the fact that the primary goals in Child Welfare are to reunite children with their families whenever possible, family reunification was often not seen as an option for gay and lesbian children. One Child Welfare professional in New York gave this detailed overview of young people's estrangement from their families:

> Gay and lesbian kids have no way back. So while we talk about family reunification with somebody because they couldn't take their mother's drinking anymore, or their mother's boyfriend would come in and beat the hell out of them and they couldn't take it anymore. You can refer people like that to counseling and say you can all work this out. But where there was an issue of a kid being homosexual, forget it and it was so sad, because this kid was like painted into a corner and they needed somewhere they could not only receive validation of their own humanity again, but they needed some way that they could see past the present, they had to learn that their lives were not defined by their sexuality.

Young people recounted numerous stories of physical abuse by family members. Albert, a Canadian young man, recalled the pain he felt this way:

> When I came out, my stepmother hit me. I had never been hit before. And I just stood there and I was like shocked and then she hit me again and I was just like, why are you hitting me . . . I couldn't believe it. Things were never the same after that. I couldn't deal with it. I kept running away.

The stories of the young women interviewed suggest that family violence was a hardship that they also endured. As Wilma's story illustrates:

> When my family found out that I was a lesbian, they just went crazy. Even my brothers saw it as a reason to hit on me. My mother watched me constantly. She wouldn't even let me out by myself. We used to get into huge fights about my being gay, real physical: Hitting, punching, the works. Finally one day, I just thought, they are never gonna accept me and I left. I couldn't take it anymore, anywhere would have been better than there.

Physical Violence by Peers

The negative impact of peer culture within out-of-home care settings is well documented (Berkley, 1996; Mayer et al., 1978; Polsky,
1962; Schaefer, 1980) and powerful for all young people in placement.
Many of the most serious attempts at victimizing gay and lesbian
young people occurred during the evening hours when there were
fewer staff on duty and when young people knew that they could take
action against someone who was perceived to have stepped out of line.
Jose recalled this incident:

> At St. Peter's, they were all bullies there, I was getting beat up all
> the time, I was terrified at school and where I lived. I slept in the
> basement in the group home and one night this kid who had been
> bothering me took my pillow while I was sleeping and tried to
> suffocate me and then a whole bunch of other guys just started
> joining in, beating me, throwing stuff at me, I was crying and I
> was screaming–why don't you just kill me, why don't you just
> kill me? Because to tell you the truth, right then and there, at that
> point, I just wanted to die. This all started about me being gay, in
> fact the kid that they told to beat me up, was one that I was going
> out with. When I was younger it was worse, I would be sitting
> watching TV and older guys would come up to me and put their
> dick in my face, or they would slap my ass, or pinch it . . . I just
> got to a point that I thought–I'm just not going to take it anymore.

A common theme throughout these interviews was that young
people reported that peers who are questioning their own orientation,
or those who are very invested in hiding and who may be trying to
"pass" as heterosexual were often the most abusive. Maura, a young
lesbian, reported this:

> I had three kids who used to harass me, the worst ones, and I
> knew they were gay too, they are all in the life, I see them in the
> Village, they are in the closet and they are so scared to get bashed
> that they join in the bashing themselves, they make it so much
> more violent for the out people.

Physical Violence by Staff

Violence perpetrated by Child Welfare staff members was not uncommon. Since staff within Child Welfare settings have a great deal of

power over the lives of the young people for whom they care, they also have many opportunities to exploit this power. One Child Welfare veteran, reflecting on the perceived incidence of institutional abuse, made the following observations about the incidence of violence directed toward gay and lesbian youths:

> Then we send them to places like Mount Laurel to protect them from their families and what happens? They are beaten up there too! Not just by their peers, by the way, but also by the staff who are paid to care for them. So in lots of ways these young people are victimized twice, first by their families and then by the Child Welfare system.

Both young people and professionals interviewed reported that physical abuse carried out by staff was frequent. Sharte, a young man from New York, suggested that alleged physical restraints by staff members frequently escalated into episodes of physical violence:

> This one staff member is so homophobic. He and I never got along. We were always getting into these physical confrontations that ended with him restraining me, I guess it never went like it was supposed to go because he was always calling the cops on me and then I'd have to go to the station house, fill out all of this paperwork and go through these changes. It was really more like an assault than a restraint, a personal vendetta.

Although not all staff people participated in violence which was this flagrant, young people reported that some staff played an indirect role, by standing by and permitting the abuse to occur. Professional respondents from all three cities corroborated the accounts of physical abuse over and over again in interviews.

STAFF REFUSAL TO INTERVENE

Young people reported that they were not likely to receive help from staff when they brought verbal harassment or physical abuse issues to their attention, as Gerald's comments suggest:

> When I told the staff that I just couldn't take it anymore, that all of the guys were picking on me, they said why are they picking

on you? I said they're all calling me a faggot and a homo. They said–well, you shouldn't have told them that you're gay–what do you expect?

Several staff members corroborated these accounts and remarked that, on occasion, staff members sanctioned the violence by allowing it to happen, as was the case in this narrative:

I've heard situations where a child care worker sent other kids to really beat them up. We have one kid here who was actually beat up by other kids in his group home because of his orientation. He said to us that workers knew it was happening. They said there was nothing they could do about it. It was actually that there was nothing that they would do about it. There's a big difference.

RAPE OF YOUNG PEOPLE

The worst cases of staff perpetrating violence, however, were heard from those young people who reported being raped by staff members. Rape is not an uncommon form of violence directed at both lesbians and gay men (Comstock, 1991, pp. 198-203). The young people interviewed for this study were no exception. Of the 54 interviewed, four young people reported actual rapes; three young women and one young man. Several others reported that they lived in constant fear of this harrowing possibility. In recounting her experience with being raped by a male staff member, Sharice vividly recalled:

I had a man counselor and he knew about me, you know, about seeing women and all, and one day when everybody else was out on a trip he said I had an appointment with him and said that I had to stay behind. And we was talking and talking and talking, and so he asked me if I had ever been with a man and I was like, no and then he started to put his hands all over me and you know tried to molest me. When I resisted he started beating me up, but someone came in and stopped him. But he had already beat me up, I had all knots all over my head. He just kept telling me that I was not supposed to be with women, I was supposed to be with men and that this is not the life you is suppose to live. We had to take him to court and everything, he lost his job. Then when I went to another group home, they tried to do that again, and then after that I decided that I would not go to no more group homes.

Wilma, who was also raped by a staff member, reflected on her experience:

> I was abused in the group home by the male staff. I would get beat up, and you know I got raped in the group home by a staff member, by the custodian, by a man who worked there, you know the ones who clean up. When I told the counselors they would say oh, we don't believe you, you probably just wanted it, you was probably hot anyway, look at the kind of girl you are, cause you in here aren't you? It was just real bad. I ran away a lot because I got tired of being raped. I want to say that I don't understand why it is that every time in a group home, I see gays get raped more than straight people, especially like gay females, but the gay guys also, they get raped more than straight people do.

Rape was perpetrated by men on the women who were interviewed as a corrective for lesbianism. Perpetrators were under the delusion that if women whom they perceived to be lesbians had a sexual experience with one good man, which they believed themselves to be, then their "impediment" would be remedied.

The act of rape, one of the most disparaging experiences that one can endure, was also recounted by Ralph:

> The first place I was sent to, I was eight, was in _____. I was raped there by this counselor. He told me that if I told anybody that they would just keep me there or put me in another group home. I was there for five months and then I ran away, I was tired of being raped, I was repeatedly raped. Then I went to a foster home and it was real strict, I left there and went to another group home and there somebody tried to set me on fire. I was sleeping and they put lighter fluid on my bed and threw a match on me, I got burned on the leg [he points to an eight inch burn mark]. The staff didn't do nothing, they knew about it, they just moved my bed, but that's staff, you know? I didn't feel safe there, you kinda had to sleep with one eye open. I finally left. I was tired of that shit.

In an earlier interview, an advocate for gay and lesbian adolescents corroborated the above story, noting that this terrible case of abuse was a catalyst for starting an agency to "protect" gay and lesbian youths.

RECOMMENDATIONS

Professionals interested in creating safe environments for gay and lesbian youths must be prepared to work toward nothing less than organizational transformation. Transforming an organization from one that is overtly hostile to gay and lesbians to one which is affirming toward their identity is a process that takes time. Listed below are a few recommendations that can assist those interested in beginning the shift.

1. Work on developing an organization that has a zero level tolerance for violence.
2. Make clear in written policies that your organization has a no slur policy.
3. Provide a written sexual harassment and anti-discrimination policy for all staff and program clients.
4. Contract with outside consultants to provide on-going training for staff that focuses on gay and lesbian issues.
5. Speak to the needs of gay and lesbian clients in your organization's literature.
6. Make sure that visible signs of safety (i.e., gay and lesbian affirming posters) are posted in your organization's waiting room.
7. Recruit, hire, and train openly gay and lesbian staff at all levels of your organization.
8. Keep working at becoming a gay and lesbian affirming organization through continuous quality improvement efforts.

CONCLUSION

The life stories collected for this study depicted vivid illustrations of gay and lesbian young people's tribulations as they embarked on a constant search for environments that could provide them with "a good fit." When, and if, young people found a responsive environment, they suspended the search and recommenced with their lives. Conversely, when, and if, the young gay or lesbian person found themselves to be negotiating a life within a stress-filled, unnurturing and hostile environment, he or she either attempted to make an adaptation to that inhospitable environment or migrated to the next level in search of those environments that he or she perceived as sustaining and nourishing. They searched for a good fit on two tiers: internally and externally. On an internal plane, young people searched for fit within the context of their personal identity development; externally, they searched on three levels: within their family systems; within the out-of-home care Child Welfare systems; and, finally, on the streets where more than half dodged environments that were, for them, the quintessence of poor fit. Young people in the three cities from which the sample was drawn reported to have had both positive and negative experiences within all three external environments.

The dominant features of a good fit for gay and lesbian adolescents, as evidenced by the data presented in this study, are threefold: (1) Safety from physical violence or verbal harassment; (2) A chance to live within the context of an environment which provides the nutrients necessary for integrating one's gay or lesbian identity into all other areas of one's life without hiding or fear of differential treatment should one decide to disclose his or her gay or lesbian sexual orientation; and (3) The prospect of interacting with adults and peers who were affirming and nurturing of a gay or lesbian sexual orientation. Concurrently, these are basic human rights and elements of good child welfare practice, and not necessarily unique to caring for gay and lesbian adolescents.

Raped, beaten, and living under the virtually constant threat of violence, the stories of these 54 young people more resemble narratives from convicted felons in a State Penitentiary than of those who have had the experience of being placed in out-of-home Child Welfare systems.

Verbal harassment was, at some point in time, an every day occurrence for 98% of the gay and lesbian young people interviewed for this study. Physical violence perpetrated by peers, staff, families, and the community is also commonplace for more than half of them (52%), and led equally as many (50%) to seek the perceived "safety" of the streets when they determined that they had had enough. The concept of "caring" for or "protecting" young people in need, with respect to gay and lesbian adolescents in care, seemed, in hearing these stories, to be improbable. Discrimination, bias, and the absence of written policies appear to have allowed these environments to go unchecked. Excusing the perpetrators for the violence and not holding them accountable for their negative actions, the gay youngster is victimized twice, first by the young people and staff who are permitted to act on their hate and second by the system who silently sanctions the activity by not working to create a more gay/lesbian affirming environment for all young people to live in.

REFERENCES

Berkley, S. (1996, January/February). Homophobia in the group home: Overcoming my fear of gays. *Foster Care Youth United*, 17-19.

Comstock, G. D. (1991). *Violence against lesbians and gay men*. New York: Columbia University Press.

D'Augelli, A. R., & Hershberger, S. L. (1993). Lesbian, gay, and bisexual youth in community settings: Personal challenges and mental health problems, *American Journal of Community Psychology, 21*(4), 421-448.

Fitzgerald, M. D. (1996). Homeless youths and the child welfare system: Implications for policy and service. *Child Welfare, 75*(3), 717-730.

Fraser, M., Pecora, P., & Haapala, D. (1991). *Families in crisis*. New York: Aldine de Gruyter.

Garnets, L., Herek, G. M., & Levy, B. (1992). Violence and victimization of lesbians and gay men: Mental health consequences. In G. M. Herek & K. T. Berrill (Eds.), *Hate crimes* (pp. 207-226). Newbury Park, CA: Sage.

Goffman, E. (1963). *Stigma: Notes of the management of a spoiled identity*. Englewood Cliffs, NJ: Prentice-Hall.

Herek, G. M. (1990). The context of anti-gay violence: Notes on cultural psychological heterosexism. *Journal of Interpersonal Violence, 5*(3), 316-333.

Herek, G. M., & Berrill, K. T. (Eds.). (1992). *Hate crimes: Confronting violence against lesbians and gay men*. Newbury Park, CA: Sage.

Hetrick, E., & Martin, A. D. (1987). Developmental issues and their resolution for gay and lesbian adolescents. *Journal of Homosexuality, 13*(4), 25-43.

Holdway, D. M., & Ray, J. (1992). Attitudes of street kids toward foster care. *Child & Adolescent Social Work, 9*(4), 307-317.

Hunter, J. (1990). Violence against lesbian and gay male youths. *Journal of Interpersonal Violence, 5*(3), 295-300.

Hunter, J., & Schaecher, R. (1987). Stresses on lesbian and gay adolescents in schools. *Social Work in Education, 9*(3), 180-188.

Janus, M. D., Archambault, F. X., & Brown, S. M. (1995). Physical abuse in Canadian runaway adolescents. *Child Abuse and Neglect, 19*, 433-447.

Mallon, G. P. (1998). *We don't exactly get the welcome wagon: The experience of gay and lesbian adolescents in child welfare systems.* New York: Columbia University Press.

Mayer, M. F., Richman, L. H., & Balcerzak, E. A. (1978). *Group care of children in crossroads and transitions.* New York: Child Welfare League of America.

Meston, J. (1988). Preparing young people in Canada for emancipation from child welfare care. *Child Welfare, 67*(5), 625-34.

Meyer, C. (1996). Reflection. *Reflections: Narratives of Professional Helping, 2*(2), 49-65.

Miranda, D. (1996). I hated myself. In P. Kay, A. Estepa, & A. Desetta (Eds.), *Out with it: Gay and straight teens write about homosexuality* (pp. 34-39). New York: Youth Communications.

Pharr, S. (1988). *Homophobia: A weapon of sexism.* Little Rock, AK: Chardon Press.

Polsky, H. (1962). *Cottage six: The social system of delinquent boys in residential treatment.* New York: Russell Sage Foundation.

Rindfleisch, N. (1993). Combatting institutional abuse. In C. E. Schaefer & A. Swanson (Eds.), *Children in residential care: Critical issues in treatment* (pp. 263-283). Northvale, NJ: Jason Aronson.

Savin-Williams, R. C. (1994). Verbal and physical abuse as stressors in the lives of lesbian, gay male and bisexual youths: Associations with school problems, running away, substance abuse, prostitution, suicide. *Journal of Consulting and Clinical Practice, 62*, 261-269.

Schaefer, C. E. (1980). The impact of peer culture in the residential treatment of youth. *Adolescence, 15*(60), 831-845.

Wadley, C. (1996a). Shunned, insulted, threatened. In P. Kay, A. Estepa, & A. Desetta (Eds.), *Out with it: Gay and straight teens write about homosexuality* (pp. 57-60). New York: Youth Communications.

Wadley, C. (1996b). Kicked out because she was a lesbian. In P. Kay, A. Estepa, & A. Desetta (Eds.), *Out with it: Gay and straight teens write about homosexuality* (pp. 58-60). New York: Youth Communications.

Webber, M. (1991). *Street kids: The tragedy of Canada's runaways.* Toronto, ON: University of Toronto Press.

Zide, M. R., & Cherry, A. L. (1992). A typology of runaway youths: An empirically based definition. *Child & Adolescent Social Work, 9*(2), 155-16.

Domestic Violence:
The Ultimate Betrayal of Human Rights

Carol T. Tully

SUMMARY. Domestic violence in same-sex relationships is still a rarely spoken about phenomenon that occurs far too often. This article explores this heinous behavior as a gross violation of human rights and explores how and why domestic violence may happen. Strategies for professional social work intervention for both the victim and the perpetrator are explored, and myths about same-sex domestic violence are exploded. *[Article copies available for a fee from The Haworth Document Delivery Service: 1-800-342-9678. E-mail address: <getinfo@haworthpressinc. com> Website: <http://www.HaworthPress.com> © 2001 by The Haworth Press, Inc. All rights reserved.]*

KEYWORDS. Lesbian, gay, homosexual, queer, domestic violence, hate crimes, violence, human rights

INTRODUCTION

Discussions about domestic violence in the lesbian and gay community as a violation of the most basic of human rights are seldom articulated. While the gay and lesbian community seems anxious to delineate what it characterizes as human rights violations to the homo-

Carol T. Tully is Professor and Associate Dean, Kent School of Social Work, University of Louisville.

[Haworth co-indexing entry note]: "Domestic Violence: The Ultimate Betrayal of Human Rights." Tully, Carol T. Co-published simultaneously in *Journal of Gay & Lesbian Social Services* (Harrington Park Press, an imprint of The Haworth Press, Inc.) Vol. 13, No. 1/2, 2001, pp. 83-98; and: *From Hate Crimes to Human Rights: A Tribute to Matthew Shepard* (ed: Mary E. Swigonski, Robin S. Mama, and Kelly Ward) Harrington Park Press, an imprint of The Haworth Press, Inc., 2001, pp. 83-98. Single or multiple copies of this article are available for a fee from The Haworth Document Delivery Service [1-800-342-9678, 9:00 a.m. - 5:00 p.m. (EST). E-mail address: getinfo@haworthpressinc.com].

centric lifestyle in terms of heterocentrism and homophobia, there has been a generalized reluctance in the community to acknowledge and confront same-sex domestic violence. Yet, domestic violence within lesbian and gay relationships does exist (Renzetti, 1992; Shernoff, 1995; Zawitz, 1994). This article focuses on domestic violence within the gay and lesbian community as a significant violation of basic human rights. The concepts of domestic violence and human rights will be defined, prevailing explanations for domestic violence will be explored, and treatment alternatives for victims and perpetrators will be discussed.

HUMAN RIGHTS AND DOMESTIC VIOLENCE: DEFINITIONS

The *Universal Declaration of Human Rights* (United Nations, 1948) is considered the seminal document related to those rights defined as "human rights"–or rights accorded to individuals simply on the basis of being human. They include both legally mandated civil rights, such as freedom from arbitrary arrest, detention, or exile; life, liberty, and personal security; the right to fair and public hearings by impartial tribunals; freedom of thought, conscious, and religion; and freedom of peaceful association and legally unenforceable cultural, economic, and social rights, such as the right to work and participate in the cultural community (Barker, 1995; United Nations, 1948; Wronka, 1995). Written following the atrocities of the German Holocaust, where 10 million people (mostly Jews but also including homosexuals, gypsies, Poles, and those with disabilities) were systematically slaughtered, the *Universal Declaration of Human Rights* affirmed the dignity and worth of every human being, promoted social justice, and sought to ensure that legal remedies would be developed for each defined human right (United Nations, 1948). Although legal remedies for each human right have yet to be established, the *Declaration* continues as the cornerstone of defining the concept of human rights.

Articles 3 and 5 of the declaration speak simply but eloquently to the issue of safety. Article 3 simple states, "Everyone has the right to life, liberty, and security of person" (United Nations, 1948), and Article 5 says, "No one shall be subjected to torture or to cruel, inhuman or degrading treatment or punishment" (United Nations, 1948). Although written for another time and with a more macro-level focus, these two articles also have relevance for lesbians and gay men caught in the tangle of domestic violence. Such violence may be seen as particularly vile as it occurs between persons who purportedly love one another and denies human rights at its core.

The *Violent Crime and Control and Law Enforcement Act* of 1994 defines a hate crime as "a crime in which the defendant intentionally selects a victim, or in the case of a property crime, the property that is the object of the crime because of the actual or perceived race, color, national origin, ethnicity, gender, disability, or sexual orientation of any person" (Leadership Conference on Civil Rights, 1994). The victims of these hate crimes generally do not know their attackers well if they know them at all (Leadership Conference on Civil Rights, 1996). In contrast to these "hate" crimes, a more sinister type of violence exists in the gay and lesbian community–domestic violence. Domestic violence, while statistically counted as a "hate" crime, is defined a bit differently. At a micro-level, domestic violence has been defined as abuse that occurs in the home and is committed by family members on spouses, children, older persons, or others living in the home (Barker, 1995). At a higher social institutional level, domestic violence has also been called a societal problem where the health or property of a family member are endangered or harmed because of the intentional behavior of another family member (Barker, 1995). The terms spouse abuse, spousal battery, family violence, and domestic violence tend to be used interchangeably, but all constitute variables within the overall construct of domestic violence.

Vickers (1996) noted that domestic violence was related to the use of illegitimate power and coercive control by one partner over the other. Such power is used to control the behaviors, thoughts, actions, or conduct of the less powerful partner and may involve psychological or physical abuse or damage to property. Although in some areas there are differences between gay men and lesbians, the definitions for domestic violence apply to both. Domestic violence in lesbian relationships has been defined by Vickers (1996) as a behavior pattern of violence and coercion where one lesbian partner seeks to control her partner's conduct, thoughts, or beliefs and seeks to punish her partner for resisting the control. Gay male domestic violence is defined as unwanted psychological abuse, physical abuse, or damage to personal or material property (Vickers, 1996).

Just as there are subtle differences between hate crimes and domestic violence, there are differences between the concepts of domestic arguments and domestic violence. Domestic arguments are those inevitable conflicts that arise in any relationship of two people. They may erupt in relation to job stress, financial worries, childcare issues, health, career, etc., but are seen as being solved by two partners who have equal power. Such arguments may be viewed as helpful and positive in the growth and development of the relationship. Domestic violence occurs when there is an imbalance of power between the partners where one partner is afraid of the other or has been physically or psychologically harmed by the other (Women's Issues and Social Empowerment, 1998a, 1998d). Domestic violence is never seen as a positive way of dealing with conflict, and once domestic violence becomes part of a relationship, the more likely it is to recur (Vickers, 1996).

Domestic violence takes the form of verbal, physical, emotional, psychological, sexual, economic, social, or spiritual abuse and may involve the destruction or damage of personal property, including belongings or pets (Appleby & Anastas, 1998; Trimble, 1994; Women's Issues and Social Empowerment, 1998b, 1998d). Much domestic violence, occurs within the context of drug or alcohol abuse (Shernoff, 1998) and occurs within the privacy of the gay or lesbian home. Neither the victim nor the perpetrator is eager to discuss or report domestic violence, and there is no common profile for either victims or perpetrators. It remains a largely invisible issue within both the gay and lesbian communities as well as the non-gay society, and most victims do not voluntarily seek treatment or social services (Appleby & Anastas, 1998).

Adequate statistics on the number and kinds of domestic violence are not readily available, but it has been estimated that there may be as many as 500,000 battered men in the United States. Further, estimates indicate that between 22-44% of all lesbians have been in relationships where violence occurred and that perhaps 15-20% of all gay or lesbian couples are abusive (Appleby & Anastas, 1998; Vickers, 1996). Based on current estimates of the total number of lesbians and gay men in the United States (somewhere between 3-10% of the population or between 7 and 23 million gay men and lesbians), this means that there are potentially anywhere from 1 million to 4.6 million victims of gay or lesbian domestic violence in the country.

In sum, domestic violence is a type of hate crime that occurs within the intimate relationships of lesbian and gay couples and families, differs from domestic arguments, and is related to power differentials between partners. One partner is more powerful and seeks to dominate the less powerful partner through physical or psychological abuse or though damaging property. Domestic violence is seen as an inappropriate means of dealing with conflict and is likely to recur once unleashed. It is a betrayal and violation of the most basic of human rights as it occurs between intimate partners in the privacy of the home. It is infrequently discussed and few wish to acknowledge its existence. But, even for the limited amount of information about same-sex domestic violence, there are some data that explore why it exists and how its victims (both the abuser and the abused) can be assisted.

DOMESTIC VIOLENCE: HOW AND WHY?

As noted, hate crimes and domestic violence are different. And, although statistically counted as a hate crime, domestic violence seems more horrific in that it occurs in relationships where the victim and perpetrator are intimately known to one another and in the context of "loving" relationships. Domestic violence in same-sex relationships is similar to domestic violence in non-gay relationships–there is a fundamental imbalance of power between the partners where one partner is weaker than the other, more dominant partner. Domestic violence is the ultimate denial of human rights.

There are various conceptual models that depict the cycle of domestic violence (Trimble, 1994; Women's Issues and Social Empowerment, 1998a), and most depict the cycle as circular. The model proposed here is a spiral where each episode of domestic violence moves up the spiral until there is resolution (see Figure 1). Starting at the bottom, the first phase of domestic violence lies in one partner's ability to gain power and control over the other partner. This may be a testing phase where one partner is pushing to have her or his way. It may be noticed in small things like screening phone calls or setting curfews. If tensions around these issues begin to mount and are not resolved, this development of an unequal power base may lead to the more powerful partner's inappropriate use of power. If a partner becomes sullen or angry when he or she does not get her way most of the time, it may be a signal that the relationship is not as healthy as it

FIGURE 1. The Spiral of Domestic Violence

Violence has its own pattern that emerges and expands in a spiral fashion where the episodes are of increasing strength and likely to continue until some permanent resolution is determined.

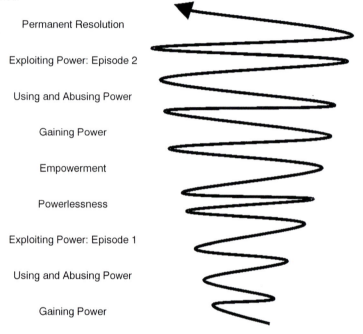

Permanent Resolution

Exploiting Power: Episode 2

Using and Abusing Power

Gaining Power

Empowerment

Powerlessness

Exploiting Power: Episode 1

Using and Abusing Power

Gaining Power

should be. After the initial phase of gaining power, the more dominant partner begins to use and abuse power; it may lead into a more volatile phase where there is an actual violent eruption.

For example, Cecelia and Carla had been partners for four years before Cecelia realized that Carla monitored all Cecelia's phone calls, demanded to know where Cecelia was at all times, and insisted on defining Cecelia's role in the relationship. The relationship rules had been incrementally developed over the four-year relationship and all done in the name of "love." When Cecelia broke one of the rules, Carla became angry and argumentative. Because Cecelia deeply believed that Carla loved her and that the relationship was a good one, she overlooked the signs of a power differential. As the relationship entered its seventh year Cecelia had become convinced that she was no good and could do nothing right. This belief was reinforced by

Carla who daily reminded Cecelia of her shortcomings. Cecelia was told of her inability to properly take out the trash, hang a picture, or mow the lawn. Her self-esteem at a low point, an almost suicidal Cecelia went into therapy. It was suggested that Carla also get therapeutic intervention, but this sparked the most violent eruption in the relationship to that point. The result of this argument, which turned into a physical brawl, was a black eye for Cecelia and seventeen stitches in Carla's leg–the result of a wineglass that shattered on the table and landed in her leg.

Following the violence, both Cecelia and Carla felt remorse, sorrow, and profound guilt over their behavior. Separately, both went into therapy, and they entered a new honeymoon phase of their long-term relationship. Both sensed a loss of their control and not being able to curb their violence, and each empowered the other to forgive and forget. Their sexual activity increased, they had romantic dinners, each gave the other love presents, and both promised that domestic violence would not ever be part of their lives again. This honeymoon lasted several months, but slowly old behavior patterns began to reappear and the cycle, evolving from the first episode, began again. Only after Cecelia and Carla had moved up the spiral through several episodes of domestic violence (that included physical abuse and psychological abuse) did Cecelia finally realize that the only way to end the abuse was to end the relationship, which, after 12 years, she did. Her decision to end the relationship came as a surprise to the lesbian and gay community because to many Cecelia and Carla had been outwardly viewed as the "perfect couple": happy, well educated, and financially secure.

Cecelia and Carla provide one example of how an abusive relationship can move through the spiral of domestic violence. This example is not atypical, but it is not as horrible as other cases of same sex domestic violence where the final resolution of the problem results in the death of one of the partners. The common thread about how domestic violence occurs is the unequal power distribution between partners that results in emotional, psychic, spiritual, or physical trauma or abuse to one of the partners at the hands of the other. Domestic violence is a hideous form of control that seems to move through identifiable phases and does not discriminate on the basis of socioeconomic status, sex, religion, race, ethnicity, or physical ability. And, although it may be possible to explore *how* domestic violence occurs, the more sinister root of domestic violence is *why* it occurs.

Trying to uncover why acts of domestic violence in same-sex relationships occur is a daunting, if not impossible task. Searching for quantifiable reasons as to why particular patterns of behavior exist has been seen as futile and non-productive, but there seems to be some correlation between domestic violence and particular variables even if causality can never be established. Some data demonstrate that domestic violence may occur when substance abuse is part of the relationship, when low self-esteem exists, when poor relationship skills exist, when members in the relationship have been involved in prior domestic violence (either in families of origin or families of choice), or when homophobia plays a significant role in the relationship. Some say that those who tend to be the perpetrators in domestic violence situations tend to: have issues with domination, power, and control; have poor self-concepts; and have been victims of domestic violence or child abuse. Most agree that there is not one profile that fits either the perpetrator or victim of domestic violence (Appleby & Anastas, 1998; Lobel, 1986; Renzetti, 1992; Robson, 1997). Since domestic violence takes place in the privacy of the home and since those that are involved with it tend not to discuss it, the reasons behind its cause remain hidden. What is no longer hidden is the reality that domestic violence between same-sex couples and in same-sex families is an ongoing phenomenon that must be addressed by the social service community.

SOCIAL WORK WITH VICTIMS AND PERPETRATORS

That same-sex domestic violence exists is not in question. What is in question is the depth and breadth of social services designed to address this significantly insidious, underreported social problem. The reality of same-sex domestic violence was not an issue for social services until the 1980s simply because the violence was invisible and, therefore, services were not considered necessary (Lobel, 1986). And, although same-sex domestic violence is at least recognized as a social problem requiring intervention, agencies have been slow to provide services to lesbian victims of same-sex violence and even slower to acknowledge domestic violence in gay male relationships (Appleby & Anastas, 1998; Renzetti, 1992). This section explores services necessary for dealing with both victims and perpetrators of same-sex domestic violence, identifies possible sources of support, and suggests pragmatic ways of stemming the violence and ensuring human rights.

Social Services and Victims

Victims of same-sex domestic violence include both women and men. Men tend to be more reluctant to report such domestic violence, but both lesbians and gay men still cover up the majority of incidents related to same-sex domestic violence. The reasons for the continuing cloak of invisibility stem from a pervasive fear of being ignored, berated, ridiculed, or even abused by police, physicians, nurses, and even social workers if the secret were made known (Family Violence Awareness Page, 1998; Lobel, 1986; Renzetti, 1992). Additionally, victims may be fearful of making their secret known in a public setting because, as a member of an already marginalized minority, they have known the sting of institutionalized homophobia (Vickers, 1996). In sum, victims seem to feel their human rights would be violated were the truth to be told–a sad commentary given the apparent lack of protections of basic human rights by social service providers, but an apparently realistic one.

Coupled with this fear of disclosure is the alarming reality that services for victims of same-sex domestic violence in the late 1990s are still woefully inadequate. This may be because of the lingering myth that lesbians and gay men do not engage in domestic violence, the inability to overcome institutional homophobia, or the insensitivity of the social service community to this issue (Appleby & Anastas, 1998; Renzetti, 1992; Vickers, 1996). But, if services do exist and the victim manages to connect with existing services, there are still barriers that must be overcome.

One of the first hurdles facing both the victim of same-sex domestic violence and the social worker facing the victim is that of homophobia. Questions confronting the victim may include: "Is it safe to tell this social worker I am not heterosexual?" "Will the social worker allow me to tell my story and accept my position?" "Why should I come out?" "Do I dare divulge that my lover beats me?" Social workers must avoid the "heterosexual assumption" and should encourage the development of a trusting relationship based on non-judgmental attitudes and client self-determination. Establishing that a client is a lesbian, gay, bisexual, or transgender may be easier than getting them to acknowledge their being a victim of same-sex domestic violence.

Given the reluctance of same-sex domestic violence victims to step forward and openly acknowledge their plight, social workers may need to become detectives. Like their non-gay counterparts, victims of same-sex domestic violence may demonstrate obvious and recurring signs of physical violence, including such things as burns, bite marks, bruises, swellings, lacerations, cuts, or broken bones. As isolated incidents, there may be little reason for alarm; however, if there is repeated evidence of physical harm, the social worker must suspect domestic violence. Physical violence and its effects are not the only forms of domestic violence. Other forms include psychological or emotional abuse. Victims of psychological or emotional domestic violence may suffer depression, suicidal ideation, withdrawal, isolation, anxiety, substance abuse, or even symptoms of post-traumatic stress disorder (Family Violence Awareness Page, 1998; Lobel, 1986; Renzetti, 1992). It is imperative for social workers working with clients who are presenting such symptoms to uncover the root cause of the symptom–it may be related to domestic violence.

Once the barriers have been overcome and the victim of same-sex domestic violence has acknowledged that reality (or at least the reality that he or she has been brutalized by an intimate partner of undetermined sex), services must be immediately related to the crisis. Ensuring the physical and emotional safety of the client and attending to necessary medical treatment must come first. Only when the client is safe from harm can other services be provided. Since domestic violence is generally viewed as related to a power imbalance within the relationship, such crisis intervention techniques as positive reinforcement of appropriate responses to the violence, providing needed information about same-sex domestic violence, making appropriate referrals, and empowering the victim to move toward resolution and removal of all threats of violence are appropriate (Appleby & Anastas, 1998; Women's Issues and Social Empowerment, 1998c).

Such services can only be provided if the social worker can develop a supportive and trusting relationship with the victim where the practical issues associated with the violence are addressed before other needs. To create such a relationship, social work practitioners need to have an understanding of issues associated with not only domestic violence, but also lesbian- and gay-related issues. Such might include knowledge of gay and lesbian history, homophobia and its forms, and resources available not only to lesbians and gays but to battered lesbians and gays. Practitioners also must overcome and challenge stereotypes that lead us to believe women do not engage in violence or men who get beaten up are "wimps." Some of the more prevalent myths associated with same-sex domestic violence are seen in Figure 2. In addition to freeing themselves of stereotypes and myths, practitioners must also realize that in same-sex domestic violence situations there are often two victims–the one who is battered or emotionally damaged

FIGURE 2. Stereotypes, Myths, and Realities about Same-Sex Domestic Violence

When providing services to victims and perpetrators of same-sex domestic violence, social workers need to be aware of some of the prevalent stereotypes and myths associated with this almost invisible, disenfranchised minority.

Myths and Stereotypes*
- Domestic violence does not occur in lesbian relationships because women are not violent.
- Gay men are not the victims of domestic violence because gay men do not really "fight" they merely rough-house for fun.
- Lesbians and gay men have equal power in relationships so there could never be a power imbalance between the couple.
- The abuser/batterer is always larger and more physically powerful than the victim.
- Domestic violence in lesbian couples occurs only in the context of sado-masochistic (S/M) relationships.
- Domestic violence occurs mostly between gay or lesbian couples who frequent the bars, who are poor, or who are members of ethnic minorities.
- Domestic violence in same-sex relationships is an enjoyable form of sexual entertainment.
- The victims of domestic violence get what they deserve as they provoke the violence.

Realities
- Women are and may become violent. Lesbians are not immune from domestic violence.
- Gay men are also at risk of domestic violence and do engage in physically or psychologically damaging acts.
- While ideally there would be an equal balance in lesbian and gay relationships (and all relationships), this may not be the case. Power imbalances do exist that may lead to domestic violence.
- There is no correlation between size and the perpetrators of domestic violence–they come in all sizes and shapes.
- Domestic violence and S/M lesbian relationships are not correlated–domestic violence can and does occur in any kind of lesbian relationship.
- Domestic violence occurs in every socioeconomic strata and across all races.
- Domestic violence is never viewed as enjoyable.
- Victims of domestic violence never deserve psychological or physical harm.

*Stereotypes and myths were paraphrased from L. Vickers (1996).

and the one who is inflicting the harm. Figure 3 offers suggestions for providing services to victims of same-sex domestic violence. Figure 4 offers suggestions for working with perpetrators.

Social Services and Perpetrators

If identifying and providing services to victims of same-sex domestic violence seems like a daunting task with few available resources, identifying and providing services to the perpetrators of those violent acts is even more difficult. Little data on the perpetrators of same-sex domestic violence exist, but anecdotal information characterizes these individuals as blaming the victim for the abuse, denying involvement in the violence, and being unwilling to seek necessary services (Lobel, 1986; Renzetti, 1992; Vickers, 1996).

Because inadequate data exist on same-sex perpetrators of domestic violence, there has been a tendency to equate lesbian and gay batterers with heterosexual male perpetrators of domestic violence and abuse. While there may be similar characteristics related to issues of power

FIGURE 3. Providing Services to Victims of Same-Sex Domestic Violence

When providing services to victims of same-sex domestic violence social work practitioners should consider the following:

Services and the Victim

- Ensure the immediate physical safety of the individual and get appropriate medical intervention as needed.

- Assess the emotional reactions of the victim by being sensitive to the horror of the violence and allowing the person to ventilate and regain self-esteem.

- Help reinforce a positive self-image and focus on internal and external coping mechanisms.

- Encourage the victim to take steps to ensure that she or he will be in a violence-free environment.

- To counter feelings of powerlessness, assist the victim to regain a sense of personal identity and personal control.

- Act as an advocate with police, medical personnel, and the legal system.

- Provide adequate information and referrals as to where safe services can be obtained.

- Decrease victim isolation by developing appropriate social support networks from the individual's formal and informal networks.

- Do not believe stereotypes and myths associated with same-sex domestic violence.

FIGURE 4. Providing Services to the Perpetrators of Same-Sex Domestic Violence

When providing services to the perpetrators of same-sex domestic violence, social work practitioners should consider the following:

Services and the Perpetrator

- Perpetrators of same-sex domestic violence may be of any sex, ethnic minority, and socioeconomic status–avoid stereotypes and myths.

- Because they do not usually voluntarily seek services their patterns of violence may have existed across several relationships.

- Perpetrators must openly acknowledge and own the violence.

- Appropriate measures (such as separating the victim and perpetrator, therapeutic intervention, anger management, etc.) must be taken to ensure that the violence is extinguished and that the perpetrator is able to live in a violence-free environment.

- Exploration of the perpetrator's needs and feelings about violence is important.

- Issues associated with power, dominance, and control need to be examined and addressed.

- Because substance abuse and domestic violence are correlated, the context in which the violence occurred should be defined.

- Issues of substance abuse must be addressed.

- Whether or not the perpetrator has been a victim of child abuse, sexual abuse, or other forms of discrimination needs elaboration.

- The role of violence in the perpetrator's family of origin may provide clues as to current issues of self-esteem.

and domination, some data indicate that lesbians who batter are not similarly situated with heterosexual male batterers (Robson, 1997). Lesbians who engage in domestic violence are more likely to have been the victim of childhood abuse or discrimination and may believe they have little or no actual perceived power. Additionally, they may suffer from low self-esteem and use domination and control within the relationship to feel powerful (Appleby & Anastas, 1998; Renzetti, 1992).

There are only scant bits of information about lesbian perpetrators of domestic violence and even less information exists about gay male abusers. What information does exist tends to support the premise that much male same-sex domestic violence occurs in the context of alcohol or drugs, issues with power and control, and low impulse control (Appleby & Anastas, 1998; Shernoff, 1998; Vickers, 1996). In sum, little is known about either lesbian or gay male abusers, but there is some consensus about appropriate service interventions when dealing with a perpetrator of same-sex domestic violence.

It is generally agreed that when working with an abusive partner, the goals should first include having the perpetrator assume responsibility for her or his actions and acknowledge the violence. Once that is accomplished, appropriate methods for controlling the violence need to be incorporated. This may be done through an examination of the client's needs and feelings as well as through an exploration of the role violence has played in his or her life. By exploring the nature of the role violence has played in her or his family structure, it may be possible to relate that to current issues of self-image, power, and control (Appleby & Anastas, 1998; Trimble, 1994).

In sum, while there may be some similarities between non-gay batterers and lesbian or gay perpetrators of domestic violence, there are also differences. It is with these differences that the social work practitioner must become familiar. The best way to become familiar with the nuances of gay and lesbian clients is to learn about their communities, the role of homophobia in their lives, and the safe resources available to them.

Stemming the Violence: Some Concluding Thoughts

It has been repeatedly stated that same-sex domestic violence is the most degrading form of human rights violation that can occur because it takes place in the context of a supposed "loving" and intimate relationship. A first step in stemming this violence is to openly acknowledge its existence. A logical next step is to ensure adequate social service supports for the problem, and, finally, to ensure that legal protections for same-sex victims and perpetrators are in place.

To openly acknowledge the reality of same-sex domestic violence seems simple enough until one factors in homophobia: institutional homophobia prevents agencies from developing and implementing adequate services; individual homophobia prevents social workers from acknowledging the extent of the problem; internal homophobia prevents the victims and perpetrators from revealing their secret. Creating solutions to homophobia will encourage agencies to be more inclusive in providing services, practitioners to be more capable of dealing with same-sex domestic violence, and clients to be more open and honest. But, confronting and combating homophobia in a society currently preoccupied with the religious right and conservative values is no easy task. It is there as a challenge for those willing to support one of the social work profession's most basic tenets–advocacy.

There are some agencies willing to address the issue of same-sex domestic violence, but these are almost exclusively available to victims of lesbian domestic violence, as the reality of gay men engaging in such violence is still mostly unrecognized. Generally situated within existing shelters for battered women, some services for battered lesbians are emerging, but services in many locales are extremely limited or nonexistent. This has to change. All social service agencies must recognize the reality of the horror of same-sex domestic violence, provide training for workers on the issue, monitor the implementation of such services, and support necessary measures to ensure the safety of the victim and the needs of the perpetrator.

Finally, legal protections need to be implemented to provide for both the victim and the perpetrator of same-sex domestic violence. Sexual orientation needs to be included as a protected category in each state's statutes, and victims need to be encouraged to report such crimes. Training on how to appropriately treat both victims and perpetrators of same-sex domestic violence must be mandated for local and state police, jail staff, medical personnel, judges, legal advocates, and social service providers. And legal protections must be included in policies and procedures at all levels within the social service safety network.

In sum, same-sex domestic violence is a vile and despicable reality that must be addressed at a number of levels. The first is making it visible as the ultimate violation of human rights.

REFERENCES

Appleby, G. A., & Anastas, J. W. (1998). *Not just a passing phase: Social work with gay, lesbian, and bisexual people.* New York: Columbia University Press.

Barker, R. L. (1995). *The social work dictionary (3rd edition).* Washington, DC: NASW Press.

Family Violence Awareness Page. (1998). *A handbook to stop violence–domestic violence: The facts. (http://www.famvi.com/dv_facts.htm).*

Leadership Conference on Civil Rights. (1994). Hate crimes: A definition. *(http://www.civilrights.org/lcef/hcpc/define.html).*

Leadership Conference on Civil Rights. (1996). Hate crime statistics. *(http://www.civilrights.org/lcef/hcpc/stats/table1.htm).*

Lobel, K. (Ed.). (1986). *Naming the violence: Speaking out about lesbian battering.* Seattle: The Seal Press.

Renzetti, C. M. (1992). *Violent betrayal: Partner abuse in lesbian relationships.* Thousand Oaks, CA: Sage.

Robson, R. (1997). Convictions: Theorizing lesbians and criminal justice. In M. Duberman (Ed.), *A queer world* (pp. 418-430). New York: New York University Press.

Shernoff, M. (1995). Gay men: Direct practice. In R. L. Edwards (Ed.-in Chief), *Encyclopedia of social work 19th edition* (1: 1075-1085). Washington DC: National Association of Social Workers.

Shernoff, M. (1998). Individual practice with gay men. In G. P. Mallon (Ed.), *Foundations of social work practice with lesbian and gay persons* (pp. 77-103). New York: Harrington Park Press.

Trimble, D. (1994). Confronting responsibility: Men who batter their wives. In A. Gitterman & L. Shulman (Eds.), *Mutual aid groups, vulnerable populations, and the life cycle* (pp. 257-271). New York: Columbia University Press.

United Nations. (1948). *Universal Declaration of Human Rights.* In H. O. Dahlke, T. O. Carlton, C. Itzkovitz, & T. M. Madison (Eds.), (1980), *A foundation for social policy analysis (Revised Edition)* (pp. 76-80). Lexington, MA: Ginn Custom Publishing.

Vickers, L. (1996). The second closet: Domestic violence in lesbian and gay relationships: A Western Australian perspective. *(http://www.murdoch.edu.au/elaw/issues/v3n4/vickers.html).*

Women's Issues and Social Empowerment. (1998a). Domestic violence information manual: The dynamics of domestic violence. *(http://www.infoxchange.net.au. wise/dvim/dvdynamics.htm).*

Women's Issues and Social Empowerment. (1998b). Domestic violence information manual: Forms of domestic violence. *(http://www.infoxchange.net.au.wise/dvim/ dvabuse.htm).*

Women's Issues and Social Empowerment. (1998c). Domestic violence information manual: Interpreting the signs of domestic violence. *(http://www.infoxchange. net.au.wise/dvim/dvsigns.htm).*

Women's Issues and Social Empowerment. (1998d). Domestic violence information manual: What is domestic violence. *(http://www.infoxchange.net.au.wise/dvim/ dviml.htm).*

Wronka, J. (1995). Human rights. In R. L. Edwards (Ed.-in Chief), *Encyclopedia of social work 19th edition* (2: 1405-1418). Washington DC: National Association of Social Workers.

Zawitz, M. W. (1994). U.S. Department of Justice: Violence between intimates: Domestic violence. *(http://www.ojp.usdoj.gov/pub/bjs/ascii/vbi.txt).*

Economic Rights, Economic Myths, and Economic Realities

Jeane W. Anastas

SUMMARY. Although the myth is that gay and lesbian people, especially gay men, are affluent and are faring well in the workplace, research shows that they in fact experience wage discrimination and lack many other fundamental rights related to employment. This article reviews the literature addressing gay, lesbian, bisexual, and transgendered people as workers, showing the ways in which their economic rights are still compromised in the United States today. The social work profession must understand these realities and seek ways to address them. *[Article copies available for a fee from The Haworth Document Delivery Service: 1-800-342-9678. E-mail address: <getinfo@haworthpressinc.com> Website: <http://www.HaworthPress.com> © 2001 by The Haworth Press, Inc. All rights reserved.]*

KEYWORDS. Gays, lesbians, economic myths, economic rights, employment, wage discrimination, employment benefits, gay rights, social work

1. Everyone has the right to work, to free choice of employment, to just and favorable conditions of work and to protection against unemployment.
2. Everyone, without any discrimination, has the right to equal pay for equal work.

Jeane W. Anastas, MSW, PhD, is affiliated with Ehrenkranz School of Social Work, New York University.

[Haworth co-indexing entry note]: "Economic Rights, Economic Myths, and Economic Realities." Anastas, Jeane W. Co-published simultaneously in *Journal of Gay & Lesbian Social Services* (Harrington Park Press, an imprint of The Haworth Press, Inc.) Vol. 13, No. 1/2, 2001, pp. 99-116; and: *From Hate Crimes to Human Rights: A Tribute to Matthew Shepard* (ed: Mary E. Swigonski, Robin S. Mama, and Kelly Ward) Harrington Park Press, an imprint of The Haworth Press, Inc., 2001, pp. 99-116. Single or multiple copies of this article are available for a fee from The Haworth Document Delivery Service [1-800-342-9678, 9:00 a.m. - 5:00 p.m. (EST). E-mail address: getinfo@haworthpressinc.com].

3. Everyone who works has the right to just and favorable remuneration ensuring for himself and his [sic] family an existence worthy of human dignity, and supplemented, if necessary, by other means of social protection.

United Nations *Universal Declaration of Human Rights*, 1948
Article 23

The right to work and the right to equal treatment in the workplace are fundamental. Opinion polls for some time have shown that average United States citizens overwhelmingly support equal treatment of gays and lesbians in the workplace (Human Rights Campaign, 1999b). However, the realities of gay, lesbian, bisexual, and transgendered people as workers are poorly understood. Prevalent myth assumes that gays and lesbians, especially gay men, are affluent and that economic and personal problems related to work are not important issues for them in the United States today (Badgett, 1999). In addition, most Americans do not know that gay and lesbian people's rights to equal treatment at work are not currently protected on a national level (Human Rights Campaign, 1999c).

This article will review evidence which suggests that the economic rights of gay, lesbian, bisexual, and transgendered[1] people as workers are not presently secure. This situation has many implications for social workers. The National Association of Social Workers (NASW) currently estimates that approximately 10% of its membership identify as gay, lesbian, or bisexual. It also, of course, has implications for clients and their families. In fact, I have argued elsewhere that, from an ecological perspective (Van Soest & Bryant, 1995), "homophobia and heterosexism in the workplace do violence to the gay, lesbian and bisexual people directly affected as well as to their families and communities" (Anastas, 1998, p. 84). Finally, as Badgett (1997) explains, ". . . . even in a modern market economy, work is a virtuous activity and is an important part of our economic foundation" (p. 383). Thus, attending to the roles of gay, lesbian, bisexual, and transgendered people as producers rather than consumers helps to promote a positive image of us as a group (Badgett, 1997).[2]

ECONOMIC MYTHS

Badgett (1999) has written the most comprehensive analysis to date of the belief, common in both the heterosexual and the gay and lesbian communities, that gay and lesbian individuals and/or gay and lesbian households are more affluent on average than heterosexual ones. However, the statistics used to support this belief come from marketing surveys and are not at all representative of gay and lesbian individuals or households in general. In addition, the marketing survey data depict gay, lesbian, and bisexual people as consumers rather than as producers, as earners in the labor force and productive members of society (Badgett, 1997). This myth of affluence is also destructive because the spurious data on affluence are often cited by those who oppose gay civil rights initiatives on the grounds that gay, lesbian, and bisexual people obviously do not need protections (Badgett, 1997, 1999). The small amount of representative data that does exist suggests that working gay, lesbian, and bisexual people are no better off and in some ways are disadvantaged economically in relation to comparable heterosexual people (Badgett, 1995; Klawitter & Flatt, 1998).

Because people in representative surveys are not routinely asked about sexual orientation, there are only a few sources of reliable data to compare the economic well-being of gay and lesbian people to others. The few representative surveys available that examine gay, lesbian, and/or bisexual earnings in comparison to that of heterosexuals show consistently that gay, lesbian, and bisexual people are no different from heterosexual ones. Gay, lesbian, and bisexual individuals and households are found at all levels of the earnings spectrum, from the very poor to the very rich. In fact, data from three surveys suggests that gay men earn less than comparable heterosexual men (Badgett, 1999). Also, when it comes to households, those composed of two women have lower incomes than others because of the fact that women are still disadvantaged in earnings as compared to men. The households of lesbian and bisexual women do not benefit from the higher average earnings of men (Badgett, 1995, 1999; Klawitter & Flatt, 1998). Thus the representative data that exist suggest not an advantage but a systematic disadvantage in the workplace.[3]

Part of the logic of this myth of gay affluence is based in the heterosexist assumption that gay and lesbian people do not involve themselves in child rearing and thus have more disposable income than comparable heterosexual people do (Badgett, 1999). Badgett discussed one poll showing that 31% of lesbians, 37% of heterosexual women, 23% of gay men, and 33% of heterosexual men had children under 18 living at home with them. In another, 67% of lesbians and 72% of heterosexual women were parents, and 32% of lesbians and 36% of heterosexual women had children under 18 living at home. While these percentages are indeed lower among gays and lesbians than among heterosexuals, child rearing is far more common among gay and lesbian people than is usually supposed.

THE RIGHT TO WORK

There is no federal guarantee of basic civil rights for gay and lesbian people, and only 10 states (Human Rights Campaign, 1999b, 1999c) and some localities have ordinances protecting the right to public and/or private employment for gay and lesbian people.[4] Because of this lack of protection and the criminalization of certain sexual activities in many states,[5] it is unreasonable to assume that a question about sexual orientation could be simply asked and would be honestly answered in any general survey of workers (Klawitter & Flatt, 1998). Therefore, there have only been a few studies to date of gay and lesbian earnings that utilize representative samples (Badgett, 1995; Klawitter & Flatt, 1998).

Gay and lesbian people participate in the labor market at perhaps even higher rates than heterosexual people do (Elliott, 1993; Fassinger, 1995; Morgan & Brown, 1991). However, no systematic national data exist on the percentages of gay or lesbian people in the workforce. Badgett's (1999) summary of findings compares people working full time to each other and does not address the question of the percentage of labor force participation between the groups. However, Klawitter and Flatt (1998) analyzed 1990 Census data describing the incomes of women (and men) in same-gender households. While not a representative sample of all lesbians, their data show that part of the reason for higher individual incomes among women in same-gender households compared to that of women who are currently married reflects more weeks and hours worked per year (Klawitter & Flatt, 1998).

Employer practices in relation to sexual orientation vary widely. Some employers have stated in surveys that they would not hire, would fire, or would not promote a gay or lesbian employee (Badgett, 1996; Woods, 1993). Others state that they make employment decisions strictly on performance and ability, not addressing or not inquiring about sexual orientation, embracing what Woods (1993) has termed the "asexual imperative" of the corporate workplace. Such practices resemble the "don't ask, don't tell" policy current in the United States military. Others state that they take action based on sexual orientation "when sexual orientation interferes with job performance, disrupts other employees or adversely affects the company" (Elliott, 1993, p. 217). As Woods (1993) notes, the argument that sexual orientation is disruptive in the workplace ". . . is a brutal, circular form of prejudice: A gay man's sexuality is disruptive because others despise him for it" (p. 214). Finally, because some employers state that they will do what the law requires them to do, public policy on this issue has a powerful impact.

Because discrimination based on sexual orientation has been well-documented, 10 states have acted to protect the rights of gays and lesbians at work (9 of them extending these basic rights to other areas such as housing and credit as well). Another 7 states have executive orders banning such discrimination in *public* employment, and two others have state civil service rules prohibiting discrimination based on sexual orientation. This leaves 31 of 50 states with no state-level workplace protection at all. Some localities (cities and towns) have enacted civil rights ordinances of their own addressing sexual orientation. In addition, an increasing number of employers have recognized the value of their gay and lesbian employees by developing and implementing their own policies of non-discrimination based on sexual orientation (Zuckerman & Simons, 1996). Advocacy organizations such as the Human Rights Campaign and others maintain up-to-date lists of such organizations, both corporate and non-profit. The limited data available suggest that these state- and local-level ordinances do not have a measurable effect on the earnings of people in same-gender households (Klawitter & Flatt, 1998), perhaps because there has not been effective enforcement of them. However, interestingly, *all* men and women in these areas–those in mixed-gender households and those in same-gender households–have higher incomes than those who live in areas without such antidiscrimination policies.

Because the importance of workplace protection is recognized even in a society in which attitudes toward same-gender sexuality and same-gender relationships are commonly very negative (Wolff, 1998), Congress has been considering specific national legislation to protect the rights of gay and lesbian people in the workplace: The Economic Nondiscrimination Act (ENDA). This act would extend the fair employment practices now guaranteed based on race, religion, sex, national origin, age, and disability to sexual orientation (gay, lesbian, bisexual, and/or heterosexual). In others words employment decisions such as hiring, firing, promotion, or compensation could not be based on sexual orientation. It is in fact a more limited guarantee in some areas (not allowing for "disparate impact" provisions and exempting most employees of religious organizations and all employees of the United States military) (Human Rights Campaign, 1999c). Thus, although it falls short of the kind of guarantee of work rights recommended by the United Nations, enacting ENDA would move the nation much further toward that goal.

Equal Pay for Equal Work

The most basic issue regarding equal pay for equal work is, of course, wage discrimination. As already noted, the representative data available suggest that such discrimination does in fact occur (Badgett, 1995, 1996, 1999; Klawitter & Flatt, 1998). This conclusion is only drawn after data comparing men and/or women to their heterosexual counterparts and after controlling for such factors as region of the country, the nature of the employment, hours worked, and the like. Although more research is needed in this area, any difference between groups that cannot be explained by these other factors known to affect earnings can be attributed to discrimination. Both Badgett (1995) and Klawitter and Flatt (1998) had two major findings on earnings. The first is that gay men[6] earn less than comparable men who are not gay. This effect reduces gay mens' earnings compared to those of heterosexual men by as much as 24% and seems to reflect differences within broad occupational categories. The second major finding is that lesbian couples have less income than other household types (married couples, unmarried heterosexual couples, and gay male couples). Thus gender discrimination in earnings is a major factor affecting lesbians. There is some evidence of occupational "crowding" among lesbian women (Badgett, 1995); that is, individual lesbian women tend to be in lower-paid occupations than their heterosexual counterparts but appear to be compensated like their heterosexual counterparts within each broad occupational category.

How same-gender *couples* are treated under the law and in the workplace is another source of inequity in compensation (Appleby & Anastas, 1998; Elbin, 1990; Human Rights Campaign, 1999a; McNaught, 1993; Poverny & Finch, 1988; Seck, Finch, Mor-Barak, & Poverny, 1993; Spielman & Winfeld, 1996). Fringe benefits, such as health insurance, life insurance, and pension plan participation, commonly represent as much as 40% of a worker's total compensation package (HRC, 1999a; Spielman & Winfeld, 1996). However, these benefits are a privilege, not a right, of employment. Men and women with same-gender partners (including partners with children) usually cannot share their employee benefits with them as married couples do, representing a tangible reduction in the value of their earnings to them. The larger question of the legal recognition of same-gender couples is addressed more fully elsewhere (Appleby & Anastas, 1998; Eskridge, 1996; Sullivan, 1995; Tully, 1994). However, the lack of legal recognition for same-gender couples is a major factor contributing to disadvantage in compensation for men and women in same-gender couples. Even existing state civil rights laws and the proposed federal measure to address sexual orientation discrimination in the workplace (ENDA) do not address this issue (Human Rights Campaign, 1999a).

Despite the obstacles, many employers have in recent years begun to offer such benefits, as many as one in ten organizations in one survey (Human Rights Campaign, 1999a). They have done so in order to compete for the best-qualified employees at a time of relatively low unemployment (Spielman & Winfeld, 1996). Despite fears to the contrary, studies of the organizations that have instituted such benefits in recent years have shown that there is no significant increase in costs to employers; that only about 1% of employees take advantage of the benefits because there are so many two-earner households among same-gender couples; that expenses related to AIDS have not been significant (a premature birth and the treatment of cancer, for example, can be much more expensive); and that there are well-accepted definitions of a domestic partnership that can be used to define who is and is not eligible to participate (Human Rights Campaign, 1999a; Spielman & Winfeld, 1996). A major focus of the development of anti-discriminatory policies in the workplace, therefore, must be on overcoming the heterosexist bias that defines "couples" in a way that prevents gay and lesbian workers with partners from enjoying the same access to employment-related benefits as their heterosexual counterparts.

FREE CHOICE OF EMPLOYMENT

If some employers would not knowingly hire a gay or lesbian person, free choice of employment has not been achieved. However, overtly discriminatory practices such as these are only the tip of the iceberg. While not enough is yet known about how being lesbian, gay, bisexual, or transgendered affects occupational choices and employment decisions (Ellis, 1996), it is well known that some occupations and vocations are more hostile to gay and lesbian people than others. These include teaching, especially teaching young children (Fassinger, 1993; Kitzinger, 1991; Olson, 1987); medicine, especially pediatrics (Fassinger, 1993; Fiskar, 1992; Parker, 1994); the military, where the well-known "don't ask, don't tell" policy makes service impossible for those who openly declare their gay or lesbian orientation; and the clergy, although it should be noted that religious organizations and denominations vary greatly in their attitudes and practices related to gay and lesbian clerics and congregation members (Anderson & Smith, 1993; Chung, 1995; McSpadden, 1993). The systematic exclusion of gay, lesbian, and bisexual people from such service professions as medicine, teaching, and the clergy affects how open people in these occupations are likely to be about their sexual orientation on the job. It is also likely to affect the ability of those gay, lesbian, and bisexual people who would prefer to receive services from a provider like themselves to find one. Finally, how gay, lesbian, bisexual, and transgendered students fare in the secondary schools and institutions of higher education that help prepare them for their careers is discussed elsewhere (see, for example, Grossman, 1997; Harris, 1997; Morgan & Brown, 1991; Pope, 1996).

JUST AND FAVORABLE CONDITIONS OF WORK

Surveys of self-identified gay and lesbian people conducted since 1980 suggest that many gay and lesbian people report experiencing incidents of discrimination at work. Gay or lesbian people may not get a job or may be fired from a job simply because of their sexual orientation (Badgett, 1996, 1997; Elliott, 1993; Friskopp & Silverstein, 1995; Krieger & Sidney, 1997; Poverny & Finch, 1988; Terry, 1992; Woods, 1993).[7] Self-report surveys suggest that between 13% and 62% of gay and lesbian people have encountered discrimination in employment or promotion because of their sexual orientation (Woods, 1993; Badgett, 1996). Many gay, lesbian, and bisexual workers worry about a "lavender ceiling" that prevents them from achieving their full potential (Friskopp & Silverstein, 1995).

Anti-gay prejudice in the workplace can often be both subtle and pervasive (Friskopp & Silverstein, 1995; Powers, 1996), resulting in powerful forms of marginalization. As Woods (1993) has described it:

> In prejudicial compensation practices, the forced invisibility of gay employees, the social validation of heterosexual mating rituals, the anti-gay commentary and imagery that circulate through company channels, even the masculine nature of the bureaucratic organization itself, a certain kind of heterosexuality is routinely displayed and rewarded . . . [resulting in] more subtle, unseen ways in which lesbians and gay men are stigmatized, excluded, and denied the support given to their heterosexual peers.
>
> (pp. 9-10)

Many messages about sexual orientation are displayed in the workplace (Powers, 1996). Engagements and marriages are celebrated; photographs of spouses and children are often displayed in offices; and even the décor in common spaces may depict heterosexual images. Many casual conversations in the workplace address themselves to private and social life, like dating and what one did the past weekend. A partnered gay or lesbian worker must decide whether to attend work-related social events that include spouses with or without the partner. Anti-gay jokes may be part of office or e-mail banter. Thus when surveys ask not just about hiring, firing, or compensation problems but also about whether a gay or lesbian sexual orientation ever creates stressful situations at work, a great many gay, lesbian, and bisexual people report this often occurs. The assumption of heterosexuality often creates many interpersonal stresses and strains in the workplace that heterosexual people do not face (Chung, 1995; Powers, 1996).

"Coming Out," or Identity Management on the Job

Schneider (1984/1998) describes lesbians as having a form of out-siders' "double vision" in relation to their participation in and rela-tionship to work: "an acute awareness of the strength and force of an oppressive ideology of heterosexuality and its structural manifesta-tions, coupled with an active accommodation and creation of a livable working environment" (p. 387). In other words, gay and lesbian people do not just accept the strains of the workplace; they endeavor to cope with them. One major strategy for coping with workplace dis-crimination is identity management, that is, making choices about if, when, and to whom to disclose a gay, lesbian, or bisexual identity in the workplace.

The strategies chosen by gay and lesbian workers vary, and both disclosure and nondisclosure appear to be adaptive for different people in different situations (Hetherington et al., 1989). Many gay, lesbian, or bisexual people who are open about their sexual orientation in their private lives are not "out" on the job, believing many aspects of private life to be irrelevant in the work setting (Woods, 1993). Howev-er, the strains associated with active or passive concealment are often considerable (Powers, 1996).

Coming out is not a one-time or one-context event; the decision about what to say about oneself must continually be made and remade as co-workers, clients or customers, and supervisors change over time (Griffin & Zuckas, 1993; Hall, 1986; Kitzinger, 1991). Thus lesbian, gay, and bisexual workers are often in some intermediate state of uncertainty about exactly what people at work know or assume about their sexual orientation (Griffin & Zuckas, 1993; Gonsiorek, 1993; Kitzinger, 1991). This uncertainty in turn can lead to confusion about how to interpret events and interactions at work: Is homophobia or heterosexism a factor or not?

Context is extremely important. One study (Ellis & Riggle, 1995) showed that gay and lesbian workers who lived in a city with civil rights protection were more likely to report that their employers had anti-discrimination policies that included sexual orientation. These workers were also more likely to be open about their sexual orienta-tion and to have higher levels of life satisfaction when more open on the job. By contrast, those who lived in a city without civil rights protection had higher levels of life satisfaction when they were *less* open on the job. Another study of gay and lesbian schoolteachers found that "coming out fitted the lifestyle only of those (predominantly men) who took on the role of crusaders for gay liberation" (Dankmeijer, 1993, p. 95). Thus gay, lesbian, and bisexual people struggle to cope rationally and appropriately with heterosexism and homophobia in the workplace by selecting the identity management strategies that will allow them to function most productively and comfortably at work.

ADDITIONAL CHALLENGES

Race and Ethnicity

Unfortunately, as already observed, very little is systematically known about how gay, lesbian, and bisexual people of color fare in the workplace. It is known, however, that race, ethnicity, gender, and sexual orientation interact in the workplace in complex gender- and culture-specific ways (Appleby & Anastas, 1998; deMonteflores, 1986; Friskopp & Silverstein, 1995; Martinez, 1998; Rosabal, 1996). Gay, lesbian, and bisexual people of a non-dominant race or ethnicity may experience discrimination in the workplace on several levels (Martinez, 1998; Rosabal, 1996). In Friskopp and Silverstein's (1995) study of graduates of the Harvard Business School, they made special efforts to identify and interview respondents of color. In general, their respondents felt that race had more often been a problem for them than sexual orientation largely because many successfully concealed a gay, lesbian, or bisexual identity at work. Moreover, they reported that being gay or lesbian sometimes compromised their ability to draw support outside the workplace from their racial and ethnic communities, and being a person of color sometimes limited the support they felt from the gay and lesbian community. Creating social support networks on and off the job is an important coping strategy (Schneider, 1984/1998), underlining the importance of such a pervasive experience of marginalization.

Transgender Issues

As defined by the Human Rights Campaign (1999d),

"transgendered" is a broad term that encompasses cross-dressers, intersexed people, transsexuals, and people who live sub-

> stantial portions of their lives as other than their birth gender. Generally speaking, a transgendered person manifests a sense of self, the physical characteristics and/or personal expression commonly associated with a sex other than the one he or she was assigned at birth. (p. 1)

There are even fewer protections for transgendered workers than for gay, lesbian, or bisexual ones: currently only 5 states and a handful of localities offer even limited safeguards, usually based on the diagnosis of gender identity disorder (GID) and its definition as a disability. Only one state (Minnesota) has defined its statute banning discrimination based on sexual orientation to include "self-image or identity" (Human Rights Campaign, 1999d, p. 6). Those workers who maintain the same job while in the process of transitioning in their gender presentation, which includes all pre-operative transsexuals, face a number of special challenges that have to be artfully negotiated (Human Rights Campaign, 1999d). Peer support from other workers can be essential in such a process. Generally speaking, employers have a right "to regulate employee appearance and behavior in the workplace for reasonable business purposes" and to "require conformity to accepted community standards of dress and behavior" (Human Rights Campaign, 1999d). These gender norms can make maintaining employment a challenge for transgendered people, including those transsexuals in transition. However, with proper education and support in the workplace, transitioning, transsexual, and other transgendered employees can continue to function effectively at work (Human Rights Campaign, 1999d, McNaught, 1993).

CONCLUSION

> Sexual orientation does not affect a person's ability to contribute to society . . . Gay people have an overall potential to contribute to society similar to that of heterosexual people, including in the workplace.
>
>
>
> Brief of amicus curiae
> American Psychological Association
> in *Watkins v. United States Army*
> (Gary B. Melton, 1989, 9. 936).
>
>

Discrimination against gay, lesbian, bisexual, and transgendered people in the workplace does not just diminish them; it diminishes what they can contribute to society as a whole. In advanced industrial economies, participation in the labor market is essential economically to individuals and their families. However, work is not just about making money. As Schneider (1984/1998) notes, "work and one's relationship to it is considered a major source of economic and social status, personal validation, and life purpose . . . in this society" (p. 377). Thus the kinds of barriers to fair and equitable treatment in the workplace described here do not just affect economic well-being, both individual and collective, but they also likely contribute to the erosion of personal and social well-being as well.

What do gay, lesbian, bisexual, and transgendered people want at work? An often-quoted passage sums it up:

1. An explicit employment policy that prohibits discrimination based upon sexual orientation;
2. Creation of a safe work environment that is free of heterosexist, homophobic, and AIDS-phobic behaviors;
3. Company-wide education about gay issues in the workplace and about AIDS;
4. An equitable benefit program that recognizes the domestic partners of gay, lesbian, and bisexual employees;
5. Support of a gay/lesbian/bisexual employee support group;
6. Freedom for all employees to participate fully in all aspects of corporate (organizational) life;
7. Public support of gay issues.

(McNaught, 1993, p. 66)

Since this was written, a few additional points can be added. There is a new awareness of the special challenges that transgendered people face on the job (Human Rights Campaign, 1999d). In terms of public support, some corporations have found that advertising in gay or lesbian markets has been good for business as well as affirming to employees. ENDA was first introduced in Congress in 1996, but at this writing it has yet to pass in either the Senate or the House despite support from many major United States corporations (Human Rights Campaign, 1999b). Finally, data to refute the myths about gay and lesbian affluence are only now emerging (Badgett, 1999), myths that have been used to challenge the need for basic human and civil rights protections for gay, lesbian, and bisexual people. However, guaranteeing all gay, lesbian, bisexual, and transgendered people in the United States the right to work, to equal pay for equal work, and to just and favorable conditions of work remains, alas, a vision for the future.

There are many implications of this situation for the social work profession. We need to base our practice with gay, lesbian, bisexual, and transgendered people and their families on an understanding of their realities, not on myth. This means facing the realities of workplace discrimination as well as knowing about those legislative and employer-based initiatives that can make a positive difference. In particular, social workers who practice in Employee Assistance Programs (EAPs), unions, and other work-related settings are often in a position to assist in the achievement of equal treatment and favorable working conditions for gay, lesbian, bisexual, and transgendered employees at all levels. We need to participate in advocacy efforts at local, state, and national levels until basic protections are in place for all gay, lesbian, bisexual, and transgendered people. However, because so little is now known about the extent and nature of direct and indirect forms of workplace discrimination, we need to contribute to knowledge-building efforts in that area.

In fact, we know very little about ourselves. Despite an avowed ideology of egalitarianism and antidiscrimination, women in the social work profession do not get fair and equal treatment in employment (Gibelman & Schervish, 1993, 1995, 1997). How do gay, lesbian, bisexual, and transgendered students fare in our schools and departments of social work that prepare them for social work jobs? The one study published to date on the issue suggests that very few social work graduate and/or undergraduate programs place much emphasis on recruiting or retaining gay and lesbian faculty members or students. In addition, the self-reported amount of curriculum emphasis on sexual orientation lags far behind that on women or people of color (Mackleprang, Ray, & Hernandez-Peck, 1996). How do gay, lesbian, bisexual, and/or transgendered social workers fare on their jobs? No such large-scale study has ever been done. Well-designed research on the issue would tell us more about how homophobia and heterosexism can affect social workers' employment and earnings both directly and indirectly. It might also shed some light on how these forces affect employment and earnings in general, thus suggesting ways to benefit our clients and their families as well.

NOTES

1. Most of the existing research on the workplace addresses the situations of gay men and/or lesbians. This article will try to make clear which groups are being addressed, but it should be noted at the outset that very little is known about how bisexual and transgendered people fare at work.

2. This analysis, based as it is on the available published literature, is confined to the pursuit of income through employment. I know of no studies that address the effects of sexual orientation on self-employment and other forms of economic self-maintenance.

3. Because the numbers of gay, lesbian, and/or bisexual respondents in all of the samples analyzed was very small (1%-10%), it was not possible to examine differences in earnings within the gay and lesbian group for anything other than gender. Thus the joint effects of race and ethnicity along with sexual orientation have yet to be systematically studied.

4. According to the National Gay and Lesbian Task Force (NGLTF) Public Policy Institute (1998), these states are California (private employment only), Connecticut, the District of Columbia, Illinois (public employment only), Hawaii, Massachusetts, Minnesota, New Hampshire, New Jersey, Rhode Island, Vermont, and Wisconsin.

5. In 1998, there were 19 states with sodomy statutes, 5 of them targeting only same-gender activity (NGLTF, 1998).

6. Being gay was defined by self-reported sexual behavior in the Badgett (1995) study and in the Klawitter and Flatt (1998) study by the use of the Census category of "unmarried partner" in households where both of the partners were male or female.

7. Most of the studies cited here did not ask about or sample bisexual or transgendered people.

REFERENCES

Anastas, J. W. (1998). Working against discrimination: Gay, lesbian and bisexual people on the job. *Journal of Gay & Lesbian Social Services, 8*(3), 83-98.

Anderson, C. W., & Smith, H. R. (1993). Stigma and honor: Gay, lesbian, and bisexual people in the U. S. military. In L. Diamant (Ed.), *Homosexual issues in the workplace* (pp. 65-69). Washington, DC: Taylor & Francis.

Appleby, G. A., & Anastas, J. W. (1998). *Not just a passing phase: Social work with gay, lesbian and bisexual people.* New York: Columbia University Press.

Badgett, M. V. L. (1995). The wage effects of sexual orientation discrimination. *Industrial and Labor Relations Review, 48*(4), 726-739.

Badgett. M. V. L. (1996). Employment and sexual orientation: Disclosure and discrimination in the workplace. *Journal of Gay & Lesbian Social Services, 4*(4), 29-52.

Badgett, M. V. L. (1997). Thinking homo/economically. In J. T. Sears & W. L. Williams (Eds.), *Overcoming heterosexism and homophobia: Strategies that work* (pp. 380-390). New York: Columbia University Press.

Badgett, M. V. L. (1999). *Income inflation: The myth of affluence among gay, lesbian, and bisexual Americans.* Washington, DC: Policy Institute of the National Gay and Lesbian Task Force and the Institute for Gay and Lesbian Strategic Studies.

Chung, Y. B. (1995). Career decision-making of lesbian, gay, and bisexual individuals. *Career Development Quarterly, 44*(2), 178-190.

Dankmeijer, P. (1993). The construction of identities as a means of survival: The case of gay and lesbian teachers. *Journal of Homosexuality, 24*(3/4), 95-105.

deMonteflores, C. (1986). Notes on the management of difference. In Stein & Cohen (Eds.), *Contemporary perspectives on psychotherapy with lesbians and gay men* (pp. 73-101). New York: Plenum Press.

Elbin, R. L. (1990). Domestic partnership recognition in the workplace: Equitable employee benefits for gay couples (and others). *Ohio State Law Journal, 51*(4), 1067-1087.

Elliott, J. E. (1993). Career development with gay and lesbian clients. *Career Development Quarterly, 41*(3), 210-226.

Ellis, A. I. (1996). Sexual identity issues in the workplace: Past and present. *Journal of Gay & Lesbian Social Services, 4*(4), 1-16.

Ellis, A. L., & Riggle, E. D. D. (1995). The relation of job satisfaction and degree openness about one's sexual orientation for lesbians and gay men. *Journal of Homosexuality, 30*(2), 75-85.

Eskridge, W. N., Jr. (1996). *The case for same-sex marriage: From sexual liberty to civilized commitment.* New York: The Free Press.

Fassinger, R. E. (1995). From invisibility to integration: Lesbian identity in the workplace. *Career Development Quarterly, 44*(2), 148-167.

Fiskar, C. R. (1992). The gay pediatrician: A report. *Journal of Homosexuality, 23*(3), 53-63.

Friskopp, H., & Silverstein, S. (1995). *Straight jobs, gay lives: Gay and lesbian professionals, the Harvard Business School, and the American workplace.* New York: Scribner.

Gibelman, M., & Schervish, P. H. (1993). The glass ceiling in social work: Is it shatterproof? *Affilia, 8,* 442-455.

Gibelman, M., & Schervish, P. H. (1995). Pay equity in social work: Not! *Social Work, 40,* 622-629.

Gibelman, M., & Schervish, P. H. (1997). *Who we are: A second look.* Washington, DC: NASW Press.

Gonsiorek, J. C. (1993). Threat, stress, and adjustment: Mental health and the workplace for gay and lesbian individuals. In L. Diamant (Ed.), *Homosexual issues in the workplace.* Washington, DC: Taylor & Francis.

Griffin, C., & Zuckas, M. (1993). Coming out in psychology: Lesbian psychologists talk. *Feminism and Psychology, 3*(1), 111-133.

Grossman, A. H. (1997). Growing up with a "spoiled identity": Lesbian, gay, and bisexual youth at risk. *Journal of Gay & Lesbian Social Services, 6*(3), 45-56.

Hall, M. (1986). The lesbian corporate experience. *Journal of Homosexuality, 12* (3/4), 59-75.

Harris, M. B. (Ed.). *School experiences of lesbian and gay youth: The invisible minority.* New York: The Haworth Press, Inc. (Simultaneously published as Volume 7, Number 4 of the *Journal of Gay & Lesbian Social Services*).

Hetherington, C. E., Hillerbrand, E., & Etringer, B. (1989). Career counseling with gay men: Issues and recommendations. *Journal of Counseling and Development, 14*(1/2), 25-42.

Human Rights Campaign. (1999a). *Domestic partnership benefits for same-sex couples.* Washington, DC: Human Rights Campaign. *(http://www.hrc.org/issues/workplace/dp/index.html).*

Human Rights Campaign. (1999b). *Employment Non-Discrimination Act (ENDA): Fact Sheet.* Washington, DC: Human Rights Campaign. *(http://www.hrc.org/issues/leg/enda/endafact.html).*

Human Rights Campaign. (1999c). *Non-discrimination in the workplace.* Washington, DC: Human Rights Campaign. *(http://www.hrc.org/issues/workplace/nd/index.html).*

Human Rights Campaign. (1999d). *Transgenderism and transition in the workplace.* Washington, DC: Human Rights Campaign. *(http://www.hrc.org/issues/trans/dana2. html).*

Kitzinger, C. (1991). Lesbian and gay men in the workplace: Psychological issues. In M. J. Davidson & J. Earnshaw (Eds.), *Vulnerable workers: Psychosocial and legal issues* (pp. 223-240). New York: Wiley.

Klawitter, M. M., & Flatt, V. (1998). The effect of state and local antidiscrimination policies on earnings for gays and lesbians. *Journal of Policy Analysis and Management, 17*(4), 658-686.

Krieger, N., & Sidney, S. (1997). Prevalence and health implications of anti-gay discrimination: A study of black and white women and men in the CARDIA cohort. *International Journal of Health Services, 27*(1), 157-176.

Mackleprang, R. W., Ray, J., & Hernandez-Peck, M. (1996). Social work education and sexual orientation: Faculty, student, and curriculum issues. *Journal of Gay & Lesbian Social Services, 5*(4), 17-31.

Martinez, D. G. (1998). Mujer, Latina, lesbiana–Notes on the multidimensionality of economic and sociopolitical injustice. *Journal of Gay & Lesbian Social Services, 8*(3), 99-112.

McNaught, B. (1993). *Gay issues in the workplace.* New York: St. Martin's.

McSpadden, J. R. (1993). Homosexuality and the church. In L. Diamant (Ed.), *Homosexual issues in the workplace* (pp. 91-103). Washington, DC: Taylor & Francis.

Melton, G. B. (1989). Public policy and private prejudice: Psychology and law on gay rights. *American Psychologist, 44*(6), 933-40.

Morgan, K. S., & Brown, L. S. (1991). Lesbian career development, work behavior, and vocational counseling. *Counseling Psychologist, 19*(2), 273-291.

National Gay and Lesbian Task Force Policy Institute. (1998). *Gay, lesbian, bisexual and transgender civil rights laws in the United States.* Washington, DC: Author.

Olson, M. R. (1987). A study of gay and lesbian teachers. *Journal of Homosexuality, 13*(4), 73-81.

Parker, S. G. (1994). Curing homophobia. *The New Physician, 43*(3), 13-19.

Pope, M. (1996). Gay and lesbian career counseling: Special career counseling issues. *Journal of Gay & Lesbian Social Services, 4*(4), 91-105.

Poverny, L. M., & Finch, W. A. (1988). Integrating work-related issues on gay and lesbian employees into occupational social work practice. *Employee Assistance Quarterly, 4*(2), 15-29.

Powers, B. (1996). The impact of gay, lesbian and bisexual workplace issues on productivity. *Journal of Gay & Lesbian Social Services, 4*(4), 17-28.

Rosabal, G. S. (1996). Multicultural existence in the workplace: Including how I thrive as a Latina lesbian feminist. *Journal of Gay & Lesbian Social Services, 4*(4), 17-28.

Schneider, B. E. (1984/1998). Peril and promise: Lesbians' workplace participation. In P. M. Nardi & B. E. Schneider (Eds.), *Social perspectives in lesbian and gay studies: A reader* (pp. 377-389). London and New York: Routledge. Originally published in T. Darty & S. Potter (Eds.), *Women-identified women* (pp. 211-230). Palo Alto, CA: Mayfield Publishers.

Seck, E. T., Finch, W. A., Mor-Barak, M. E., & Poverny, L. M. (1993). Managing a diverse workforce. *Administration in Social Work, 17*(2), 67-79.

Spielman, S., & Winfeld, L. (1996). Domestic partner benefits: A bottom line discussion. *Journal of Gay & Lesbian Social Services 4*(4), 53-78.

Sullivan, A. (1995). *Virtually normal: An argument about homosexuality.* New York: Knopf.

Terry, P. (1992). Entitlement not privilege: The right of employment and advancement. In N. Woodman (Ed.), *Lesbian and gay lifestyles: A guide for counseling and education* (pp. 133-143). New York: Irvington.

Tully, C. T. (1994). To boldly go where no one has gone before: The legalization of lesbian and gay marriage. *Journal of Gay & Lesbian Social Services, 1*(1), 73-87.

Van Soest, D., & Bryant, A. S. (1995). Violence reconceptualized for social work: The urban dilemma. *Social Work, 40*(4), 549-57.

Wolff, A. (1998). *One nation, after all.* New York: Viking Press.

Woods, J. D. (1993). *The corporate closet: The professional lives of gay men in America.* New York: Free Press.

Zuckerman, A. J., & Simons, G. F. (1996). *Sexual orientation in the workplace: Gay men, lesbians, bisexuals and heterosexuals working together.* Thousand Oaks, CA: Sage.

Who Gets to Drink
from the Fountain of Freedom?:
Homophobia in Communities of Color

Pat Washington

SUMMARY. The question "Who Gets to Drink from the Fountain of Freedom?" is designed to evoke the image of the "Whites Only" water fountains of the segregated South and to provoke discomfort and dissonance among those who, having claimed the right to drink from the fountain of freedom, would deny this right to others. Homophobia in families and communities of color is explored, and discrimination against gays and lesbians within those communities is analyzed. Commonalties in the oppression experienced across communities of color and lesbians and gays of color are explored. Finally, some progressive initiatives occurring within racialized communities are examined, including recommendations for necessary institutional and individual changes for broadening the definition of community to fully incorporate lesbians and gay men of color. *[Article copies available for a fee from The Haworth Document Delivery Service: 1-800-342-9678. E-mail address: <getinfo@ haworthpressinc.com> Website: <http://www.HaworthPress.com> © 2001 by The Haworth Press, Inc. All rights reserved.]*

KEYWORDS. Communities of color, homophobia, discrimination, lesbians, gay men

---

Pat Washington is affiliated with the Department of Women's Studies, San Diego State University.

[Haworth co-indexing entry note]: "Who Gets to Drink from the Fountain of Freedom?: Homophobia in Communities of Color." Washington, Pat. Co-published simultaneously in *Journal of Gay & Lesbian Social Services* (Harrington Park Press, an imprint of The Haworth Press, Inc.) Vol. 13, No. 1/2, 2001, pp. 117-131; and: *From Hate Crimes to Human Rights: A Tribute to Matthew Shepard* (ed: Mary E. Swigonski, Robin S. Mama, and Kelly Ward) Harrington Park Press, an imprint of The Haworth Press, Inc., 2001, pp. 117-131. Single or multiple copies of this article are available for a fee from The Haworth Document Delivery Service [1-800-342-9678, 9:00 a.m. - 5:00 p.m. (EST). E-mail address: getinfo@ haworthpressinc.com].

INTRODUCTION

In *The Autobiography of Miss Jane Pittman*, the film's title character reveals symbolically what it means to "drink from the fountain of
freedom." The 110-year-old Jane Pittman, played by a theatrically-
aged Cicely Tyson, has suffered repeated, devastating losses throughout a century marked by slavery, failed Reconstruction, and murder-
ous Jim Crow segregation. The final loss–the blow she cannot bear
with her characteristic fortitude and forbearance–occurs when her
friend Jimmy, a young Civil Rights activist, is arrested and murdered
in his jail cell for crossing the color line to drink at a "Whites Only"
water fountain.

Jimmy's death, the capstone and culmination of all the tragedies she
has experienced in the course of a century, compels Ms. Jane to act.
Despite the threats of her White landlord that she will not be allowed
to return to the home where she has lived for the last fifty years, Ms.
Jane goes to town to confront Jimmy's murderers. Initially assisted by
another elderly Black woman, the ancient Jane Pittman purposefully
makes her way along the pavement to the courthouse. Ahead of her–
and nearly obscured by glaring, pot-bellied policemen–is the "Whites
Only" drinking fountain at which Jimmy and his friends had been
arrested a few days earlier. The elderly companion fades into the
background, and Ms. Jane is left to make her way assisted only by her
cane and the knowledge that Jimmy has left a "little piece of himself
behind." Slowly moving past the police officers, she makes her painful trek to the "Whites Only" fountain. Once there, she stoops, rests
one hand on the fountain, and–in a single moment that vanquishes a
century of racist exclusion–takes a drink, licks her lips, and (her purpose accomplished) returns to the throng of Black family and friends
awaiting her.

The "Whites Only" water fountain of the segregated South was
emblematic of a national consciousness that drew an invisible, yet
indelible, line between "White" and "Colored," "superior" and "inferior," "deserving" and "undeserving," "human" and "subhuman."
It was emblematic of a belief that one group of people deserved the
full range of human rights afforded by the U.S. Constitution, while
another group deserved only humiliation, degradation, and depriva-
tion.

The question "Who Gets to Drink from the Fountain of Freedom?" is designed to be both evocative and provocative. It is meant to evoke the image of the "Whites Only" water fountains of the segregated South. It is meant also to evoke the images of the courageous men, women, and children who dared to challenge the notion that one group was inherently superior and, thereby, had the right to dominate (degrade, humiliate, kill) another. It is meant to provoke discomfort and dissonance among those who, having claimed the right to drink from the fountain of freedom, would deny this right to others.

WHO GETS TO DRINK?: A SOCIOLOGICAL PERSPECTIVE

An important area of sociological analysis is social stratification, the concept that "any society will consist of levels that relate to each other in terms of superordination and subordination, be it in power, privilege or prestige" (Berger, 1963, p. 78). In the U.S., the most obvious systems of superordination and subordination are those based on gender, race, class, and sexual orientation (Collins, 1990; Gorelick, 1996). Less obvious–and more perplexing–are systems of superordination and subordination that occur among and within groups that are themselves subordinated (Cameron, 1983; Clarke, 1983; Collins, 1990, p. 225; Densham, 1997; Diaz, 1998). An example of this system within a system–or this oppression within and by an oppressed group–is the homophobia that is often manifested in communities of color (Cameron, 1983; Clarke, 1983; Diaz, 1998; Shukla, 1997, p. 280; Valerio, 1983, p. 44).

Defined as the fear and loathing of people perceived or known to engage in same-sex intimacy (Clarke, 1983; Eskridge, 1996; Scarce, 1997; Valerio, 1983), homophobia can be as "innocuous" as assuming a person is heterosexual (Boykin, 1996) or as toxic as anti-gay violence (Lewin & McDevitt, 1993; Scarce, 1997). It can be as viciously demeaning as schoolyard taunts or as politely "academic" as unfounded assertions that homosexuality did not exist in pre-colonial Africa (Wyatt, 1997). Like other forms of intolerance, homophobia exists on both individual and institutional levels.

Although recent studies suggest that lesbians and gay men of color may experience higher degrees of acceptance within their families and communities of origin than do their White counterparts (Vaid, 1995), such acceptance is often limited and typically means only that racialized families and communities do not, for the most part, disown or expel their lesbian and gay members (Boykin, 1996; Brown, 1989; Cameron, 1983; Clarke, 1983; Diaz, 1998; Moraga, 1983; Scott, 1991; Valerio, 1983). For instance, in his research on Latino gay males and HIV, Rafael Diaz (1998) observed, "For the majority of Latino gay men . . . their homosexuality has been culturally accepted (or rather tolerated) only if it is not mentioned or talked about and not labeled as such" (p. 61). Likewise, "[f]amily support, when reported, was mostly experienced as tolerance, parental resignation, or the absence of overt mocking and abuse" (p. 92).

By and large, racialized communities appear reluctant to address homophobia and, in fact, at times seem all too eager to fuel anti-gay sentiment (Clarke, 1983; Diaz, 1998; Shukla, 1997). As a consequence, lesbians and gay men of color are constrained by multiple levels of subordination–those emanating from the dominant culture (Badgett, 1997; Cameron, 1983; Clarke, 1983; Jenness & Broad, 1997) and those emanating from families and communities of origin (Cameron, 1983; Clarke, 1983; Cohen, 1999; Collins, 1990; Densham, 1997, p. 285; Diaz, 1998; Moraga, 1983; Shukla, 1997; Thompson, 1996; Valerio, 1983). This latter phenomenon is the starting point for this article.

In addition to exploring the persistent and seemingly entrenched homophobia in families and communities of color and analyzing how discrimination against gays and lesbians is uniquely shaped (and rationalized) by those communities, this article also explores commonalties in the oppression experienced across communities of color and lesbians and gays of color–and the resistance expressed–by both lesbians and gay men and certain racialized groups (Badgett, 1997; Jenness & Broad, 1997). I will conclude with an examination of some progressive initiatives occurring within racialized communities as well as make recommendations for necessary institutional and individual changes for broadening the definition of community to fully incorporate lesbians and gay men of color.

I will primarily examine manifestations of multiple levels of subordination emanating from homophobia within Black and Latino communities, although, when feasible, similar observations will be made regarding Asian-American and Native American groups. In writing this article, I do not mean to imply that lesbians and gays are without allies in communities of color. Nor do I mean to skirt the issue of racism in the lesbian and gay community. Both of these are important issues deserving of a much fuller treatment than they can be given here.

THEORETICAL FRAMEWORK

Many current theoretical perspectives on the oppression of lesbians and gay men in the United States are based on scholarly and activist understandings that our social institutions are grounded in beliefs that U.S. born, able-bodied, White, heterosexual, propertied Christian males are inherently superior and thereby have the right to dominate those unlike themselves (Badgett, 1997; Hearn, 1996). Fueled largely by the contributions of women of color, as well as the work of a smattering of progressive Whites and some men of color, current scholarship on social stratification is becoming increasingly rooted in understandings that gender, race, class, and sexuality are simultaneous social processes that shape all relationships (Chow, 1996; Shende, 1997; West & Fernstermaker, 1996).

The theoretical approach informing this article is an amalgam of Barbara Smith's "web of oppression" (Scott, 1991, p. 9), Marilyn Frye's "cage of oppression" (Frye, 1998, p. 149), Kimberle Crenshaw's concept of "intersectionality" (1997, pp. 551-554), and Patricia Hill Collins' definition of "Black feminist thought" (1990). The works of these four individuals are based on an understanding that people are constrained and oppressed by factors that operate both independently of and interdependently with each other. Collins in particular notes the need for developing "analyses of contemporary social phenomena that explore the connections among race, class, and gender oppression and use new reconceptualizations of family, community, and power in doing so" (p. 224). Collins' thesis that people's identities and experiences are defined by both/and, rather than either/or, realities is central to the analysis of the multiple levels of subordination experienced by lesbians and gay men of color.

COMMONALTIES IN MANIFESTATIONS OF OPPRESSION AND RESISTANCE TO OPPRESSION

Boykin (1996) writes that "Virtually all oppressed groups suffer from three types of oppression: internal oppression as the individual struggles with her or his identity, group-based oppression from others in the same category, and external oppression from those who dislike the group" (p. 56). These categories coincide with those described by Patricia Hill Collins, who writes, "People experience and resist oppression on three levels: the level of personal biography; the group or community level of the cultural context created by race, class, and gender; and the systemic level of social institutions" (p. 227). The discrimination that lesbians and gays and racialized people in the U.S. endure from mainstream, White, heterosexual culture falls within Boykin's third category of "external oppression" or Collins's "systemic level of social institutions."

Sociologists have long noted that the persecution of racialized people and the persecution of lesbians and gays serve a similar function for Whites and heterosexuals–namely, that both Whites and heterosexuals rely on the counterimage of their respective despised groups to elevate themselves (Berger, 1963; Zinn, 1996). During historical and contemporary times, both racialized men and women and lesbians and gays have labored under dominant cultural stereotypes depicting them as criminals, sexual perverts, and moral and intellectual inferiors (Berger, 1963; Boykin, 1996; Brown, 1989; Chow, 1996; Collins, 1990; Diaz, 1998; Israel, 1992; Vaid, 1995; Wyatt, 1997). Making a connection specifically between the oppression of Blacks and the oppression of lesbians and gay men, Brown (1989) notes, "Whites see Blacks as not only different but inferior. Which is also the way heterosexuals see homosexuals" (p. 75). In similar fashion, Boykin observes that the "experience of dealing with prejudice is perhaps the defining attribute of both blackness and homosexuality (1996, p. 57).

Labeling racialized groups and lesbians and gay men as inferior or deviant has allowed major social institutions of the dominant culture to neglect these groups or to otherwise act against their best interests (Badgett, 1997; Boykin, 1996; Boykin, 1999; Brown, 1989; Chow, 1996; Collins, 1990; Densham, 1997; hooks, 1994; Israel, 1992; Jenness & Broad, 1997; Scott, 1991; Vaid, 1995).

One social institution that appears to be particularly oppressive to members of racialized groups *and* lesbians and gay men is the criminal justice system. Again, we have to go no further than recent issues of the *New York Times* or the *Los Angeles Times* for examples of how men and women of color are still subjected to police brutality and/or excessive force. While accounts of police brutality against lesbians and gay men rarely make it to the front pages of mainstream U.S. newspapers, police violence against women and men for their actual or perceived sexual orientation is also an ongoing concern of predominantly gay publications (Israel, 1992). In addition to the forms of violence sanctioned within our formal social institutions, both racialized peoples and lesbians and gay men are subjected to hate crimes and bias incidents that, while directed at an individual member of a group (e.g., James Byrd or Matthew Shephard), are meant to send a message to the entire community (Brown, 1989; Lewin & McDevitt, 1993).

Since my aim here is not to provide an exhaustive analysis of oppressions shared by both racialized people and lesbians and gay men, I will conclude with just one more example of a major social institution that has actively contributed to the subjugation of lesbians and gays, as well as certain racialized groups. The Christian religion–whether Catholic or Protestant–has historically been inimical to racialized groups and to homosexuals (Stevens, 1997). In the antebellum South, for instance, the Christian Bible was used to justify slavery and to convince enslaved Blacks that their earthly suffering was a small price to pay for heavenly bliss. Today, it is used by militant White Christians to argue for an apartheid America and/or to agitate for a race war. The same Bible has been, and continues to be, used to justify discrimination against lesbians and gay men (Eskridge, 1996; Stevens, 1997). While some contemporary religious leaders and congregations have struggled through their homophobia to embrace lesbian and gay members of their faith, many have not. As a consequence, lesbians and gay men, like Black Americans before them, have either created alternative religious institutions that allow their full humanity, or settled for marginal status within traditional churches (Brown, 1989; Collins, 1991; Eskridge, 1996).

HOMOPHOBIA IN COMMUNITIES OF COLOR: WHO HAS A RIGHT TO CIVIL RIGHTS?

Examining the discourse concerning who is or is not deserving of civil rights is important to our understanding of homophobia within communities of color. As suggested earlier in this article, homophobia within communities of color is an example of "a system within a system"–of one subordinated group subordinating another.

Families and communities of color all too often mirror the dominant culture's practice of designating lesbians and gay men as acceptable targets of various forms of victimization (Diaz, 1998; Scott, 1991, pp. 42-43; Shukla, 1997, p. 280). The discrimination that lesbians and gays of color experience from families and communities of origin can be characterized as within-group oppression or "group-based oppression from others in the same category" (Boykin, 1996; Diaz, 1998; Scott, 1991; Shukla, 1997). In this case, the shared identity is race/ethnicity, while the basis for the oppression is a devalued sexual orientation that distinguishes the oppressed from the oppressors within the community.

Some of the more recognizable examples of homophobia within families and communities of color include aversion, denial, silencing, or other forms of censorship (Diaz, 1998; Scott, 1991). Gonzalez (1999) illustrates the destructive power of within-group oppression in his account of progressive Latina/o organizations that were targeted by conservative Latina/o politicians and other reactionaries for advancing "the homosexual agenda." As a consequence of these highly publicized attacks, the targeted organizations lost community acceptance and credibility, as well as financial backing and human resources, even though their so-called "homosexual agenda" was in actuality a broad-based mission to "create a world where everyone has civil rights and economic justice, where the environment is cared for, where cultures are honored and communities are safe" (p. 14).

Lesbians and gays of color are important to their communities of origin because of their contributions to civil rights and anti-war movements; their numerical presence in families and communities; their creative contributions to the artistic, musical, literary, and scholarly productions; their political and cultural leadership and advocacy; their entrepreneurship and business acumen; and their value as members of the human family (Boykin, 1999; Collins, 1990; Diaz, 1998; Jordan, 1981; Scott, 1991).

BLACK RESISTANCE TO CIVIL RIGHTS CLAIMS OF LESBIANS AND GAYS

Given this country's legacy of slavery and the ongoing racial discrimination against Blacks, it is not surprising that there is considerable Black resistance to civil rights claims of lesbians and gay men.

The rhetoric of scarce resources, a mentality that believes "whatever your group gets means my group gets less," hundreds of years of scholarly and activist teachings that Blacks are the most oppressed minority group in the U.S., and the reality that Black sacrifice and struggle opened doors of opportunity to many other oppressed groups have all contributed to the presumption on the part of some Blacks that they are the only true and rightful heirs of the tools of struggle and resistance (Anderson, 1999). This presumption often leads Blacks, as a group, to challenge other groups (among whom lesbians and gays are, arguably, the most despised) when those groups appear to be upstaging Black demands for social and economic justice.

Black resistance to the civil rights claims of lesbians and gay men is nowhere more evident than in the angry pronouncements that lesbians and gays–by seeking inclusion in a purportedly democratic socie-ty–are co-opting or misappropriating the language and strategies of civil rights. Indeed, analogies between the struggles for Black civil rights and the struggles for lesbian and gay civil rights are fiercely denounced by Blacks and neoconservatives of every hue (Sen, 1997).

It is true that, despite the existence of homophobia within the domi-nant culture, predominantly White lesbian and gay organizations en-joy a racial privilege that often results in their securing the visibility, credibility, and financial backing to which lesbian and gay organiza-tions of color have minimal, if any, access (Diaz, 1998; Jenness and Broad, 1997). It is also true, as Vaid (1995) submits, that White gays and lesbians should not adopt an ostensibly "Black" civil rights plat-form without "a broader and more inclusive commitment to cultural transformation," "a clear stand on the civil rights of Blacks, people of color, immigrants and women," and a deeper understanding of ongo-ing racial discrimination (pp. 186-189).

Nevertheless, presumption of sole ownership of civil rights strate-gies and tactics by Blacks needs to be challenged.[1] For one thing, all movement organizers and advocates construct terminology and tech-niques to further their particular causes without "re-inventing the wheel." As Jenness and Broad argue, "[A]ctivists and advocates nec-essarily relate their goals and programs to extant meanings; thus they are simultaneously consumers and producers of cultural meaning" (1997, p. 105). For another, Blacks have borrowed liberally from "the White man's Bible," the *United States Constitution* (itself copied largely from the Iroquoi), and the ideologies and strategies of individuals and groups from around the world (e.g., Mathatma Ghandi). We can point to the human and financial resources other racial-ethnic group members have expended (and often continue to expend) on behalf of Black civil rights, and we can also recognize that Blacks and other oppressed groups are part of a human family where resources are constantly shared, reshaped, redistributed, and passed along (Anderson, 1999; Cameron, 1983; Jordan, 1981). Finally, we can point to the fluid nature of social justice struggles and argue that lesbians and gays (both White and of color) who suppressed their need for sexual equality in earlier eras are less willing to do so today (Anderson, 1999; Badgett, 1997; Diaz, 1998). Ultimately, broadening the civil rights agenda to include lesbians and gays becomes integral to persistent struggles for human rights, of which the Black struggle for civil rights is a central component.

A great deal of the social science literature dealing with race suggests that achieving a just society is dependent upon eradicating racial oppression. Understanding racial oppression is certainly necessary to understanding the life experiences of racialized people, but it is not sufficient. Treating racial oppression as the single–or even most important–common denominator in the lives of oppressed people ignores the ways in which other factors (e.g., class standing, sexual orientation, gender) shape and inform individual perspectives, standpoints, experiences of oppression, and resistance to that oppression (Badgett, 1997; Diaz, 1998; hooks, 1994). For example, lesbians and gays of color in the United States military who challenge military persecution of homosexuals derive no protection from legal prohibitions against racial discrimination and little or no support from the social movement organizations of racial-ethnic groups or lesbian and gay groups (Vaid, 1995). Racial subordination, then, is clearly only one site of oppression to be eliminated in the lives of people of color.

FALSE DICHOTOMIES BETWEEN RACIALIZED GROUPS AND LESBIANS AND GAY MEN

The creation of false dichotomies between "people of color" and "lesbians and gay men" also encourages homophobia in communities of color (Collins, 1990; Diaz, 1998). These false dichotomies arise from the insistence by some within communities of color that homosexuality is "a White thing" which is essentially foreign to our respective communities, as opposed to a sustained aspect of family and community life (Scott, 1991; Smith and Smith, 1983). They also arise from the overwhelming visibility of White lesbians and gay men in highly publicized gay struggles for full citizenship and equality within the United States. Still another contributor to false dichotomies between people of color and lesbians and gay men is the way in which the contributions of lesbians and gay men of color have been hidden within the histories of both dominate and oppressed groups.

Frequently, when communities of color are compelled to acknowledge the existence of homosexuality within their racial identity groups, they treat it as an anomaly attributable to corrupting European (i.e., "White") influences (Scott, 1991; Smith and Smith, 1983). Arguably, homosexuality as a *distinct identity* is a modern phenomenon, but claiming that one or another culture did not condone homosexuality is an unsupported rewriting of history that contributes to the negative mythology surrounding the origins of homosexuality (Eskridge, 1996; Boykin, 1996).

RECOMMENDATIONS FOR CHANGE

In "A Place of Rage," June Jordan describes being asked to speak at a campus rally against Palestinian oppression one day and a rally against lesbian and gay oppression the next day. In Jordan's words, "There should have only been one rally." Rinku Sen argues that communities of color would greatly benefit from infusing our cultural institutions with a focus on gender equity. I would agree with that argument and add that communities of color can also benefit from broadening our social justice efforts to include building alliances with lesbians and gays within our communities and the dominant society (Smith & Smith, 1983). When we are battling oppression on the basis of race, gender, class, and sexual orientation, there should be one struggle whenever and wherever feasible. Alliances among oppressed people are not only desirable, coalitions among these groups may prove the ultimate strategy for achieving social justice for all people (Chow, 1996; hooks, 1994; Martinez, 1998; Shukla, 1997; Vaid, 1995).

In the interest of genuine coalition and alliance building, we must confront the Black-White Racial Dichotomy that dominates political discourse in the United States despite the reality of Latina/o, Asian, Native American presence and prominence in the United States (Chow,

1996; Diaz, 1998). In a society that relies on dichotomizing its citizens by one or another characteristic, we must forcefully assert a multiple identity which includes sexuality, class, race, gender, and any other defining characteristics that speak to the political realities of our lives (Chow, 1996; Diaz, 1998; Shende, 1997). For instance, a Black gay man with disabilities challenges the notion of someone who is oppressed solely on the basis of race. Yet, acknowledging such a multiple identity does not deny that some benefits may be derived from being male in a sexist society, even as being gay and disabled contribute to one's potential victimization in other arenas. Confronting the Black-White racial dichotomy also requires that we address the intersectionality of hate crimes and bias incidents for the interrelated racist, sexist, anti-Semitic, anti-Islamic and homophobic violence that such acts promote (Lewin & McDevitt, 1993).

We must also strive for a qualitative versus a quantitative presence in social institutions of both dominant and marginalized groups–a presence that agitates for lesbian and gay civil rights as an integral focus of human rights platforms. "Skin-color," "sexual," and "feminist" politics are hostile to the advancement of full citizenship rights when the persons striving to lead us under those banners are homophobic, racist, or sexist and simply spout the respective party line. It may be more useful– and beneficial to the whole–to have one progressive individual with inclusive politics than several whose politics are identity-specific.

We need to confront homophobia within communities of color now more than ever, because gay men and lesbians of color who are HIV positive or at risk for AIDS (or have Sexually Transmitted Diseases (STDS)) are not receiving proper medical attention from institutions of the dominant culture and are often ostracized by the service providers within communities of origin and predominantly White-run gay social service agencies (Cohen, 1999; Diaz, 1998). These issues are also important because of our young people. Studies show that lesbian and gay youths who are troubled by same-sex attractions commit suicide at higher rates than their heterosexual counterparts. With increased societal understanding that hate and bias incidents against lesbians and gays are punishable offenses, and the longstanding reality that people of color are more likely to receive the harshest penalties allowable under the law for criminal offenses, we risk losing both victims and victimizers in hate and bias incidents involving lesbians and gays of color.

Finally, these issues are important because several groups are competing with each other for full citizenship rights when alliances could prove more effective. Women's groups have always included male allies in their struggles, and the struggles of racial-ethnic and sexual minorities have always included majority members.

Progressive changes within the larger society must be paralleled by similar changes within families and communities of color. Necessary changes include, but are not limited to, openly and adequately addressing the issue of homophobia (Diaz, 1998); providing culturally specific and targeted sex education programs; disrupting rigid sex and gender role stereotypes; redefining family values to include lesbian and gay families; acknowledging that lesbians and gays span racial-ethnic backgrounds and representing that reality in the media; and, most importantly, acknowledging the rich, full, and complex humanity represented within lesbian and gay populations.

NOTES

1. I am very grateful to Isidro Ortiz of Chicana/o Studies at San Diego State University for his support, intellectual guidance, and valuable critical comments. I would also like to thank my life partner, Maggie Allington, and other colleagues at San Diego State and elsewhere, who reviewed drafts of this article: Evelyn Nakano Glenn, Ramon Gutierrez, Bethania Maria, Margo Okazawa-Rey, Charles Toombs, Ronald Young, research assistants Myra Hester, Janet Lorenzen, Joy Sapinoso, and Tracy Yen, Mary Swigonski and the editors and reviewers of the special issue of the *Journal of Gay & Lesbian Social Services* dedicated to Matthew Shepard, and The College of Arts and Letters at San Diego State University for grant funding to pursue the research for this article.

2. Boykin (1996, p. 68) cautions groups from thinking that they hold "a proprietary interest over the rhetoric of freedom" simply "because [they are] temporarily favored by society."

REFERENCES

Anderson, T. (1999). *The sixties*. Reading, MA: Addison Wesley Longman, Inc.

Badgett, M. V. L. (1997). The wage effects of sexual orientation discrimination. In C. Cohen, K. Jones, & J. Tronto (Eds.), *Women transforming politics: An alternative reader* (pp. 107-122). New York and London: New York University Press.

Berger, P. (1963). *Invitation to sociology: A humanistic perspective*. New York: Bantam Doubleday Publishing Group, Inc.

Boykin, K. (1996). *One more river to cross: Black and gay in America*. New York: Bantam Doubleday Dell Publishing Group, Inc.

Boykin, K. (1999). *Respecting the soul: Daily reflections for black lesbians and gays*. New York: Avon Books.

Brown, H., MD. (1989). *Familiar faces, hidden lives: The story of homosexual men in America today*. Orlando: Harcourt Brace Jovanovich Publishers.

Cameron, B. (1983). Gee, you don't seem like an Indian from the reservation. In C. Moraga & G. Anzaldua (Eds.), *This bridge called my back: Writings by radical women of color* (pp. 46-52). Latham, New York: Kitchen Table: Women of Color Press.

Chow, E. N-L. (1996). The development of feminist consciousness among Asian American women. In E. N-L. Chow, D. Wilkinson, & M. B. Zinn (Eds.), *Race, class, and gender: Common bonds, different voices* (pp. 251-264). Thousand Oaks, CA: Sage.

Clarke, C. (1983). Lesbianism: An act of resistance. In C. Moraga & G. Anzaldua (Eds.), *This bridge called my back: Writings by radical women of color* (pp. 128-137). Latham, NY: Kitchen Table: Women of Color Press.

Cohen, C. (1999). *The boundaries of blackness: AIDS and the breakdown of black politics*. Chicago: The University of Chicago Press.

Collins, P. H. (1990). *Black feminist thought: Knowledge, consciousness, and the politics of empowerment*. Boston: Unwin Hyman, Inc.

Crenshaw, K. W. (1997). Beyond racism and misogyny: Black feminism and 2 live crew. In C. Cohen, K. Jones, & J. Tronto (Eds.), *Women transforming politics: An alternative reader* (pp. 549-568). New York and London: New York University Press.

Densham, A. (1997). The marginalized uses of power and identity: Lesbians' participation in breast cancer and AIDS activism. In C. Cohen, K. Jones, & J. Tronto (Eds.), *Women transforming politics: An alternative reader* (pp. 284-301). New York and London: New York University Press.

Diaz, R. M. (1998). *Latino gay men and HIV*. New York: Routledge.

Eskridge, W. N., Jr. (1996). *The case for same-sex marriage: From sexual liberty to civilized commitment*. New York: The Free Press.

Frye, M. (1998). Oppression. In P. Rothenberg (Ed.), *Race, class, and gender in the United States: An integrated study* (pp. 146-149). New York: St. Martin's Press.

Gonzalez, B. R. (1999, April). Remember the Alamo part II. *Z Magazine*. pp. 13-16.

Gorelick, S. (1996). Contradictions of feminist methodology. In E. N-L. Chow, D. Wilkinson, & M. B. Zinn (Eds.), *Race, class, and gender: Common bonds, different voices* (pp. 385-401). Thousand Oaks, CA: Sage.

Hearn, J. (1996). Men's violence to known women: Men's accounts and men's policy developments. In *Violence and gender relations: Theories and interventions* (pp. 99-114.) Thousand Oaks, CA: Sage.

hooks, b. (1994). *Outlaw culture: Resisting representations*. New York: Routledge.

Israel, C. D. (1992). *Hate crimes against gay/lesbians*. Las Colinas, TX: Monument Press.

Jenness, V., & Broad, K. (1997). *Hate crimes: New social movements and the politics of violence*. New York: Aldine De Gruyter.

Jordan, J. (1981). *Civil wars*. Boston, MA: Beacon Press.

Lewin, J., & McDevitt, J. (1993). *Hate crimes: The rising tide of bigotry and bloodshed.* New York: Plenum Press.

Martinez, E. (1998). *De colores means all of us: Latina views for a multi-colored century.* Cambridge, MA: South End Press.

Moraga, C. (1983). La guera. In C. Moraga & G. Anzaldua (Eds.), *This bridge called my back: Writings by radical women of color* (pp. 27-34). Latham, NY: Kitchen Table: Women of Color Press.

Scarce, M. (1997). *Male on male rape: The hidden toll of stigma and shame.* New York, NY: Plenum Press.

Scott, K. Y. (1991). *The habit of surviving.* New York: Ballentine Books.

Sen, R. (1997). Winning action for gender equity: A plan for organizing communities of color. In C. Cohen, K. B. Jones, & J. Tronto (Eds.), *Women transforming politics: An alternative reader* (pp. 302-323). New York: New York University Press.

Shende, S. (1997). Fighting the violence against our sisters: Prosecution of pregnant women and the coercive use of norplant. In C. Cohen, K. B. Jones, & J. Tronto (Eds.), *Women transforming politics: An alternative reader* (pp. 123-135). New York: New York University Press.

Shukla, S. (1997). Feminisms of the diaspora both local and global: The politics of South Asian women against domestic violence. In C. Cohen, K. B. Jones, & J. Tronto (Eds.), *Women transforming politics: An alternative reader* (pp. 269-283). New York: New York University Press.

Smith, B., & Smith, B. (1983). Across the kitchen table: A sister-to-sister dialogue. In C. Moraga & G. Anzaldua (Eds.), *This bridge called my back: Writings by radical women of color* (pp. 113-127). Latham, NY: Kitchen Table: Women of Color Press.

Stevens, J. (1997). On the marriage question. In C. Cohen, K. B. Jones, & J. Tronto (Eds.), *Women transforming politics: An alternative reader* (pp. 62-83). New York: New York University Press.

Thompson, B. (1996). "A way out of no way": Eating problems among African American, Latina, and White women. In E. N-L. Chow, D. Wilkinson, & M. B. Zinn (Eds.), *Race, class, and gender: Common bonds, different voices* (pp. 52-69). Thousand Oaks, CA: Sage.

Vaid, U. (1995). *Virtual equality: The mainstreaming of gay and lesbian liberation.* New York: Bantam Doubleday Dell Publishing Group, Inc.

Valerio, A. (1983). It's my blood, my face–my mother's voice, the way I sweat. In C. Moraga & G. Anzaldua (Eds.), *This bridge called my back: Writings by radical women of color (pp. 41-45).* Latham, NY: Kitchen Table: Women of Color Press.

West, C., & Fernstermaker, S. (1996). Doing difference. In E. N-L. Chow, D. Wilkinson, & M. B. Zinn (Eds.), *Race, class, and gender: Common bonds, different voices* (pp. 357-384). Thousand Oaks, CA: Sage.

Wyatt, G. E. (1997). *Stolen women: Reclaiming our sexuality, taking back our lives.* New York: John Wiley and Sons, Inc.

Zinn, H. (1995). *A people's history of the United States 1492-present (rev. ed.).* New York: Harper Perennial.

Sexual Orientation Bias Experiences and Service Needs of Gay, Lesbian, Bisexual, Transgendered, and Two-Spirited American Indians

Karina L. Walters
Jane M. Simoni
Pamela F. Horwath

SUMMARY. Employing both quantitative and qualitative methodologies, this study examined: sexual orientation bias experiences among American Indians (AIs) who were gay, lesbian, bisexual, transgendered, or two-spirited (GLBTT-S); service provider attitudes toward AI GLBTT-S; and service barriers and needs with respect to AI GLBTT-S at one AI community-based organization. Among the 14 AI GLBTT-S surveyed, the percentages reporting various bias-related experiences were comparable or greater to those reported for non-AI GLBTT-S in other studies (e.g., 36% had been physically assaulted because of their sexual orientation). The 22 service providers surveyed revealed gener-

Karina L. Walters and Pamela F. Horwath are affiliated with The University of Washington, Seattle. Karina is affiliated with The School of Social Work and Jane is affiliated with The School of Social Work and Jane is affiliated with the Department of Psychology. Jane M. Simoni is affiliated with Ferkauf Graduate School of Psychology.

Address correspondence to Karina L. Walters, School of Social Work, University of Washington, 4101 15th Avenue NE, Rm. 211G, Seattle, WA 98195-6299 (E-mail: kw5@u.washington.edu).

The study was supported by a grant from the Stonewall Community Foundation.

[Haworth co-indexing entry note]: "Sexual Orientation Bias Experiences and Service Needs of Gay, Lesbian, Bisexual, Transgendered, and Two-Spirited American Indians." Walters, Karina L., Jane M. Simoni, and Pamela F. Horwath. Co-published simultaneously in *Journal of Gay & Lesbian Social Services* (Harrington Park Press, an imprint of The Haworth Press, Inc.) Vol. 13, No. 1/2, 2001, pp. 133-149; and: *From Hate Crimes to Human Rights: A Tribute to Matthew Shepard* (ed: Mary E. Swigonski, Robin S. Mama, and Kelly Ward) Harrington Park Press, an imprint of The Haworth Press, Inc., 2001, pp. 133-149. Single or multiple copies of this article are available for a fee from The Haworth Document Delivery Service [1-800-342-9678, 9:00 a.m. - 5:00 p.m. (EST). E-mail address: getinfo@haworthpressinc.com].

ally low levels of heterosexism, which was inversely related to contact and comfort with AI GLBTT-S as well as understanding of AI GLBTT-S terms. Data from 8 focus groups (7 with service providers and 1 with AI two-spirited men) yielded four main themes related to problems and barriers to service utilization for AI GLBTT-S (i.e., invisibility, discrimination, trauma, and identity) as well as ideas for community-based program planning with this population. *[Article copies available for a fee from The Haworth Document Delivery Service: 1-800-342-9678. E-mail address: <getinfo@haworthpressinc.com> Website: <http://www.HaworthPress.com>* © *2001 by The Haworth Press, Inc. All rights reserved.]*

KEYWORDS. American Indians, bias experiences, gay, lesbian, two-spirited, transgendered

[Native American] Lesbians and gay men find themselves in cities built on racism and fed on the oppression of everyone who is not heterosexual, White, and male. A White man comes up to you and mutters "squaw." Your friend is beaten up on the street and you don't know if it's because the attacker didn't like Indians or fags. (Beaver, 1992, p. 13)

Within the last century, AIs have endured a succession of traumatic assaults on their cultural and physical well-being (referred to as a "soul wound" by Duran, Duran, Yellow Horse Brave Heart, and Yellow Horse-Davis, 1998), and they continue to disproportionately experience violence and trauma. For example, during 1992-1996, AIs were victims of violent crimes at a rate (124 per 1000) that was 2.5 times the national average. The violent victimization rate was higher for urban AIs than for those residing in rural areas (207 vs. 89 per 1000). Furthermore, AI victims of violent crimes were more likely than victims of other racial groups to report interracial violence. For example, 82% of AI rape victims reported White assailants (Greenfeld & Smith, 1999).

There is limited and somewhat conflicting evidence that AI who are gay, lesbian, bisexual, transgendered, or two-spirited (GLBTT-S) are at higher risk for trauma than their heterosexual counterparts (Allison, 1998; Comstock, 1989; Pilkington & D'Augelli, 1995). AI GLBTT-S must contend with pervasive racism within non-AI lesbian and gay male communities (Walters, 1997) as well as homophobia within AI communities (Deschamps', 1998; Meyers, Calzavara, Cockerill, Marshall, & Bullock, 1993; Sullivan, 1991). Note that the term "two-spirited," which evolved from a Northern Algonquin word *niizh manitoag* (two-spirits; Anguksuar, 1997), originally referred to an identity determined less by genital contact than by culturally prescribed spiritual powers and social roles, such as dreamer, mediator, and name-giver (Jacobs, 1997; Jacobs, Thomas, & Lang, 1997). More recently, "two-spirited" has come to signify a fluidity of gender roles and sexuality beyond the dualistic Western notions of male/female and homosexual/heterosexual.

A common form of trauma is victimization based on a perceived or actual gay or lesbian sexual orientation (Pilkington & D'Augelli, 1995). Berrill (1990) found that among gay and lesbian adults, 87% reported verbal assault based on their sexual orientation. Summarizing ten victimization surveys, Berrill reported 13%-38% of GLBT individuals had been chased or followed, 9%-24% had been physically assaulted, and 4%-10% had been assaulted with a weapon. In another study among GLBT ages 15-21, over 15% reported being victimized six times or more (Pilkington & D'Augelli, 1995). Anti-gay victimization has not only been associated with physical harm but also with psychological harm, including diminished feelings of trust, safety, and self-worth; increased feelings of fear and hypervigilance; heightened internalized homophobia; and increased social distancing from other GLBTs (Garnets, Herek, & Levy, 1990; Herek, 1989; Pilkington & D'Augelli, 1995; Stermac & Sheridan, 1993).

Prejudice and related violence are enacted through heterosexism, which may be defined as "an ideological system that denies, denigrates, and stigmatizes any nonheterosexual form of behavior, identity, relationship, or community" (Herek, 1990, p. 316; Herek, 1993). Cultural and psychological heterosexism are the backbone of anti-gay attitudes and their behavioral manifestations, which include epistemic violence (e.g., assumptions of heterosexuality as normal and anything else as abnormal) as well as physical violence (Herek, 1993; Onken, 1998).

Positive contact and friendships with GLBTT-S have been associated with decreased heterosexist attitudes among non-AIs (D'Augelli, 1989; D'Augelli & Rose, 1990). Anecdotal evidence among AIs suggests that positive contact and disclosure to family members may diminish heterosexist attitudes and increase the level of acceptance and comfort level with AI GLBTT-S (Jacobs & Brown, 1997).

Prejudicial attitudes and discriminatory behaviors on the part of service practitioners may be particularly devastating to GLBTT-S. These include the avoidance and deflection of GLBTT-S issues, outing, harassment, and misinformation regarding GLBTT-S issues (Travers & Schneider, 1996); unchallenged negative perceptions of GLBTT-S in general (Foster, 1997); and lack of acceptance of GLBTT-S as professional colleagues (Rudolph, 1990). Practitioner lack of awareness and unconditional acceptance of institutionalized heterosexist practices as well as personal anti-sexual minority biases may lead to victimizing GLBTT-S clients or becoming secondary victimizers (Garnets et al., 1990).

To address the paucity of data on AI GLBTT-S and their service providers, this study examined sexual orientation bias experiences among AI GLBTT-S, service provider attitudes toward AI GLBTT-S, and service barriers and needs with respect to AI GLBTT-S at one AI community-based organization. As requested by the organization, we aimed to produce preliminary but generalizable data to inform community-based program planning around AI GLBTT-S needs.

SURVEY

Method

Survey procedures. Data collection took place at an AI community-based agency located in an urban setting in the northeastern United States. The principal investigator (the first author, who is AI) invited every employee of the Center as well as a purposive sample of AI GLBTT-S known to her from outside the Center to participate in the survey. Respondents completed the survey in private, sealed it in the envelope provided, and placed it in a box in a main hallway at the Center. No reimbursement was provided.

Survey participants. Nine community members and 22 employees (85% of the staff) returned a usable survey. The sample consisted of 16 men and 15 women, ranging in age from 18 to 64; 40% had at least a 4-year college degree. In terms of ethnic identification, 87% self-identified as Native American/American Indian/Indigenous, 6% as African American/Afro-Caribbean, 3% as White/Caucasian, and 3% as Hispanic/Latino/a. For analytical purposes, we divided the total sample of 31 respondents into overlapping groups of Center staff (*n* = 22: 11 men,

18 AI, 9 GLBTT-S) and AI GLBTT-S (*n* = 14: 11 men). Note that 5 of the Center staff, because they were AI GLBTT-S, were included in both groups.

Survey measures. In addition to standard demographics, the survey instrument was designed to assess key variables in accordance with Neuber's (1980) Community-Oriented Needs Assessment model.

To assess *sexual orientation bias experiences,* we employed an 8-item checklist (e.g., Have you ever in your lifetime been chased or followed because someone perceived you were gay or lesbian?; Pilkington & D'Augelli, 1995). For each item, respondents also indicated whether the perpetrator was AI.

Regarding provider attitudes toward GLBTT-S, providers were asked if they have any GLBTT-S friends and, if so, were any AI. They also indicated their comfort level with AI GLBTT-S from 1 (*very comfortable*) to 4 (*very uncomfortable*). Level of acceptance for six specific subgroups of the GLBTT-S population (i.e., lesbian AI women, gay AI men, bisexual AI men, FTM, MTF, bisexual AI women) was rated from 1 (*celebrate*) to 4 (*disapprove*) based on the work of Eliason & Raheim (1996) and familiarity with certain GLBTT-S terms was rated from 1 (*very limited*) to 4 (*very good*). Finally, the Attitudes Toward Lesbians and Gay Men scale (ATLG; Herek, 1984, 1988) tapped providers' level of heterosexist attitudes.

We assessed *service needs and barriers* by asking all respondents their perceptions of problems facing the AI GLBTT-S community via a 15-item checklist. Participants also rated each of 14 potential barriers in terms of service provision or utilization at the Center from 1 (*no barrier*) to 4 (*great barrier*). Based on Pelletier, Rogers, and Dellario (1985), these items included client barriers, staff-client barriers, and institutional barriers. Finally, all respondents indicated the best methods of informing the AI community regarding AI GLBTT-S issues via a 6-item checklist.

Survey Results

Below are descriptions of (a) sexual orientation bias experiences among the 14 AI GLBTT-S respondents, (b) attitudes toward AI GLBTT-S reported by the 22 service providers, and (c) suggestions regarding service provision offered by the sample of 31 respondents overall.

Sexual orientation bias experiences among AI GLBTT-S. As seen in Table 1, rates of sexual orientation bias experiences were quite high

TABLE 1. Sexual Orientation Bias Experiences Among AI GLBTT-S (N = 14)

Experience	% of respondents	% of victimized respondents indicating assailant was AI
Verbal insults	100	79
Threat of attack	79	70
Chased or followed	57	43
Objects thrown	36	60
Spat upon	36	60
Physically assaulted	36	40
Assaulted with a weapon	36	40
Sexually assaulted	29	50

among the 14 AI GLBTT-S in the study; percentages of assailants who were AI ranged from 43-79%.

Service provider attitudes toward AI GLBTT-S. Among the 22 service providers, 91% had GLBTT-S friends, and 95% of these had GLBTT-S friends who were AI. Providers reported feeling very comfortable (50%), comfortable (46%), and uncomfortable (5%) with AI GLBTT-S. Attitudes toward specific subgroups of AI GLBTT-S were comparable, with most divided fairly evenly between "celebrate" and "accept"; no provider indicated disapproval of any category. Providers indicated "very limited" or "limited" understanding most commonly (66-73%) for the transgendered terms real life test and FTM/MTF; less commonly (29-57%) for homo-negativity, internalized homophobia, heterosexism, heterosexual privilege, biphobia, homo-ignorance, transgendered, and two-spirited; and least commonly (< 25%) for the concepts of passing, heterosexism, gender identity, homophobia, and sexual orientation.

The mean ATLG score for the 22 service providers was 30.46 ($SD = 7.89$) of a possible 100, indicating low levels of heterosexism. Consistent with other studies, respondents reported more negative attitudes toward gay men than lesbians (respective $M/SD = 14.27/3.91$ vs. $11.18/4.21$), paired samples $t(21) = 4.71$, $p = .000$, and those with GLBT friends versus those without reported reduced heterosexist attitudes (respective $M/SD = 28.80/5.78$ vs. $47.00/8.49$), $t(20) = 4.13$, $p = .001$. Further analyses indicated that lower levels of heterosexism among providers were related to less discomfort with AI GLBTT-S, $r(21) = .65$, $p = .001$; a lower mean disapproval rating across the 6 AI

GLBTT-S subgroups, $r(21)$ = .58, p = .005; and a higher mean understanding of AI GLBTT-S terms, $r(21)$ = $-$.37, p = .089.

Data on service provision. The 31 respondents overall noted various problems facing the AI GLBTT-S community (displayed in Table 2) and barriers to service provision (see Table 3). As best ways to inform the AI community regarding GLBTT-S issues, respondents indicated word-of-mouth (90%), educational talks (90%), Center newsletter (90%), television (81%), radio (81%), and pamphlets (77%). For Center staff, they suggested in-service training (100%), talking circles regarding AI GLBTT-S issues (90%), pamphlets (77%), videos (71%), and supervision (65%). Finally, to best inform AI GLBTT-S, participants suggested announcements of relevant programming through a Center newsletter (100%), word-of-mouth (94%), pamphlets (94%), educational talks (87%), radio (90%), and television (77%).

QUALITATIVE INQUIRY

Method

Procedures. We conducted 8 focus groups with 3-8 people in each (total N = 34). One group consisted of AI two-spirited men, and the remaining seven consisted of Center service providers and administra-

TABLE 2. Problems Facing the AI GLBTT-S Community

Problem	%
HIV/AIDS epidemic	93
Alcohol or other drug problems	90
Homophobia in AI community	86
Shunned by AI community	73
Homelessness	71
Trauma	70
Conflict with kin network/elders	68
Racism from non-AI GLBT	57
Conflict with religion	57
Suicide	52
Anti-gay violence	50
Conflict with Native traditions	46
Problems of raising children	35

Note. N = 21 to 29 due to missing data (Sample 31: 22 staff, 14 AI GLBTT, 5 both staff & AI GLBTT)

TABLE 3. Barriers to Services Utilization by AI GLBTT-S

	% rated moderate or great
Availability of financial resources to GLBTT-S for obtaining services	74
Availability of programming specifically for Native GLBTT-S	68
Fear of what other Native community members might think	66
Fear of violation of confidentiality by staff	63
Fear of GLBTT-S clients "being outed" by accessing services	61
Stigma of "being gay" within the agency	57
Professionals' knowledge of Native GLBTT-S issues	55
Attitudes of Native GLBTT-S clients/family toward Center services	54
Support to staff by non-Native GLBTT-S agencies	54
Native GLBTT-S don't know where the Center is	45
Attitudes of staff toward Native GLBTT-S clients	41
Availability of transportation services	31
Physical accessibility/location of services and programs	25

Note. N = 26 to 29 due to missing data. (Sample 31: 22 staff, 14 AI GLBTT, 5 both staff & AI GLBTT)

tive personnel within each of the Center's departments (e.g., job training, health). The principal investigator conducted all groups with one non-AI female research assistant. Light snacks were provided and, for community members, $10.00 was given to cover transportation costs. Each focus group lasted approximately 2 hours.

The synetics technique (Osborn, 1963) was employed, whereby moderators work to create an accepting atmosphere in order to facilitate brainstorming along with more innovative and creative modes of problem analysis (Stewart & Shamdasani, 1990). The interview guide consisted of the following questions: What are the problems facing AI GLBTT-S? What are the barriers to service utilization in general? What are the program development needs at the Center? Each main question was followed by two questions designed to elicit specific responses in relation to AI community experiences and Center experiences.

Data analysis. Focus group data analysis consisted of typing all notes taken during the focus groups into a standard word processing program in preparation for a three-step analytic process using cut-and-paste techniques (Stewart & Shamdasani, 1990). First, the data were sorted according to themes that arose within each question for each group. Second, the data were sorted according to themes that arose within each question across all focus groups. Third, the data were sorted to identify the themes that cut across all groups and across the first two main questions (i.e., problems and barriers). This process involved designation analysis (i.e., counting the number of times a concept is mentioned across focus groups) and assertion analysis (i.e., noting the frequency with which persons or the community were characterized in a certain way). Thus, the problems/barriers themes were identified separately from program planning themes in the final step. The data yielded four main themes (i.e., invisibility, discrimination, trauma, and identity) embedded in the problems and barriers questions as well as program planning themes that are described in the interpretive analysis that follows.

Focus Group Results: Main Themes

Invisibility. Four of the seven focus groups specifically discussed how invisibility (both as an AI in the GLBT community and a GLBTT-S in the AI community) is a general problem as well as a barrier to accessing services. Many groups contextualized the invisibility problem as stemming from the colonization process and the entrenched stereotypes that exist within the non-AI imagination. For example, one group member stated, "So many myths and stereotypes persist . . . most [non-AI city people] think we live in the West or on a reservation." Invisibility within AI communities makes it difficult for AI GLBTT-S to identify each other for social support. Many participants commented on an "automatic heterosexual assumption–where [AI] community members just don't consider being gay or lesbian as a possibility or a Native reality."

However, for two-spirited men, invisibility appears to convey some advantages. The two-spirited focus group participants stated that some AI gay men come to urban areas to "explore one's gayness" and to "get lost." They "want some anonymity because of the oppression about being gay back home." Similarly, one service provider stated, "Gay Indians might not want to affiliate with an Indian organization as a gay person if they experienced being shunned on the rez [reservation], so, they avoid other Indians."

This invisibility fuels homophobia within the heterosexual AI community. As one participant remarked, "If no one identifies as gay within the community, then no one thinks it exists." Many stated that negotiating multiple oppressions has led to the perception that to openly identify as gay would mean "adding to your oppression." Additionally, many stated that gay-related stigma is often associated with the stigma of HIV/AIDS within AI communities. Public disclosure and visibility are, therefore, typically downplayed out of "concerns that public disclosure of your orientation leads to assumptions about your HIV status."

Related to this issue of visibility and disclosure, one participant noted how cultural values play a significant role in creating and defining the parameters regarding acceptable behaviors. He said, "The problem is drawing so much attention to yourself. Elders might not like that. So, it's not that the person is gay that the elder is responding to but it's how the person is behaving that they don't like . . . like if they are loud or something." Many participants made a distinction between a person's sexual orientation and his or her behaviors. This conflict in cultural values (see Walters, 1997) may be a barrier to accessing services at an AI-specific organization.

On a more positive note, some focus group members stated that visibility of AI GLBTT-S has led to a decrease in homophobia among AI community members and an increase in practitioner sensitivity. One AI said, "[GLBTT-S] are becoming more visible and accepting as a result of more contact between gay Indians and straights–this helps us to decrease our homophobia in the community."

Discrimination. Dealing with the racism in the non-AI GLBT community and in society in general as well as the homophobia within the AI community were identified as critical issues. As one GLBTT-S participant pointed out, "There's still gay stigma where you are seen as abnormal." The objectification and eroticization of gay AIs within the non-AI GLBT community was seen as increasing the possibilities for exploitation of AI GLBTT-S youths.

In terms of the homophobia within the AI community, many identified reservation-based attitudes as being very hurtful to AI GLBTT-S. For example, one participant stated, "Some say they [AI GLBTT-S] should be on an island of their own." Others gave specific examples of AI people being asked to leave their reservation when they publically disclosed their sexual orientation. Many discussed how it might be harder for AIs who traveled to the city from the reservation: "Urban-born gay Indians might be able to blend in some ways and read the racism in the gay and lesbian scene." Several participants stated that AI GLBTT-S youths who run away or are exiled from the reservation come to the city for support but only encounter more trauma. As one participant said, "Runaways from the rez and Mexico are easy targets for gay porn, prostitution, and survival sex. For transgender youth, there is major job discrimination."

Trauma. Nearly all participants stated that dealing with historical and cumulative traumas is a serious concern. Fear of anti-gay violence specifically was palpable in the two-spirits' focus group and was broached in other focus groups as well. Openly gay AI men were seen as particularly vulnerable. Domestic violence within the AI GLBTT-S community was also identified as another concern facing AI GLBTT-S, with one participant commenting, "Mental and emotional abuse are forms of domestic violence that are not addressed in the general population and especially not addressed among gays, lesbians, or bisexuals." Many focus group participants identified binge drinking as a way to deal with trauma: We drink to "numb the pain of being gay" and to "deal with parental and cultural anti-gay attitudes." In several focus groups, participants discussed the fear of being retraumatized by insensitive or "homo-ignorant" AI service providers as being another barrier to accessing services.

Identity. All focus groups mentioned identity as a critical issue. Some of the two-spirited participants indicated feeling lost. One stated, "Because of colonization, many of us have lost the social and spiritual context of who we are. We are always in a crisis mode in [the city], trying to hold onto traditions while dealing with the [city's] gay scene." This task of integrating a healthy, positive identity as both an AI person and as a two-spirited person was a constant theme. As one two-spirited participant stated, "We always have to transcend various levels, negotiating multiple levels of our identities with heterosexuals, with gays, with the heterosexual American Indian dominated patriarchal world, colonization, and Judeo-Christian belief systems in our communities."

Almost all the provider groups noted that difficulties arise in helping AI GLBTT-S when they are struggling to develop an integrated identity. Specifically, AI GLBTT-S who are struggling to externalize homophobia tend to present with justifiable, yet free-floating anger and rage that is, at times, difficult to properly contextualize for some of the service providers. One explained, "Old lessons from elsewhere and ways of relating stay with [GLBTT-S]. This creates fear-based reactions in interacting with the community and lots of anger." Complicating the integration process is the historical diversity in terms of tribal acceptance of AI GLBTT-S and the individual AI GLBTT-S' search for place and identity in relation to his or her specific tribal nation. Finally, a few groups discussed conflicts between AI Christian belief systems and acceptance of AI GLBTT-S. As one focus group member stated, the concern is that "Christian die-hards were raised with homophobia and that Church Lady in us."

Program planning. Four key themes emerged that may be helpful for creation of AI GLBTT-S programming at other AI centers. First, participants highlighted the need for community-based discussion to identify culturally relevant and meaningful ways to discuss sex, sexuality, gender identity, and AI GLBTT-S issues. Some focus groups proposed outreach programs targeting elders and traditional leaders to help incorporate AI GLBTT-S concerns into ongoing community dialogue. Many discussed creating cultural and educational events that integrate two-spirit issues as part of a larger discussion of health and sexuality and the importance of using culturally relevant methods, such as storytelling and talking circles, to do this.

Second, participants discussed the importance of contextualizing anti-gay violence and more general AI GLBTT-S experience within the context of AI experience of colonization, historical trauma, and the cumulative effect of anti-gay victimization and resulting trauma. As one focus group member noted, "Healing old traumas . . . especially mental and emotional stuff from family and relatives" is a critical theme.

Third, all focus groups suggested in-service training for AI staff regardless of sexual orientation. They suggested a specific focus on increasing cultural competence in working with AI GLBTT-S clients and in creating a service delivery system that is safe and healing for all involved. One AI GLBTT-S community member noted that we "need to develop leadership within [AI organizations] to set an example for professional conduct and behavior."

Finally, men in the two-spirit focus group emphasized the need to develop programs that focus on health and mental health issues and to create a safe space for AI GLBTT-S youths. Additionally, they suggested that GLBTT-S-specific programming should be integrated within AI service organizations and should be "pro-active not reactive" not "focused on pathology or problems."

DISCUSSION

This study of the sexual orientation bias experiences and service needs of AI GLBTT-S provides some of the first empirical and qualitative data on this topic. Findings revealed the percentages of AI GLBTT-S who had experienced various kinds of sexual orientation bias experiences were equal to or greater than those reported in studies of non-AI GLBT populations: verbal harassment (100% vs. 52-87%), target of objects thrown (36% vs. 25-38%), being chased (57% vs. 13%-38%), physical assault (36% vs. 9%-24%), assault with a weapon (36% vs. 4-10%); and sexual assault (29% vs. 5-14%) (Berrill, 1990; Pilkington & D'Augelli, 1995). Of utmost concern is the very high rates of Type III violence (Dean, Wu, & Martin, 1992)–physical assault, sexual assault, and assault with a weapon.

Previous research has demonstrated that anti-gay sexual assault has particular psychological and interpersonal ramifications for GLBTs. For example, anti-gay sexual assault tends to trigger in the victim a sense of degradation of sexual intimacy and leads to difficulties with intimate partners (Garnets et al., 1990). Internalized homophobia is often exacerbated by interpreting the assault as a punishment for one's sexual orientation. Survivors often struggle to understand their physiological response during the assault (e.g., involuntary ejaculation may be confused with personal consent to the assault) (Garnets et al., 1990). For AI GLBTT-S, the interconnectedness of anti-gay violence and racial violence makes the recovery from victimization even more psychologically complex. An increase in internalized racism and heterosexism in response to an assault poses a particular challenge to AI service providers. Attending to both GLBTT-S and AI identity processes simultaneously will help keep AI GLBTT-S from splitting off aspects of the self or isolating themselves from important community supports (GLBT and AI) in the post-trauma recovery process (Walters, 1997).

Consistent with overall assault patterns among AIs in urban areas, physical assault and assault with a weapon were perceived to be primarily perpetrated by non-AIs, suggesting that interracial assault is a major concern for intervention development at individual and community levels. These preliminary findings suggest future research should consider contextualizing interracial violence, in part, as another extension of the continuous pattern of violence associated with the colonization that AIs have endured over the last 500 years. Overall, the findings suggest that sexual orientation bias experiences among urban AI GLBTT-S merit serious future research attention. Studies should examine prevalence rates as well as social, cultural, community, and regional (i.e., urban vs. reservation) contexts of victimization.

Findings related to service provider attitudes toward AI GLBTT-S were generally encouraging. Specifically, service providers were found to be knowledgeable and accepting of AI GLBTT-S. Consistent with other studies, respondents reported more negative attitudes toward gay men than lesbians, although their overall attitudes still tended to be more accepting and less heterosexist than attitudes of heterosexuals found in other studies (e.g., D'Augelli, 1989; Simoni, 1996). Not surprisingly, less heterosexist attitudes were related to greater contact, comfort, acceptance, and understanding with respect to AI GLBTT-S populations. Future research will need to discern the temporal relationship between heterosexist attitudes and these variables, as we can not know from our cross-sectional data whether providers with more accepting attitudes were more likely to seek out contact with GLBTT-S or whether initial contact subsequently decreased heterosexism.

The results of the study are subject to methodological limitations. Most importantly, our design was cross-sectional and nonrandom, precluding any clear identification of causal relationships as well as limiting the generalizability of the findings, especially in respect to the rates of anti-gay victimization. Future research will need to address how best to sample this population, perhaps using multiplicity sampling methods (Rothbart, Fine, & Sudman, 1989). Second, our assessment of sexual orientation bias and corresponding race of perpetrator were mainly dichotomous and measured over the lifetime, and, as a result, these measures did not provide any important details related to the frequency, chronicity, or severity of the traumas, the social or environmental context of the traumas, or any information related to the number of perpetrators per event.

Despite its methodological limitations, the study has some relevance for the field. First, the findings indicate trauma is a major factor in the lives of AI GLBTT-S that should be addressed in agency-based practice during both assessment and intervention. Additionally, focus group data suggested that unintended secondary victimization is a potential problem if AI service providers are not aware of their own heterosexist biases. Additionally, findings suggest that the cycle of invisibility (at a societal level for all AIs and in the AI community for AI GLBTT-S), discrimination (i.e., racism within non-AI GLBT institutions and society at large as well as heterosexism within AI communities and institutions), and intended (as in anti-gay bias crimes) and unintended (unchecked psychological heterosexism of AI practitioners) trauma inflicted upon AI GLBTT-S have reciprocal effects on their identity processes, sense of self-worth, and service utilization. Creating a safe space at AI agencies will help decrease the likelihood of further trauma to AI GLBTT-S.

Finally, the findings suggest that community outreach through culturally relevant educational talks are key to changing AI community attitudes. Clearly, AI community responsibility for disseminating knowledge and creating professional agency-based models for culturally relevant service delivery is seen as a priority among all of the participants. Most importantly, incorporating AI GLBTT-S issues into community process benefits all in the AI community–from elders to youths, both the two-spirited and others, and tribal nations in all four directions. By restoring, and in some cases creating, a place for AI GLBTT-S within AI space and traditions, community healing truly begins for the community as a whole.

REFERENCES

Allison, K. W. (1998). Stress and oppressed social category membership. In J. K. Swim, & C. Stangor (Eds.), *Prejudice: The target's perspective* (pp. 145-170). CA: Academic Press.

Beaver, S. (1992). Report to the Royal Commission on Aboriginal Peoples. In Deschamps' (1998), *We are part of a tradition* (pp. 12-16). Toronto, Ontario: Two-Spirited People of the 1st Nations.

Berrill, K. (1990). Anti-gay violence and victimization in the United States: An overview. *Journal of Interpersonal Violence, 5*, 274-294.

Comstock, G. D. (1989). Victims of anti-gay/lesbian violence. *Journal of Interpersonal Violence, 4*, 101-106.

D'Augelli, A. R. (1989). Homophobia in a university community: Views of prospective resident assistants. *Journal of College Student Development, 30*, 546-552.

D'Augelli, A. R., & Rose, M. L. (1990). Homophobia in a university community: Attitudes and experiences of heterosexual freshmen. *Journal of College Student Development, 31*, 484-491.

Dean, L., Wu, S., & Martin, J. L. (1992). Trends in violence and discrimination against gay men in New York City: 1984-1990. In G. M. Herek & K. T. Berrill (Eds.), *Hate crimes: Confronting violence against lesbians and gay men* (pp. 46-64). Newbury Park, CA: Sage.

Deschamps', G. (1998). *We are part of a tradition.* Toronto, Ontario: Two-Spirited People of the 1st Nations.

Duran, E., Duran, B., Yellow Horse Brave Heart, M., & Yellow Horse-Davis, S. (1998). Healing the American Indian soul wound. In Y. Danieli (Ed.), *Intergenerational handbook of multigenerational legacies of trauma* (pp. 341-354). New York: Plenum.

Eliason, M. J., & Raheim, S. (1996). Categorical measurement of attitudes about lesbian, gay, and bisexual people. *Journal of Gay & Lesbian Social Services, 4(3),* 51-65.

Foster, S. J. (1997). Rural lesbians and gays: Public perceptions, worker perceptions, and service delivery. *Journal of Gay & Lesbian Social Services, 6,* 23-35.

Garnets, L., Herek, G. M., & Levy, B. (1990). Violence and victimization of lesbians and gay men: Mental health consequences. *Journal of Interpersonal Violence, 5,* 366-383.

Greenfeld, L. A., & Smith, S. K. (1999). *American Indians and crime.* Washington, D.C.: U.S. Department of Justice.

Herek, G. M. (1984). Attitudes toward lesbians and gay men: A factor-analytic study. *Journal of Homosexuality, 10,* 39-51.

Herek, G. M. (1988). Heterosexuals' attitudes toward lesbians and gay men: Correlates and gender differences. *The Journal of Sex Research, 25,* 451-477.

Herek, G. M. (1989). Hate crimes against lesbians and gay men: Issues for research and policy. *American Psychologist, 44(6),* 948-955.

Herek, G. M. (1990). The context of Anti-gay violence: Notes on cultural and psychological heterosexism. *Journal of Interpersonal Violence, 5,* 316-333.

Herek, G. M. (1993). The context of anti-gay violence: Notes on cultural and psychological heterosexism. In R. Cleaver & P. Meyers (Eds.), *A certain terror: Heterosexism, militarism, violence, and change-up* (pp. 221-233). Chicago: American Friends Service Committee.

Jacobs, M. A., & Brown, L. B. (1997). American Indian lesbians and gays: An exploratory study. *Journal of Gay & Lesbian Social Services, 6(2),* 29-41.

Meyers, T., Calzavara, L. M., Cockerill, R., Marshall, V. W., & Bullock, S. L. (1993). *Ontario First Nations AIDS and Healthy Lifestyle Survey.* National AIDS Clearinghouse, Canadian Public Health Association: Ottowa, Ontario.

Neuber, K. A. (1980). *Needs assessment: A model for community planning.* Newbury Park, CA: Sage.

Onken, S. J. (1998). Conceptualizing violence against gay, lesbian, bisexual, intersexual and transgendered people. *Journal of Gay & Lesbian Social Services, 8(3),* 5-24.

Osborn, A. F. (1963). *Applied imagination* (3rd ed.). New York: Charles Scribner's Sons.

Pelletier, J. R., Rogers, E. S., & Dellario, D. J. (1985). Barriers to the provision of mental health services to individuals with severe physical disability. *Journal of Counseling Psychology, 32,* 422-430.

Pilkington, N. W., & D'Augelli, A. R. (1995). Victimization of lesbian, gay, and bisexual youth in community settings. *Journal of Community Psychology, 23,* 34-56.

Rothbart, G. S., Fine, M., & Sudman, S. (1989). On finding and interviewing the needles in the haystack: The use of multiplicity sampling. In E. Singer & S. Presser (Eds.), *Survey research methods: A reader* (pp. 18-31). Chicago: University of Chicago.

Rudolph, J. (1990). Counselors' attitudes toward homosexuality: Some tentative findings. *Psychological Reports, 66,* 1352-1354.

Simoni, J. (1996). Pathways to prejudice: Predicting students' heterosexist attitudes with demographics, self-esteem, and contact with lesbians and gay men. *Journal of College Students Development, 37,* 68-78.

Stermac, L. E., & Sheridan, P. M. (1993). Antigay/lesbian violence: Treatment issues. *Canadian Journal of Human Sexuality, 2,* 33-38.

Stewart, D. W., & Shamdasani, P. N. (1990). *Focus groups: Theory and practice.* Newbury Park, CA: Sage.

Sullivan, C. (1991). Pathways to infection: AIDS vulnerability among the Navajo. *AIDS Education and Prevention, 3,* 241-257.

Travers, R., & Schneider, M. (1996). Barriers to accessibility for lesbian and gay youth needing addictions services. *Youth and Society, 27,* 356-378.

Walters, K. L. (1997). Urban lesbian and gay American Indian identity: Implications for mental health service delivery. *Journal of Gay & Lesbian Social Services, 6(2),* 43-65.

Older Gays and Lesbians: Surviving a Generation of Hate and Violence

Deana F. Morrow

SUMMARY. This article discusses the impact that coming of age in the Pre-Stonewall era has had on older gays and lesbians. Anti-gay hate and violence, within a historical context of homophobia and heterosexism, are examined. Risk factors, as well as coping capacities, for older lesbians and gays are explored. Research on the psychological adjustment and well-being of older gays and lesbians is reviewed, and suggestions for intervention with this population are proposed. *[Article copies available for a fee from The Haworth Document Delivery Service: 1-800-342-9678. E-mail address: <getinfo@haworthpressinc.com> Website: <http://www.HaworthPress.com> © 2001 by The Haworth Press, Inc. All rights reserved.]*

KEYWORDS. Aging, gays, lesbians, hate crimes, heterosexism, homophobia, violence

The current cohort of older gay and lesbian Americans (i.e., those who are 65 years old or older) came of age in an era when gay-related hate and violence were even more pervasive than they are today. Many

Deana F. Morrow, PhD, LPC, LCSW, ACSW, is affiliated with the Social Work Department, The University of North Carolina at Charlotte, 9201 University City Boulevard, Charlotte, NC 28223-0001 (E-mail: dmorrow@email.uncc.edu).

[Haworth co-indexing entry note]: "Older Gays and Lesbians: Surviving a Generation of Hate and Violence." Morrow, Deana F. Co-published simultaneously in *Journal of Gay & Lesbian Social Services* (Harrington Park Press, an imprint of The Haworth Press, Inc.) Vol. 13, No. 1/2, 2001, pp. 151-169; and: *From Hate Crimes to Human Rights: A Tribute to Matthew Shepard* (ed: Mary E. Swigonski, Robin S. Mama, and Kelly Ward) Harrington Park Press, an imprint of The Haworth Press, Inc., 2001, pp. 151-169. Single or multiple copies of this article are available for a fee from The Haworth Document Delivery Service [1-800-342-9678, 9:00 a.m. - 5:00 p.m. (EST). E-mail address: getinfo@haworthpressinc.com].

of these 3.5 million Americans (Dawson, 1982; Slusher, Mayer, & Dunkle, 1996) led clandestine lives in an effort to avoid the harm and violence that could befall them because of their sexual orientation (Adelman, 1990; Appleby & Anastas, 1998; Deevey, 1990; Kehoe, 1986; Kimmel, 1979). They learned to conceal their sexual identity as a means of survival (Grossman, 1995; Martin & Lyon, 1992; McLeod, 1997; Shenk & Fullmer, 1996). Others, pioneers in what would become the "modern" lesbian and gay rights movement, dared to push the envelope of visibility in order to challenge the societal homophobia and heterosexism that defined them as sick, sinful, and criminal. This article explores the impact that coming of age in the Pre-Stonewall era has had on older gay and lesbian adults. It includes an examination of older gays and lesbians as survivors of a hostile, and many times violent, anti-gay American culture. The social forces that have abused and oppressed this generation are explored and their abilities to cope and respond to such forces are addressed. In addition, suggestions for social work intervention with this population are proposed.

HISTORICAL CONTEXT

A historical perspective is a useful starting point for understanding the anti-gay social and cultural oppression that has impacted the lives of the current cohort of older gay and lesbian Americans. Their development from youth into adulthood has occurred within a context of severe homophobia and heterosexism. Homophobia is defined as the fear and hatred of those who are, or are presumed to be, gay or lesbian (Weinberg, 1972), and heterosexism is defined as the belief in the superiority of heterosexuality over other forms of sexual orientation identities (Morrow, 1996a). Homophobia and heterosexism are interlocking forms of oppression that are institutionalized in major social systems (e.g., laws, employment benefits, marriage, health care, etc.). Homophobia arises out of heterosexist beliefs which serve to systematically privilege those who have a heterosexual identity while simultaneously oppressing those who have a gay or lesbian identity. The historical events to be highlighted here were selected because of their influence on societal attitudes toward lesbian and gay people. These events became the social/cultural framework within which this cohort came of age.

Stonewall Rebellion

The Stonewall Inn rebellion, which occurred on June 27, 1969, has been identified as the watershed event initiating the modern lesbian and gay civil rights movement in the United States (Duberman, 1993; Getzel, 1998; Poindexter, 1997; Weiss & Schiller, 1988). The Stonewall Inn was a gay bar in the Greenwich Village area of New York City. It was common in the 1960s for police to raid gay bars and arrest the patrons. On the night of June 27, 1969, the police arrived to raid the Stonewall Inn. Instead of acquiescing, the bar patrons fought back and rioting ensued for the next three days (Poindexter, 1997; Weiss & Schiller, 1988). The Stonewall Inn rebellion is a significant historical event for gay and lesbian culture in that it signifies movement from submission to active resistance in responding to institutionalized anti-gay violence.

While the Stonewall Inn rebellion is a major event in the history of the gay and lesbian liberation movement, it is important to recognize that older lesbians and gays grew into adulthood primarily in the Pre-Stonewall historical period. For example, gays and lesbians who are now in their 70s were in their 40s at the time of Stonewall. Thus, the Pre-Stonewall years (i.e., the years prior to 1969) are especially important in understanding the historical context of today's older lesbian and gay cohort.

Pre-Stonewall Era

Studies have found that many of today's older gays and lesbians felt alone and isolated in the Pre-Stonewall decades of the 1920s through the mid-1960s (Berger, 1982; Friend, 1987). Accurate information, as we know it today, about homosexuality was not available at that time. Research on sexual orientation and the psychological health of lesbians and gays was in its infancy, and opportunities for social supports and meeting other gays and lesbians were few.

Psychoanalytic Theory. During the 1920s and 1930s, the decades in which many in the current cohort of older Americans were born, psychoanalysis was emerging as the dominant theory of psychological development (Fadiman & Frager, 1994). In his essays on sexuality, Sigmund Freud portrayed an ambivalent stance on homosexuality. He viewed it as both a natural feature of human sexuality and also as arrested development representing a fixation in the Oedipal stage of psychosexual development (Bayer, 1981). Psychoanalytic theory continued to grow and dominate psychological literature into the 1960s, and homosexuality came to be widely viewed as pathological, resulting from dysfunctional parent-child relationships (Bieber, 1962; Socarides, 1968). Based on this social construction of homosexuality as abnormal, many lesbians and gays living in the first half of the twentieth century dared not disclose their sexual orientation (come out) for fear of being institutionalized as mentally ill.

Early Research. While psychoanalytic perspectives dominated popular discourse on homosexuality in the first half of the twentieth century, several other researchers began the process of investigating sexual identity and the psychological adjustment of gays and lesbians. In the 1930s, Dr. Magnus Hirschfield founded the Institute for Sexual Science in Germany (Plant, 1986; Weiss & Schiller, 1988). His research initially proposed that lesbians and gays constituted a "third sex." Hirschfield's work, however, ended prematurely when his Institute for Sexual Science was destroyed by Nazi forces during Hitler's ascent to power in Germany (Nardi & Bolton, 1998).

In the United States, Kinsey and his associates (Kinsey, Pomeroy, & Martin, 1948; Kinsey, Pomeroy, Martin, & Gebhard, 1953) developed the classic research studies commonly known as the Kinsey Studies. Based on interviews with 5,300 men and 5,940 women, the Kinsey researchers proposed that sexual orientation was much broader and more variable than the heretofore presumed heterosexual norm. They proposed a seven point continuum of sexual orientation identities (The Kinsey Scale) ranging from heterosexuality to bisexuality to homosexuality. They argued that homosexuality was as normative as heterosexuality:

> In view of the data we now have on the incidence and frequency of the homosexual, and in particular on its co-existence with the heterosexual in the lives of a considerable portion of the male population, it is difficult to maintain the view that psychosexual reactions between individuals of the same sex are rare and therefore abnormal or unnatural, or that they constitute within themselves evidence of neuroses or even psychoses. (Kinsey, Pomeroy, & Martin, 1948, p. 659)

Building upon Kinsey's argument that homosexuality per se was not indicative of abnormality, Dr. Evelyn Hooker conducted research on the psychological health of gay men in the 1950s (Gonsiorek, 1982; Hooker, 1957). In comparing the mental health of heterosexual men and gay men, Hooker found no distinction between the groups in relation to psychological well-being, thus challenging the popular notion that homosexuality was a form of mental illness.

American Culture. Despite the work of Kinsey and Hooker, American culture held fast to the social construction of homosexuality as mental illness and moral depravity. Homophobia and heterosexism were becoming increasingly embedded in American mainstream culture. The Motion Picture Code had banned all references to homosexuality in motion pictures as early as 1935 (Weiss & Schiller, 1988). By the late 1940s and into the 1950s, the House UnAmerican Activities Committee, in tandem with the McCarthy Hearings in the Senate, targeted gays and lesbians, along with presumed Communists and others, as threats to the stability of the country (D'Emilio & Berube, 1984; Poindexter, 1997). Popular magazines, including *Time, LOOK,* and *Life,* ran articles about gay men (women were often completely ignored) depicting them as poorly adjusted individuals who were lonely, isolated, and interested in seducing innocent others into their "lifestyle" (Weiss & Schiller, 1988). In the book, *Everything You Always Wanted to Know About Sex But Were Afraid to Ask,* physician David Reuben labeled homosexuality as "tragic" and urged gays to "convert" to heterosexuality: "If a homosexual who wants to renounce homosexuality finds a psychiatrist who knows how to cure homosexuality, he has every chance of becoming a happy, well-adjusted, heterosexual" (Reuben, 1969, p. 162).

The United States government fired gays and lesbians from federal jobs based on the rationale that the threat of having their homosexuality revealed made them susceptible to blackmail and a security threat to the government (Poindexter, 1997). While the presence of gays and lesbians in military service during the critical years of World War II was, for the most part, a non-issue, gays and lesbians were dismissed from the military after the war was over (Appleby & Anastas, 1998; Weiss & Schiller, 1988). By the late 1940s, the military was discharging an average of 1,000 gays and lesbians per year; by the 1950s, that number rose to over 2,000 per year (D'Emilio & Berube, 1984). Lesbians and gays terminated from military service were given "undesirable" discharges which precluded their receiving future military benefits and marred their reputations for seeking civilian employment. Mandatory lectures on the pathology of homosexuality were instituted for new military troops.

Thus, the Pre-Stonewall era was an oppressive time to be gay or lesbian in America. Gays and lesbians were portrayed only in negative terms by mainstream media. Medical authorities depicted homosexuality as an illness to be cured, and religious authorities viewed it as a lapse of moral conviction. Furthermore, the legal system provided no options for the protection of the civil liberties of gays and lesbians. In fact, being gay or lesbian meant living with the risk of being arrested or institutionalized because of one's sexual orientation. Although the forces of homophobia and heterosexism remain rampant today, one must recognize the even greater pervasiveness and maliciousness of those social forces for lesbians and gays who came of age during the Pre-Stonewall years.

HATE AND VIOLENCE

The Hate Crimes Statistics Act of 1990 defines hate crimes as, "Crimes in which the defendant's conduct was motivated by hatred, bias, or prejudice based on the actual or perceived race, color, religion, national origin, ethnicity, gender or sexual orientation of another individual or group of individuals" (U.S. Congress, 1992). Hate crimes are also referred to as "bias crimes." Such crimes serve to victimize and intimidate not only individuals, but also entire groups of people. The threat of being victimized because of some status characteristic, such as sexual orientation, promotes silence and invisibility among members of the target group.

Clearly violence and the threat of violence–in the form of both psychological harm, such as hate and discrimination, and physical harm–perpetuated invisibility among older gays and lesbians of the Pre-Stonewall era. There were no hate crime laws during those decades. Furthermore, hate and violence against gays and lesbians were institutionalized into American culture in the form of felony imprisonment, forced psychiatric treatment, termination from employment, religious persecution, and widespread social ostracism (Katz, 1976).

Research on the incidence of anti-gay hate crimes was not initiated until after Stonewall. Nonetheless, studies on violence against lesbian and gay adults in the 1970s and 1980s provide clues to its prevalence during the middle adulthood years of today's older gay and lesbian cohort. Jay and Young (1977) found that 27% of 4,400 gay males and 14% of 1,000 lesbians had experienced physical assault in connection with their homosexuality. In the same study, 77% of the men and 71% of the women had experienced verbal abuse because of their sexual orientation. In a sample of 289 gay men, Anderson (1982) found that 72% had experienced verbal assault and 23% has experienced physical assault because of being gay. In a study of 291 gay men and 146 lesbians in the Philadelphia area, Gross, Aurand, and Adessa (1988) found that 73% of the men and 42% of the women had experienced criminal violence because of their sexual orientation. In that study, 92% of the men and 81% of the women reported having experienced anti-gay verbal abuse. In a study by the National Gay and Lesbian Task Force (1986), results showed that nearly all of the 654 lesbians and 1,429 gay men in their sample had experienced some type of anti-gay harassment, threat, or assault. Marcus (1992) has suggested that gays and lesbians who adopted manners of dress that made them readily targeted as gay or lesbian by society were particularly at risk of physical violence.

Studies have also shown that the emotional and psychological consequences of enduring a lifetime of hate and violence can be exhausting. Outcomes reported in the literature include depression, anxiety, anger, and symptoms of Post-Traumatic Stress Disorder (Barnes, 1994; Herek, Gillis, & Cogan, 1997); hiding one's lesbian or gay orientation in order to avoid harm (Cook-Daniels, 1997; Herek, 1989); and relocation to minimize the likelihood of becoming a target for violence (Barnes, 1994).

The limited data available on gay-hate crimes likely underestimate the severity and pervasiveness of hate and violence endured over a lifetime for the current cohort of older gays and lesbians. The invisibility needed for survival in this Pre-Stonewall generation made sample attainment and data gathering difficult; and, police authorities did not view bias crimes, particularly those involving gays and lesbians, as a serious problem (Berrill, 1986; Herek, 1989; Finn & McNeil, 1987).

PSYCHOLOGICAL WELL-BEING OF OLDER LESBIANS AND GAYS

The impact of coming into adulthood in the Pre-Stonewall era has created mixed results for older lesbians and gays. Studies have identified the challenges encountered by some older gays and lesbians as including loneliness, isolation, fear of coming out (disclosure), and fear of losing family, friends, and jobs because of their sexual orientation (Kehoe, 1986; Kelly, 1977; Minnigerode & Adelman, 1978). Yet, the bulk of the literature suggests that the majority of older gays and lesbians are psychologically healthy, happy, and well-adjusted (Almvig, 1982; Berger, 1980, 1982; Dunker, 1987; Friend, 1980, 1990; Francher & Henkin, 1973; Kehoe, 1986; Kimmel, 1978; Raphael & Robinson, 1980). This section will explore the psychological health and well-being of older lesbians and gays.

Impact of Oppression

Older lesbian and gay adults must contend with the negative impact of multiple layers of oppression, including homophobia and heterosexism, ageism, racism for lesbians and gays of color, and sexism for lesbians. These multiple layers of oppression are intersecting social and cultural forces whose impact over time is cumulative. As a result, a primary challenge for this cohort has been learning how to manage anti-gay hate and discrimination over a lifetime (Berger, 1984; Hamburger, 1997; Kelly, 1977; Kimmel, 1978; Minnigerode & Adelman, 1978; Whitford, 1997).

Friend (1991) identified two options for lesbians and gays in managing the socially constructed negative identity of homosexuality: internalization and resistance. Internalization relates to internalizing societal homophobia and heterosexism (i.e., internalized homophobia). Resistance pertains to resisting society's negative image of gays and lesbians. Friend identifies resistance as the most desirable of the two options in that it leads to deconstructing negative stereotypes of homosexuality and reconstructing a positive sense of self as gay or lesbian. Both options, nonetheless, require significant emotional energy expenditures on a daily basis.

We may never know the full toll of internalized homophobia for older lesbian and gay Americans. We do know, however, that one consequence of chronic internal stress can include alcohol and drug abuse, and research has shown that substance abuse is more common among gays and lesbians than heterosexuals (Fifield, 1975; Saghir & Robins, 1973). The "gay bar" was the primary social gathering place for gays and lesbians of the Pre-Stonewall era. Thus, the presence of alcohol became not only one option for coping with the stress of stigma, but also a staple of socializing within the gay and lesbian community.

Another consequence of stress related to the internalization of societal homophobia and heterosexism can be an increased risk of suicide. Numerous researchers have identified the suicide risk for lesbians and gays as from two to four times the risk for heterosexual people (Climent, Ervin, Rollings, Plutchik, & Batinelli, 1977; Motto, 1977; Saghir & Robins, 1973; Saunders & Valente, 1987; Woodruff, Clayton, & Guze, 1972). Saunders and Valente (1987) found that vulnerability for interrupted social ties was a risk factor for suicide among gays and lesbians. Older gays and lesbians came of age in a time when the risk of broken social and family ties resulting from homophobic rejection was possibly even more pervasive than today.

Identity Development

A primary challenge for older gays and lesbians has been to develop a positive sense of self as gay or lesbian within the context of severe cultural homophobia and heterosexism. Friend (1990, 1991) identified three categories for understanding gay/lesbian identity among older gays and lesbians. The first, "stereotypic" older lesbians and gays, includes those who have severe internalized homophobia. Their sense of self mirrors their internalization of homophobic and heterosexist ideology. They are described as unhappy, lonely, depressed, and socially alienated. Stereotypic gays and lesbians tend toward isolation and invisibility and may be at greater risk for suicide and substance abuse due to their low self-esteem and self-hatred. They are secretive about their sexual orientation and remain socially "closeted" regarding their sexual identity.

The second identity category is known as "passing" older gays and lesbians (Friend, 1990, 1991). Individuals in this category may identify themselves as gay or lesbian within certain contexts (e.g., among gay or lesbian friendship circles), yet they also seek to "pass" as heterosexual in other contexts (e.g., with family members, at work, etc.). While their identity as gay or lesbian may not be as severely impaired as that of the stereotypic person, they still experience internalized homophobia so that their full sense of self-acceptance remains compromised. Friend's passing category is similar to Cass's (1979) stage of "identity tolerance." Gays and lesbians in the identity tolerance stage have learned to tolerate (rather than accept) the reality that they are gay or lesbian. As a result, they are likely to have some context within which they relate with other gays and lesbians. Yet, their gay or lesbian identity remains fairly compartmentalized and hidden within a broader social presentation of presumed heterosexuality.

The third identity category is described as "affirmative" older gays and lesbians (Friend, 1990, 1991). Those in the affirmative stage have successfully reconstructed a socially defined negative lesbian or gay identity into one that is positive and affirming. Affirmative lesbians and gays have challenged their own internalized homophobia and societal heterosexism, and they are more likely to be "out," or open, regarding their sexual orientation. This category corresponds to the stage of "identity acceptance" in the Cass (1979) model. Individuals in identity acceptance realize that being lesbian or gay is not, in itself, inherently flawed and that homophobia and heterosexism are negative social forces that engender oppression of gays and lesbians.

Both the Friend and Cass models make assumptions that progression in identity development for gays and lesbians is related to deconstructing negative images of homosexuality into images that are more positive. Experiencing episodes of hate and violence, or even living with the threat of hate and violence, can intensify and perpetuate internalized homophobia, which can inhibit the identity development process.

Erikson (1968) proposed stages of psychosocial development over the life span. He suggested that, within each life stage, there is a predictable and challenging psychosocial crisis with which each individual must contend. The psychosocial crisis for older adulthood is depicted as "ego integrity versus despair." Older adults who arrive at the outcome of integrity exhibit positive beliefs about their inherent goodness and perceive their lives as meaningful overall. The negative outcome of this psychosocial crisis is despair, the sense that one's life has been essentially meaningless, significantly flawed, and not worth living.

Given that the social construction of homophobia and heterosexism has resulted in an image of lesbians and gays as abnormal and immoral, it can be inferred that arriving at the outcome of integrity can be a formidable challenge for older lesbians and gays. Internalized homophobia can hinder movement toward the desired psychosocial outcome of integrity. Yet, research studies suggest an amazing resilience and resistance to the negative social constructions of homosexuality for many older gays and lesbians (Appleby & Anastas, 1998; Berger, 1982; Dorfman, Walters, & Burke, 1995; Friend, 1990; Kimmel, 1978). Despite the anti-gay culture of their time, older gays and lesbians have emerged, for the most part, as psychologically healthy and well-adjusted people.

Strengths Perspective

A number of psychosocial strengths have been documented as helpful for the experience of aging among older gays and lesbians. Those strengths, including crisis competence, gender role flexibility, and resilience and independence, will be reviewed in this section.

Crisis Competence. Crisis competence in older gays and lesbians is the learned ability to manage crisis-type events (Friend, 1991; Kimmel, 1978). Throughout their lives, older gays and lesbians have had to manage numerous social crisis experiences related to others' reactions to their sexual orientation. Many older gays and lesbians have been ostracized and rejected by family members, co-workers, and neighbors. Coming of age as a lesbian or gay person in the Pre-Stonewall era meant living with the threat of physical harm and coping with homophobia, heterosexism, and discrimination based on sexual orientation. Friend (1991) suggests that, because of their experiences in managing social stress related to prejudice and discrimination, older lesbians and gays may be even more prepared than heterosexual people to cope with the losses and social discrimination that come with aging.

Gender Role Flexibility. Some researchers have suggested that lesbians and gays are less dichotomized into rigid gender roles compared to most heterosexual people (Lee, 1987; Whitford, 1997). People who are multi-task oriented (i.e., those who can perform a variety of roles across gender defined expectations) may be better prepared for the changing roles that can accompany the aging process, especially the loss of a partner. This gender role flexibility, often present in lesbians and gays, can facilitate adjustment to the changes encountered by people as they grow older. Thus, it can be an important strength for older gays and lesbians.

Resilience and Independence. While many older lesbians and gays share warm, supportive relationships with their kinship network, others have learned to not expect their families to care for them in old age

(Cook-Daniels, 1997). Many older gays and lesbians have lost significant family, friends, and community supports because of homophobia and heterosexism. Virtually all older lesbians and gays have suffered social reproach from larger society, including the media, religion, and the legal system. As a result, members of this cohort can be described as resilient survivors. Many have not only survived, but thrived despite a social culture that condemned them. In reality, it is today's cohort of older gays and lesbians who initiated the beginnings of the gay civil rights movement as a response to their societal oppression in the United States. This is the generation that in the 1950s developed the first gay activist groups, including One, Inc., the Mattachine Society, and the Daughters of Bilitis (Weiss & Schiller, 1988).

Older gays and lesbians have also learned the importance of personal independence in planning for their own futures. In a study of 50 lesbians between the ages of 65 and 85, Kehoe (1986) found that these older women were independent survivors who had learned to make their own way in life. In the absence of supportive traditional family systems, some older lesbians and gays have constructed chosen families consisting of partners and friends who agree to share care and support needs interdependently (Weston, 1991). The strengths of resilience and independence cultivated by gays and lesbians over a lifetime can advantage them in coping with the changes and challenges that arise as a result of the aging process.

IMPLICATIONS FOR SOCIAL WORK PRACTICE

Social work intervention with older gays and lesbians must recognize the historical context of homophobia, heterosexism, and violence within which this generation came of age. It is important for social workers to respect the oppression and discrimination older gays and lesbians have endured and to honor their capabilities for survival. This section will offer strategies to consider when delivering social work services to older lesbians and gays.

Diversity. It is important for social workers to recognize the diversity among older lesbians and gays. Even though older gays and lesbians share in common a sexual identity status and an age status that carry certain predictable reactions from the larger society, they also vary greatly in terms of individual abilities, resources, support systems, political views, values, and life perspectives. For example, the life experiences, and thus social needs, for an older urban Latino lesbian would be significantly different from those of an older rural European American white gay man. Thus, while sexual orientation may be thought of as a commonality among all older gays and lesbians, it remains essential that social workers view older gay and lesbian clients from a multi-faceted and individualistic perspective.

Assessment. A broad examination of support systems is useful when assessing older lesbian and gay clients. It is important to assess the quality of not only traditional family supports (parents, siblings, and children), but also "chosen" family systems which clients may have created over the years. The client's life partner should be treated with the same dignity and respect that would be accorded legally recognized married spouses.

Another important area of assessment includes the client's identity related to being gay or lesbian (Cass, 1979; Friend, 1991; Morrow, 1996b). For many older clients, keeping their sexual orientation a secret has been adaptive given the punitive social climate in which they have lived. In such cases, pressuring them to be more open about their sexual orientation could be construed as a lack of respect and a devaluing of their right to self-determine. In contrast, many older gays and lesbians embark on the journey of coming out in their 60s, 70s, or even later in life. In these situations, it becomes important for the worker to support and assist clients in the coming out process. For information on assisting clients with coming out, the reader is referred to Boykin (1996), Kaufman and Raphael (1996), Marcus (1993), Morrow (1996b), and Signorile (1995).

Yet another aspect of assessment in working with older lesbians and gays lies in assessing for substance abuse, depression, and suicidality. Research suggests that, given the social stress, including overt hate and violence, endured by many older gays and lesbians, they are at higher risk for these maladies compared to the broader population (Rothblum, 1990; Sandmaier, 1980; Saunders & Valente, 1987). In particular, patterns of isolation and internalized homophobia, as precipitators of high risk behaviors, should be assessed.

And finally, workers should assess for a history of hate-related violence among older gay and lesbian clients. A descriptive understanding of the violence, including when it occurred, its severity, and its resulting impact on the client, should be established. This information can be particularly useful in that violence can be a risk factor for the development of depression, substance abuse, and post-trauma reaction symptoms, all of which may benefit from intervention. In addition, the impact of anti-gay violence can produce difficulties related to self-esteem, gay or lesbian identity development, degree of "outness," and effective coping skills, which may also be improved through supportive intervention.

Empowerment. Working with older members of the gay and lesbian community involves providing services to people who can be considered, to some degree, disempowered relative to a dominant youth-centered, heterocentric culture. Thus, seeking to empower older gay and lesbian clients is critical to the social work process. Solomon (1976) defines empowerment as "the process whereby persons who belong to a stigmatized social category throughout their lives can be assisted to develop and increase skills in the exercise of interpersonal influence and the performance of valued social roles" (p. 6). McWirter (1991) builds on this definition by suggesting that empowerment has to do with helping people become aware of the dynamics of power in their lives and with helping them take action toward gaining control over their lives. Older gays and lesbians are in need of becoming empowered in order to respond to the inequities of prejudice and discrimination (e.g., ageism, heterosexism, sexism, racism) that influence their lives.

Advocacy. The social work profession is grounded on principles of social justice. Social workers must recognize the lack of social justice for older gay and lesbian clients in areas such as insurance benefits, health care decision-making, inheritance laws, and marriage laws. Workers must advocate at the micro level on behalf of individual clients and at the macro level for passage of laws preventing discrimination based on sexual orientation.

Resource Development. Few community resources for serving the needs of older lesbians and gays exist. Yoakam (1997) states, "Because an older generation of gay and lesbian clients were secretive about their sexual orientation, no one talked about homosexuality or made provisions for same gender couples" (p. 28). Thus, current needs extend beyond available services. Kochman (1997) reports that traditional senior programs are often not open and affirming places for lesbian and gay clients. A few community supports have been developed in states such as New York, California, and Minnesota (Berger & Kelly, 1992; Martin & Lyon, 1992; Yoakam, 1997). Yet, there are virtually no community services for older gays and lesbians in most areas of the country. Particular resource development needs for older lesbians and gays include socialization opportunities, gay-affirmative housing, and gay-affirmative health care.

CONCLUSION

This article has presented an overview of the impact that coming of age in a Pre-Stonewall era has had on older gays and lesbians. Historical events which framed homophobia and heterosexism, and concomitant hate and violence, toward lesbians and gays were identified. The resilience and coping capacities of older lesbians and gays were explored. Despite enduring a generation of severe oppression and violence related to homophobia and heterosexism, older gays and lesbians appear to have emerged as a relatively psychologically healthy and well-adjusted group. The psychological adjustment of older lesbians and gays, including risks and strengths, was explored, and suggestions for intervention with this client population were offered.

REFERENCES

Adelman, M. (1990). Stigma, gay lifestyles, and adjustment to aging: A study of later-life gay men and lesbians. *Journal of Homosexuality, 20* (3/4), 7-32.

Amvig, C. (1982). *The invisible minority: Aging lesbianism.* New York: Utica College of Syracuse University.

Anderson, C.L. (1982). Males as sexual assault victims: Multiple levels of trauma. *Journal of Homosexuality, 7,* 145-162.

Appleby, G.G., & Anastas, J.W. (1998). *Not just a passing phase.* New York: Columbia University Press.

Barnes, A. (1994). The impact of hate violence on victims: Emotional and behavioral responses to attacks. *Social Work, 39*(3), 247-251.

Bayer, R. (1981). *Homosexuality and American psychiatry.* New York: Basic Books.

Berger, R.M. (1980). Psychological adaptation of the older male. *Journal of Homosexuality, 5*(3), 161-175.

Berger, R.M. (1982). *Gay and gray: The older homosexual man.* Urbana, IL: University of Illinois Press.

Berger, R.M. (1984). Realities of gay and lesbian aging. *Social Work, 29*(1), 57-62.

Berger, R.M., & Kelly, J.J. (1992). The older gay man. In B. Berzon (Ed.), *Positively gay* (pp. 121-129). Berkeley, CA: Celestial Arts

Berrill, K. (1986). *Anti-gay violence: Causes, consequences, responses.* Washington, D.C.: National Gay and Lesbian Task Force.

Bieber, I. (1962). *Homosexuality: A psychoanalytic study.* New York: Basic Books.

Boykin, K. (1996). *One more river to cross: Black and gay in America.* New York: Doubleday.

Cass, V.C. (1979). Homosexual identity formation: A theoretical model. *Journal of Homosexuality, 4,* 219-135.

Climent, C.E., Ervin, F.R., Rollings, A., Plutchik, R., & Batinelli, C.J. (1997). Epidemiological studies of female prisoners. *Journal of Nervous and Mental Diseases, 164*(1), 25-29.

Cook-Daniels, L. (1997). Lesbian, gay male, bisexual, and transgendered elders: Elder abuse and neglect issues. *Journal of Elder Abuse & Neglect, 9*(2), 35-49.

Dawson, K. (1982). Serving the older gay community. *SEICUS Report* (Nov.), 5-6.

D'Emilio, J., & Berube, A. (1984). The military and lesbians during the McCarthy years. *Journal of Women in Culture and Society, 9*(4), 759-775.

Deevey, S. (1990). Older lesbian women: An invisible minority. *Journal of Gerontological Nursing, 16*(5), 35-39.

Dorfman, R.A., Walters, K., & Burke, P. (1995). Old, sad, and alone: The myth of the aging homosexual. *Journal of Gerontological Social Work, 24*(1/2), 29-44.

Duberman, M. (1993). *Stonewall.* New York: Dutton.

Dunker, B. (1987). Aging lesbians: Observations and speculations. In the Boston Lesbian Psychologies Collective (Ed.), *Lesbian Psychologies* (pp. 72-82). Chicago: University of Illinois Press.

Erikson, E.H. (1968). *Identity, youth and crisis.* New York: W.W. Norton.

Fadiman, J., & Frager, R. (1994). *Personality and personal growth.* New York: Harper Collins.

Fifield, L. (1975). *On my way to nowhere: Alienated, drunk.* Los Angeles: The Gay Community Services Center.

Finn, P., & McNeil, T. (1987). *The response of the criminal justice system to bias crime: An exploratory review.* Submitted to the U.S. Department of Justice. Cambridge, MA: Abt. Associates.

Francher, S.J., & Henkin, J. (1973). The menopausal queen. *American Journal of Orthopsychiatry, 43,* 670-674.

Friend, R.A. (1980). GAYging: Adjustment and the older gay male. *Alternative Lifestyles, 3,* 231-248.

Friend, R.A. (1987). The individual and social psychology of aging: Clinical implications for lesbians and gay men. *Journal of Homosexuality, 4*(1/2), 307-331.

Friend, R.A. (1990). Older lesbians and gay people: Responding to homophobia. *Marriage & Family Review, 14*(3/4), 241-263.

Friend, R.A. (1991). Older lesbian and gay people: A theory of successful aging. *Journal of Homosexuality, 20*(3/4), 99-118.

Getzel, G.S. (1998). Group work practice with gay men and lesbians. In G.P. Mallon (Ed.), *Foundations of social work practice with lesbian and gay persons.* New York: Harrington Park Press.

Gonsiorek, J.C. (1982). *Homosexuality and psychotherapy.* New York: The Haworth Press, Inc.

Gross, L., Aurand, S.K., & Adessa, R. (1988). *Violence and discrimination against lesbian and gay people in Philadelphia and the Commonwealth of Pennsylvania.*

Philadelphia: Philadelphia Gay and Lesbian Task Force (1501 Cherry St., Philadelphia, PA 19102).

Grossman, A.H. (1995). At risk, infected, and invisible: Older gay men and HIV/ AIDS. *Journal of Association of Nurses in AIDS Care, 6*(6), 13-19.

Hamburger, L.J. (1997). The wisdom of non-heterosexually based senior housing and related services. *Journal of Gay & Lesbian Social Services, 6*(1), 79-95.

Herek, G. (1989). Hate crimes against lesbians and gay men. *American Psychologist, 44*(6), 948-955.

Herek, G.M., Gillis, J.R., & Cogan, J.C. (1997). Hate crime victimization among lesbian, gay, and bisexual adults: Prevalence, psychological correlates, and methodological issues. *Journal of Interpersonal Violence, 12*, 195-215.

Hooker, E.E. (1957). The adjustment of the male overt homosexual. *Journal of Projective Techniques, 21*(1), 18-31.

Jay, K., & Young, A. (1977). *The gay report.* New York: Summit.

Katz, J. (1976). *Gay American history.* New York: Crowell.

Kaufman, G., & Raphael, L. (1996). *Coming out of shame: Transforming gay and lesbian lives.* New York: Doubleday.

Kehoe, M. (1986). A portrait of the older lesbian. *Journal of Homosexuality, 12*(3/4), 157-161.

Kelly, J. (1997). The aging male homosexual: Myth and reality. *Gerontologist, 17*(4), 328-332.

Kimmel, D.C. (1978). Adult development and aging: A gay perspective. *Journal of Social Issues, 34*(3), 113-130.

Kimmel, D.C. (1979). Adjustments to aging among gay men. In B. Berzon (Ed.), *Positively gay* (pp. 146-170). Milbrae, CA: Celestial Arts.

Kinsey, A.C., Pomeroy, W.B., & Martin, C.E. (1948). *Sexual behavior in the human male.* Philadelphia: W.B. Saunders Co.

Kinsey, A.C., Pomeroy, W.B., Martin, C.E., & Gebhard, P.H. (1953). *Sexual behavior in the human female.* Philadelphia: W.B. Saunders Co.

Kochman, A. (1997). Gay and lesbian elderly: Historical overview and implications for social work practice. *Journal of Gay & Lesbian Social Services, 6*(1), 1-10.

Lee, J.A. (1987). What can homosexual aging studies contribute to theories of aging? *Journal of Homosexuality, 13*, 43-71.

Marcus, E. (1992). *Making history: The struggle for gay and lesbian elder rights, 1945-1970: An oral history.* New York: Harper Collins.

Marcus, E. (1993). *Is it a choice? Answers to 300 of the most frequently asked questions about gays and lesbians.* New York: Harper Collins.

Martin, D., & Lyon, P. (1992). The older lesbian. In B. Berzon (Ed.), *Positively gay* (pp. 111-120). Berkeley, CA: Celestial Arts.

McLeod, B. (1997). Yvonne and Helen: Finding a way to trust. *Journal of Gay & Lesbian Social Services, 6*(1), 105-107.

McWirter, E.H. (1991). Empowerment in counseling. *Journal of Counseling and Development, 69*(3), 222-227.

Minnigerode, F.A., & Adelman, M.R. (1978). Elderly homosexual women and men: Report on a pilot study. *The Family Coordinator, 27*(4), 451-456.

Morrow, D.F. (1996a). Heterosexism: Hidden discrimination in social work educa-tion. *Journal of Gay & Lesbian Social Services, 5*(4), 1-16.

Morrow, D.F. (1996b). Coming out issues for adult lesbians: A group intervention. *Social Work, 41*(6), 647-656.

Motto, G. (1977). Estimation of suicide risk by use of clinical models. *Suicide and Life Threatening Behavior, 7*(4), 236-245.

Nardi, P.M., & Bolton, R. (1998). Gay-bashing: Violence and aggression against gay men and lesbians. In P.M. Nardi & B.E. Schneider (Eds.), *Social perspectives in lesbian and gay studies* (pp. 412-433). New York: Routledge.

National Gay and Lesbian Task Force. (1986). Antigay violence: Homosexual vic-tims of assault and murder. *Qualitative Sociology, 3*(3), 169-185.

Plant, R. (1986). *The pink triangle: The Nazi war against homosexuals*. New York: Henry Holt & Co.

Poindexter, D.D. (1997). Sociopolitical antecedents to Stonewall: Analysis of the origins of the gay rights movement. *Social Work, 42*(6), 607-615.

Raphael, S.M., & Robinson, M.K. (1980). The older lesbian. *Alternative Lifestyles, 3*, 207-229.

Reuben, D. (1969). *Everything you always wanted to know about sex but were afraid to ask*. New York: Bantam.

Rothblum, E.D. (1990). Depression among lesbians: An invisible and unresearched phenomenon. *Journal of Gay & Lesbian Psychotherapy, 1*(3), 67-87.

Saghir, M.T., & Robins, E. (1973). *Male and female homosexuality: A comprehensive investigation*. Baltimore: Williams and Wilkins.

Sandmaier, M. (1980). *The invisible alcoholics: Women and alcohol abuse in Ameri-ca*. New York: McGraw Hill.

Saunders, J.M., & Valente, S.M. (1987). Suicide risk among gay men and lesbians: A review. *Death Studies, 11*, 1-23.

Shenk, D., & Fullmer, E. (1996). Significant relationships among older women: Cultural and personal constructions of lesbianism. *Journal of Women & Aging, 8*(3/4), 75-89.

Signorile, M. (1995). *Outing yourself*. New York: Simon & Schuster.

Slusher, M.P., Mayer, C.J., & Dunkle, R.E. (1996). Gays and lesbians older and wiser (GLOW): A support group for older gay people. *The Gerontologist, 36*(1), 118-123.

Socarides, C.W. (1968). *The overt homosexual*. New York: Grune and Stratton.

Solomon, B.B. (1976). *Black empowerment social work in oppressed communities*. New York: Columbia University Press.

United States Congress. (1992). H.R. 4797. 102nd Congress, 2nd Session.

Weinberg, G. (1972). *Society and the healthy homosexual*. New York: St. Martin's Press.

Weiss, A., & Schiller, G. (1988). *Before Stonewall: The making of a gay and lesbian community*. Tallahassee, FL: Naiad Press.

Weston, K. (1991). *Families we choose: Lesbians, gays, kinship*. New York: Colum-bia University Press.

Whitford, G.S. (1997). Realities and hopes for older gay males. *Journal of Gay & Lesbian Social Services, 6*(1), 79-95.

Woodruff, R.A., Clayton, P.J., & Guze, S.B. (1972). Suicide attempts and psychiatric diagnosis. *Diseases of the Nervous System, 33*(2), 617-622.

Yoakam, J. (1997). Playing bingo with the best of them: Community initiated programs for older gay and lesbian adults. *Journal of Gay & Lesbian Social Services, 6*(1), 27-34.

The University's Role
in Promoting Human Rights
Through Nurturing Human Diversities

Thomas M. Diehm
Marceline M. Lazzari

SUMMARY. This qualitative study explored those components that contribute to an atmosphere which promotes and nurtures human diversities at a new expansion campus of a public university. Semi-structured interviews were conducted with a snowball sample of faculty, staff, and administrators who were identified by other participants as having had

Thomas M. Diehm, MSW, MA, is Senior Lecturer, and Marceline M. Lazzari, PhD, MSW, is Professor and Program Director for the Alternative MSW Program at the University of Washington, Tacoma.

The authors acknowledge Sondra Perdue, DrPH, Jean Jacobson, Kim Larkey, and Betty Spadoni for their assistance in the planning and completion of this study.

Address correspondence to: Thomas M. Diehm, MSW, MA, Social Work Program, Box 358425, University of Washington, Tacoma, 1900 Commerce Street, Tacoma, WA 98402 (E-mail: tdiehm@u.washington.edu or mlazzari@u.washington.edu).

[Haworth co-indexing entry note]: "The University's Role in Promoting Human Rights Through Nurturing Human Diversities." Diehm, Thomas M., and Marceline M. Lazzari. Co-published simultaneously in *Journal of Gay & Lesbian Social Services* (Harrington Park Press, an imprint of The Haworth Press, Inc.) Vol. 13, No. 1/2, 2001, pp. 171-189; and: *From Hate Crimes to Human Rights: A Tribute to Matthew Shepard* (ed: Mary E. Swigonski, Robin S. Mama, and Kelly Ward) Harrington Park Press, an imprint of The Haworth Press, Inc., 2001, pp. 171-189. Single or multiple copies of this article are available for a fee from The Haworth Document Delivery Service [1-800-342-9678, 9:00 a.m. - 5:00 p.m. (EST). E-mail address: getinfo@haworthpressinc.com].

171

a positive impact on the creation and maintenance of such an atmosphere. Using grounded theory, a preliminary data analysis indicated a mixed picture of the institution's success at this endeavor. Although many individual and collaborative efforts are already in place, they are not coordinated in any campus-wide manner. Intentional and shared responsibility across the university community was identified as the core component of turning diversity rhetoric into action. Administrative sanction, visibility, and support (modeling) were identified as critical to facilitating the kind of ongoing communication and systematic planning necessary for this intentional effort to succeed. *[Article copies available for a fee from The Haworth Document Delivery Service: 1-800-342-9678. E-mail address: <getinfo@haworthpressinc.com> Website: <http://www.HaworthPress.com> © 2001 by The Haworth Press, Inc. All rights reserved.]*

KEYWORDS. Human diversity, higher education, hate crimes, human rights, nondiscrimination, heterosexism, homophobia

Prejudice, bigotry, and hate-related violence (often referred to as "hate crimes") sparked by strong feelings about some aspect of human diversity have been part of human attitude and behavior for all of recorded history. In recent years we have seen appalling acts perpetrated against individuals and communities based on religion (Ireland, Bosnia), ethnicity (Kosovo), or tribal origin (Rwanda). From the arrival of the first Europeans, American history is replete with incidents of hate-related acts ranging from individual assaults to genocidal attacks. Most recently, the murders of James Byrd, Jr. (Texas), Matthew Shepard (Wyoming), Billy Jack Gaither (Alabama), Ricky Birdsong (Illinois), and Won-Joon Soon (Indiana), as well as assaults on other marginalized people, serve as reminders that violence perpetrated against those who are somehow different from the standard set by the dominant culture continues unabated. It is the authors' belief that nurturing these differences is key to promoting human rights.

Universities are perceived to be at the forefront of the advancement of the humanities, the arts, and scientific and technical knowledge in society. Walters and Hayes (1998) point out that they are also perceived to be in the vanguard of social study and change. This has included placing significant emphasis on recruiting and retaining students, faculty, and staff who represent a wide array of human diversities. It is no longer unusual to walk through an academic building at virtually any institution and see representatives of human diversities who were rare not long ago–individuals in wheelchairs or with medical conditions who require special equipment or learning techniques, students who are significantly older than the traditional college student, a veritable United Nations of international students and faculty, and single mothers and fathers with children in tow. The list is as endless as the different people it attempts to categorize. Higher education opportunities are now available to a far wider range of people. Some institutions made a commitment from the beginning of this diversification of the student body to creating an atmosphere in which human diversity could be not just tolerated, but nurtured. Sadly, these efforts have not always succeeded. Other institutions have accepted and validated human differences only to the extent required to receive government funding such as research grants or student loan monies. In these instances, diversity may be tolerated but is unlikely to be nurtured.

It is the purpose of this article to explore the efforts made at an expansion campus of an established state university to foster an atmosphere that accepts and nurtures human diversities. The nondiscrimination policy of the institution affirms a policy of "equal opportunity regardless of race, color, creed, religion, national origin, sex, sexual orientation, age, marital status, disability, or status as a disabled veteran or a veteran of the Vietnam era." Every quarterly registration guide reaffirms the institution's commitment to "promoting respect for the rights and privileges of others, understanding and appreciation of human differences, and the constructive expression of ideas." Violations of these policies may result in "a variety of disciplinary actions."

The age of the campus provides a unique opportunity to capture the elements that appear to facilitate the creation of an open and nurturing institutional environment around issues of human diversities. By addressing historical as well as ongoing actions, approaches, and relationships, elements that appear necessary to build a foundation for the creation and maintenance of such an institutional atmosphere can be identified. These components could be used by other institutions to guide their own efforts in this important direction.

THE LITERATURE

Because of the focus and nature of the current collection of articles in this special edition, the authors have chosen to review the literature that recently has begun to accumulate related to discrimination and violence experienced by sexual minorities on college campuses. Sexual orientation is not one of the categories protected by federal law in terms of funding eligibility, making it an area which may truly indicate an institution's commitment to inclusiveness of all human diversities. As Vaid (1995) points out, attempting to address issues of human diversities in narrow and exclusive categories (e.g., race/ethnicity, disability, age, sexual orientation) may ultimately be less productive (perhaps even counterproductive) than approaching the nurturing of differences with a wide and inclusive brush.

Discrimination and violence against sexual minorities has typically been deemed a significant part of "homophobia." Research related to homophobia in educational settings has expanded greatly in the past decade. Harbeck (1992) looks at homophobia across the educational system, including college campuses, and addresses how homophobia and heterosexism are played out for students and teachers alike. In studies of these issues in higher education, Duncan (1990) concluded that gay and lesbian students were significantly more likely to experience sexual victimization than heterosexual students. Comstock's (1991) study concluded that gay and lesbian college students were victims of verbal and/or physical assault at four times the rate of the sexual majority population. A study by Rey and Gibson (1997) of college students addresses discrimination and assault from the perspective of the heterosexual perpetrators.

A number of studies addressing anti-gay/lesbian attitudes and violence at specific college campuses, including Yale (Herek cited in Berrill, 1992a), Oberlin (Norris, 1992), Pennsylvania State University (D'Augelli, 1989), Rutgers (Cavin cited in Berrill, 1992a), the University of Illinois (O'Shaughnessey cited in Berrill, 1992a), and the University of Massachusetts (Yeskel cited in Slater, 1993) support the more general research findings.

While most of the above studies focused on college students, McNaron's (1997) work addresses the experiences of sexual minority faculty from across the country, which range from stories of ruined careers and lives to acts of great support and loyalty from heterosexual colleagues and students. Tierney (1997) places individual stories of academics victimized by homophobia within the context of "cultural studies and queer theory" (p. 6).

A number of strategies for reducing levels of homophobia and heterosexism (and associated violence) at the college level, as well as classroom approaches to specific professional training, have been offered (Berrill, 1992b; Berrill & Herek, 1992; D'Augelli, 1992; D'Emilio, 1990; Mager & Sulek, 1997; Myers & Kardia, 1997; Serdahely & Ziemba, 1985; Slater, 1993; Tierney, 1997; Walters & Hayes, 1998). These writings address schools of social work (Cramer, 1997), medical schools (Wallick & Townsend, 1997), counselor training programs (Emert & Milburn, 1997), and criminal justice programs (Iasenza, 1997). The suggested university-wide strategies include implementation of policies or procedures that may help offset attitudinal homophobia, such as adding sexual orientation to institutional nondiscrimination policies; providing for an ombudsperson to investigate or advocate around sexual minority issues and incidents; domestic partner inclusion in employee benefits, etc. As important as these actions are, the implementation of even the most progressive policies and procedures geared toward eliminating homophobia do not address creating an atmosphere in which differences among people can be nurtured. Slater (1993) maintains that the creation of such an atmosphere, at least as related to sexual minorities, requires "clear-cut, non-ambivalent administrative leadership" (p. 194), so that "regardless of one's personal beliefs, discrimination is not acceptable and that the campus will be a safe, supportive environment for all students . . ." (p. 195).

With the idea of strong administrative leadership as key to creating a nurturing environment for human differences, the authors determined to explore to what extent the actions, approaches, and relationships of administrative leadership play a role in creating that environment and how other key staff, faculty, and administrators contribute both to the creation and maintenance of such an atmosphere. The attempt to describe this atmosphere and how it is fostered, if it does indeed exist, is the first part of a larger study directed toward seeking input from students and the wider campus community describing their experiences at the institution in relation to human diversities. These data could then be used to inform the institution as to whether its efforts have been effective and how future endeavors might be targeted.

THE STUDY CONTEXT

This study was conducted at the nine-year-old expansion campus of a public university located in the western United States. The subject institution provides upper division and graduate education on an urban, commuter campus to approximately 1,300 students. At the time of its founding, the institution's mission was to provide a liberal arts program in a region that was not served by any publicly funded four-year university. Several additional professional programs have been added in response to the expressed need of the region. Of the original 13 faculty of the institution, nine were white men, two were men of color, and two were white women. The student body is made up largely of working, non-traditional-aged people, most of whom are women, many with significant family responsibilities. A considerable number of classes are held in the evening to accommodate the very full lives of the majority of students. A recent voter referendum eradicated affirmative action programs at the state level, thereby eliminating any hiring or admissions decisions that might be based on such a program. This reflects the relatively conservative political climate of the state and of the social environment nationally.

METHODOLOGY

The chosen design, a modified version of the grounded-theory approach (Glaser, 1978; Glaser & Strauss, 1967; Strauss, 1987), allowed the researchers to discover meaning from the study's participants about their perceptions and ideas of the components that appear to foster a nurturing environment of human diversities in a university setting. Because of the time constraints of this study, the analysis reported here was conducted using the notes taken by both researchers during each interview, as well as summaries of each set of notes completed separately after each interview. Both researchers were present during all of the interviews. The results of this phase of the study are, thus, based upon an initial analysis of the data.

Snowball sampling was used to identify those individuals who were perceived to have played a positive role in nurturing and promoting acceptance of human diversities. Beginning with the highest level administrator, other participants were subsequently identified throughout the study. At the time of data collection, the institution employed a total of 226 faculty, staff, and administrators. Of this total, 53 names were mentioned by interviewees as potential participants for the study (23% of the total). An interview period of five weeks was established for the project with no new invitations being sent out after the fourth week. Thirty-two invitations were issued with 23 individuals (72% response rate) agreeing to confidential interviews within the allotted time period. These 23 individuals represented 10% of campus employees and were relatively representative of the four categories of employees: faculty made up 34% of the sample (40% of total employees); staff made up 52% of the sample (56% of total employees); administrators made up 3% of the sample (2% of total employees); and administrators/faculty made up 9% of the sample (2% of total employees). While fairly representative of larger employment categories, the sample was not proportionally representative of the various position classifications within the university. Individuals were identified by other employees a range of one to twelve times, with a mean of five mentions by other participants.

PRINCIPAL FINDINGS

A decision was made not to ask participants for any identifying information other than position and years at the university as well as highest educational level (Table 1). Several participants have been employed with the institution since its founding in 1990, with others employed as recently as six months ago. The mean employment period for the total sample was 4.1 years with a mean range among position categories of 3.6 to 4.6 years. The sample represented a range of diversities (Table 2), although there is no mechanism available to determine the extent to which it is representative of the diversity of the

TABLE 1. Sample Employment Duration and Education Level (N = 23)

	Average Years at Institution		Education Level		
	Years	Range	Bachelors	Masters	Doctorate
Faculty (n = 8)	4.6 yr.	6 mo.–9 yr.	0 (0%)	0 (0%)	8 (100%)
Staff (n = 12)	3.6 yr.	7 mo.–9 yr.	6 (50%)	5 (42%)	1 (8%)
Administration (n = 1)	4.0 yr.	--	0 (0%)	0 (0%)	1 (100%)
Admin/Faculty (n = 2)	4.0 yr.	3 yr.–5 yr.	0 (0%)	0 (0%)	2 (100%)
Total (N = 23)	4.1 yr.	6 mo.–9 yr.	6 (26%)	5 (22%)	12 (52%)

TABLE 2. Sample Diversity (N = 23)

	Table 2a Gender–Entire Sample		Table 2b* Other Diversity by Gender	
	Male	Female	Male	Female
Faculty (n = 8)	3 (38%)	5 (62%)	2 (25%)	2 (25%)
Staff (n = 12)	4 (33%)	8 (67%)	3 (25%)	6 (50%)
Administration (n = 1)	0 (0%)	1 (100%)	0 (0%)	0 (0%)
Admin/Faculty (n = 2)	0 (0%)	2 (100%)	0 (0%)	1 (50%)
Total (N = 23)	7 (30%)	16 (70%)	5 (22%)	9 (39%)

* Numbers and percentages in Table 2b refer to proportions of the entire sample (N = 23). Includes observed persons of color, self-disclosed persons of color, self-disclosed sexual minorities, and self-disclosed religious minorities.

institution as a whole. During the process of the interviews, the researchers were able to visually identify participants by gender and color. Of the total number of participants (N = 23), 70% were female; 60% of the total were either observed to be persons of color (30%) or self-identified during the interviews as sexual or religious minorities (34%). None of the persons of color self-identified as belonging to any other diverse groups with the exception of one who self-identified as being a religious minority as well. It was not obvious to the interviewers that this individual was a person of color.

The researchers began by considering the overall content of each semi-structured interview to determine if the participants perceived that the university is making adequate efforts to promote an accepting and nurturing environment of human diversities. Two participants said "yes"; three responded "no"; and the vast majority (n = 18) described a mixed effort based upon the realities of their experiences. Since the overall perception was so mixed, the researchers began to look at the components that were noted as being present, those that were seen as being absent (and, thus, desired), and those that were described as needing to be eliminated. What began to emerge in the process of this analysis was a picture of what might be in place in a university that took seriously the mission to nurture human diversities. Positive elements that were identified as being present by some were likewise mentioned as being absent or only minimally present by others, pointing to their importance as well as to differences in perceptions.

Core Category: Intentional and Shared Responsibility Across the University Community

In using the grounded-theory approach, one looks for a central and unifying theme, termed the *core category,* under which all of the other data can be subsumed. The notion of *theoretical saturation* is critical in understanding this method of analysis. In practice, theoretical saturation means that all of the empirical data fits conceptually under the core category. In this analysis, that did occur.

Figure 1, From Rhetoric to Action in Nurturing Human Diversities, presents the findings from this phase of the study. The title implies that there is a great deal of perceived rhetoric about how the university values human diversities and that words need to be put into action. This action is explicated under the *core category* of *intentional and shared responsibility across the university community.* Participants were clear that creating an environment which nurtures human diversities requires all members of the university community to be engaged in actions in their respective spheres of activity, influence, and responsibility. As one participant noted, "we need to live it, not just say it" (Interview 01). Figure 1 represents a dynamic, interactive, and ongoing process of intentional awareness and behaviors.

The mandate for shared responsibility was articulated in a variety of ways: "the notion of 'the other' is destructive; how do we get others to be a part of us? How do we talk about others who are different?" (Interview 14); "We need to be allies for other groups beyond ourselves. We must advocate for people who are marginalized in whatever ways; we must be visible and open" (Interview 11); "We need to be a voice for others" (Interview 17); and finally, "the majority has to change, not just the minority. This is everyone's responsibility" (Interview 16).

At this point in the analysis, a *necessary condition* for this process to occur was identified as being *administrative sanction, visibility, and support (modeling).* "It needs to be made *clear* from the *administrative level* [emphasis added] that diversity is a part of our goal" (Interview 03). "There is no vision behind our mission statement. We need to see someone model this. People who are the most visible [meaning in leadership positions] should be out there [at diversity-related events]" (Interview 19). This is not meant to imply that efforts to nurture human diversities cannot be made without such administrative

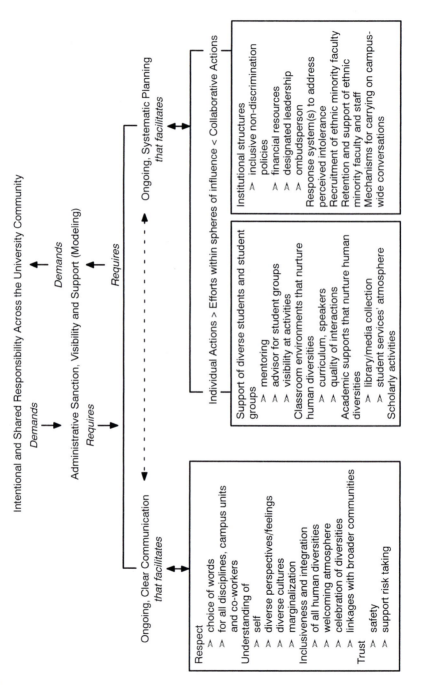

FIGURE 1. From Rhetoric to Action in Nurturing Human Diversities

Intentional and Shared Responsibility Across the University Community

Demands

Demands

Administrative Sanction, Visibility and Support (Modeling)

Requires

Requires

Ongoing, Systematic Planning
that facilitates

Individual Actions > Efforts within spheres of influence < Collaborative Actions

Institutional structures
≫ inclusive non-discrimination
policies
≫ financial resources
≫ designated leadership
≫ ombudsperson
Response system(s) to address
perceived intolerance
Recruitment of ethnic minority faculty
Retention and support of ethnic
minority faculty and staff
Mechanisms for carrying on campus-
wide conversations

Support of diverse students and student
groups
≫ mentoring
≫ advisor for student groups
≫ visibility at activities
Classroom environments that nurture
human diversities
≫ curriculum, speakers
≫ quality of interactions
Academic supports that nurture human
diversities
≫ library/media collection
≫ student services' atmosphere
Scholarly activities

Ongoing, Clear Communication
that facilitates

Respect
≫ choice of words
≫ for all disciplines, campus units
and co-workers
Understanding of
≫ self
≫ diverse perspectives/feelings
≫ diverse cultures
≫ marginalization
Inclusiveness and integration
≫ of all human diversities
≫ welcoming atmosphere
≫ celebration of diversities
≫ linkages with broader communities
Trust
≫ safety
≫ support risk taking

involvement, as indicated by the many individual actions taken by participants, but that systematic and comprehensive success cannot occur without such support. Many participants noted that what occurs within a university setting simply reflects the larger society's struggles with issues of human diversity.

Dimensions of the Core Category

Two major interactive *dimensions* (or subcategories) *of the core category* emerged from the data. The first was *ongoing, clear communication,* and the second was *ongoing, systematic planning.* Clearly, both dimensions are interdependent.

The *properties* listed under the *first dimension–ongoing, clear communication–*are self-explanatory. However, it is important to highlight several items. Perhaps most important are the meanings of diversity, which for this study's participants included all academic disciplines, campus units, and co-workers as well as the entire range of human differences (implying various physical characteristics and abilities, perspectives, feelings, and cultures). As one participant noted:

> Some kinds of diversity are considered more diverse than others. We need to be alert to who we are *excluding* [emphasis added] from the conversation. Gay and lesbian issues are intermittently and uneasily addressed. Religious diversity is not worked on all that much. The great unspoken are differing political views. I would guess that some conversations regarding ethnicity have gone underground. It is hard to create safe environments. This is tricky, complex stuff. (Interview 8)

"If you happen to be non-white, there is more discrimination and it is subtle. If you are white and middle-class, no matter what else, differences are not as readily seen and you can fit in" (Interview 13). "Issues of race tend to go underground and there is underground anger" (Interview 14). "There needs to be a place where people can safely talk about what bothers them. We need a way to talk without using 'hot words'" (Interview 09). As acknowledged by all of the participants, the challenges to creating safe environments for exploring human diversities cannot be minimized or ignored.

A second area to highlight is the need to grasp what it means to be a person who is marginalized for some reason(s) and how human diversities need to be comprehended in an integrated manner. As one participant noted, "I always try to integrate race, class, gender, and sexual identification into all of my courses" (Interview 22). "We tend to keep our understandings of diversity on an intellectual level. We need to understand the personal and day-to-day basis of how people who are marginalized struggle and feel" (Interview 03). "People need to understand how other people feel" (Interview 13). "We cannot expect marginalized people to carry the burden" (Interview 11).

The participants in this study expressed a sense of urgency about wanting *ongoing, systematic planning*, the *second dimension* of the core category. This passion must be understood within the context of the growth of the institution when even a few years ago, the smaller size was more conducive to meaningful conversations and a greater sense of community. "In the early days because we were so new, there was an energy and a willingness to go out on a limb. Now, that mind set has fizzled. I have concerns around communication and trust" (Interview 02). "We have institutional knowledge but not resources. We need an institutional method, especially in light of our growth" (Interview 07). "We are beginning to stagnate" (Interview 21).

Participants discussed the need for both *individual and collaborative actions*, which are *properties* of the *second dimension*, and described a variety of efforts within their respective spheres of influence. In the area of individual actions, respondents gave a number of examples related to working with diverse students and to bringing diversity issues into the classroom as well as academic support and student life activities. "As a teacher, I have the opportunity to create a classroom atmosphere that allows students to really explore these [diversity] issues" (Interview 23). Even though no questions were asked about students during the interviews, students were discussed, particularly as related to individual actions. The participants did not imply that working with students cannot be a collaborative effort; in fact, several participants saw their teaching and other activities with students as being collaborative endeavors. Several participants mentioned that having a non-traditional and diverse student body provides an environment that supports diversity. At the same time, another participant noted that "students don't always feel safe" (Interview 05). "The institution needs to make it clear to students where they can go if they are having problems around diversity, etc., because students might not say anything" (Interview 10). Several participants emphasized the importance of beginning to mentor ethnically diverse students when they are in elementary and high school and of serving as advisors for diverse student groups.

In relation to scholarly activities, one faculty member stressed the importance of the institution maintaining its flexibility in terms of promotion and tenure decisions. This holds salience particularly for faculty who choose to research and write about diversity-related topics such as ethnicity, feminism, classism, heterosexism, and HIV/AIDS.

Collaborative actions encompass institutional structures, such as the non-discrimination policies, that typically are in place in most universities. The university under study has an inclusive non-discrimination statement that is not characteristic of all colleges and universities. Even with this statement, numerous participants described a great deal of rhetoric and less than adequate action. One participant went so far as to express general distrust of institutions: "This university is like any other male-dominated institution. I trust no institution as it will always protect itself" (Interview 11). Related to this and referring to the gender and ethnic composition of the founding faculty, one participant noted that "there has been a contextual problem since day one. Getting people to see this as a problem, is a problem" (Interview 07). On a very serious note, thirty percent (n = 7) of the respondents made accusations of overt racism. "We have lost minority staff over issues of oppression" (Interview 21).

At the same time, there was a *pervasive* and *unanimous* description of the university being better than most of society and institutions of higher education. One participant commented that this is "probably because we're new and old structures didn't have to be dismantled" (Interview 18). Multiple participants noted that the institution has worked particularly hard around issues of disability accommodation, both with students and employees. One individual stated, "This is a great place to be a woman and working class" (Interview 23). These positive viewpoints, however, are tempered with the realization that growth has impacted the institution's continued progress in nurturing human diversity. Referring to the impact of growth, one participant provided the caveat that "positive steps need to be taken soon or it will be too late" (Interview 07). Based upon all of the interviews, there was a sense that efforts to be accepting, welcoming, and supportive of all people are not always perceived or known by others.

The need for proactive recruitment, hiring, and retention of ethnically diverse faculty and staff was mentioned by most participants, regardless of their own ethnic diversity status. "Retaining faculty, staff, and administrators of color is not a high priority on this campus; they are not nurtured to stay. New faculty-of-color do not get adequate information about promotion and tenure expectations and committee work. Also, one faculty member who was a lesbian left after one year" (Interview 04). One participant cautioned that "seeing more diversity does not necessarily mean that the atmosphere is more open" (Interview 23). Another participant noted how she "jumps at the chance to bring a diverse person [including those with physical disabilities] into her unit. The more diverse the group, the easier it is to break down stereotypes" (Interview 09). The notion of diverse people also was related to the notion of diverse perspectives and how important it is to be exposed to different ways of thinking. The demand to have avenues for faculty and staff to address perceived intolerance was emphasized. "It has taken two years to get the ombudsperson here. This is a positive step" (Interview 14).

Several areas not generally considered "diversity issues" were raised as part of a larger understanding of diversity and their importance to creating positive and nurturing environments for all. Numerous participants mentioned the degree of elitism and division of thought between and among the various academic programs. "One program in particular has a sense of important stature and wants to do things one way, and that's it. There is also the professional–staff (being less than) split. And the infrastructure does not support multidisciplinary efforts" (Interview 19). Many participants viewed staff members as taking the lead in terms of nurturing others.

The requirement to have designated leadership for diversity efforts was stressed. In the university, there is a designated "diversity position"; however, most participants were not aware of it or had very unclear understanding of its functions and responsibilities. There is also a "diversity committee," but again, most did not even know if it still exists or that it ever existed.

The above findings point to the need for mechanisms for engaging in ongoing, campus-wide conversations. We need to ask: "how are we caring for people?" (Interview 04). "Someone needs to give a damn about relationships and what is going on" (Interview 19). "There is no right answer. We need to think about issues and come to understand.

We need a place of comfort for all. There is no structure in place to facilitate communication" (Interview 20).

> We need some unit or program to hold responsibility for something being done, a group rather than a diversity czar. People come here because the campus seems a little less conventional; there is a sense of being different. People are making efforts. There is a lot of good will but not enough. Where is our diversity center? We need a focus. (Interview 08)

"It is now more complicated and harder for conversations to take place. We can't regain the early sense of what we were. I like who we are now, too. Perhaps this study will help start the conversation again" (Interview 18). "We need to do something outrageous, hold a big event to celebrate diversity" (Interview 14). "There is hope" (Interview 13).

DISCUSSION

The issues and perceptions involved in this study are varied and complex. The overall results indicate a mixed review of the efforts being made. Some efforts are seen as very positive, others as overtly negative, and most as being in need of change and refinement as the institution grows and the context changes. While all participants responded in a serious and conscientious manner, they also tended to recognize that creating a truly nurturing environment within the context of a society that does not embrace human differences is a monumental challenge. This did not, however, seem to daunt individuals in their efforts to make personal and collective efforts toward meeting these high expectations.

Clearly, the primary issue to be addressed is turning the rhetoric of honoring and nurturing diversity into ongoing, positive action. It was evident from examples provided by study participants that individuals are making principled, intentional efforts to make the campus one that is welcoming and nurturing of human differences, but these efforts tend to lack coordination. The importance of sanction and leadership for diversity related initiatives and actions from the highest levels of administration, as espoused by Slater (1993), were clearly voiced in this study. A difference in perception of the extent to which that leadership already exists may be partially attributable to the individual participant's own knowledge of campus structures and programs, which may, in turn, be attributable partially to length of employment at the university. However, the expressed need for such leadership was evident across the range of employees interviewed.

It was also clear that the responsibility for nurturing human diversity does not lie solely with administration or its policies. Participants expressed that the responsibility lies with each member of the university community and that the rhetoric is not adequate. Rather, appropriate policies and administrative leadership should provide the necessary sanction for individuals to make organized and purposeful nurturing efforts within their spheres of influence, regardless of their position at the university. Participants concomitantly emphasized that some entity within the institution must hold responsibility and accountability for the overall efforts of the university.

Based on the interview responses as well as upon the authors' personal and professional experiences, the authors are in agreement with Vaid's (1995) position that it is not appropriate to address human diversity in discrete categories. Rather, all university community members must be willing to address the myriad of ways in which individuals can be marginalized. As one study member put it, "my survival is connected to the survival of other marginalized groups. Don't ghettoize it" (Interview 11). Being willing to embrace, respect, and celebrate the differences between and among human beings is, perhaps, our greatest challenge.

These preliminary results also provide a warning that the nurturing of human diversity requires ongoing vigilance on the part of the entire university community. Respondents indicate a need to be aware of nontraditional ways of viewing human diversity, including academic discipline, role in the academic setting, and ways of perceiving education. As an institution grows, ways of relating to one another will change, becoming more complex. The institution must be prepared to address issues of communication and trust in a more intentional manner. As institution- and career-building activities absorb a larger portion of staff and faculty energy, the tight sense of community experienced by early community members becomes dissipated. In this changing environment, it becomes important that time be set aside in a safe environment for discussions to take place around the complexities of nurturing human diversities in a growing academic setting. This mandate applies not only to the university under study but to any institution that purports to honor human diversities. This is ongoing and serious work that can contribute to the reduction of hatred and intolerance in this society, and ultimately, in the world.

FUTURE RESEARCH

The findings reported in this article represent a preliminary analysis of the data collected. The interview material warrants in-depth analysis to address areas of strength and concern in a more detailed manner. Further, the snowball sampling method used lends itself to a network analysis to determine to what extent those individuals who identified one another as playing a positive role in nurturing human diversities are connected to one another through university position, social affiliation, diversity affiliation, or physical proximity on the university campus.

Only employees of the institution were solicited and interviewed for this study. It would be of significant interest to expand the project to include student perceptions of the university as a place which nurtures their differences from one another and to what extent they believe the welcoming atmosphere deemed so important by study participants exists or is lacking. Additionally, gathering information from those university employees not included in the initial study would provide a wider range of perceptions than only those provided by individuals identified as being a positive force for nurturing diversities.

REFERENCES

Berrill, K. T. (1992a). Anti-gay violence and victimization in the United States: An overview. In G. M. Herek & K. T. Berrill (Eds.), *Hate crimes: Confronting violence against lesbians and gay men* (pp. 19-45). Newbury Park, CA: Sage.

Berrill, K. T. (1992b). Organizing against hate on campus: Strategies for activists. In G. M. Herek & K. T. Berrill (Eds.), *Hate crimes: Confronting violence against lesbians and gay men* (pp. 259-269). Newbury Park, CA: Sage.

Berrill, K. T., & Herek, G. M. (1992). Primary and secondary victimization in anti-gay crimes: Official response and public policy. In G. M. Herek & K. T. Berrill (Eds.), *Hate crimes: Confronting violence against lesbians and gay men* (pp. 289-305). Newbury Park, CA: Sage.

Comstock, G. D. (1991). *Violence against lesbians and gay men.* New York: Columbia University Press.

Cramer, E. (1997). Strategies for reducing social work students' homophobia. In J. T. Sears & W. L. Williams (Eds.), *Overcoming heterosexism and homophobia* (pp. 287-298). New York: Columbia University Press.

D'Augelli, A. R. (1989). Lesbians' and gay men's experiences of discrimination and harassment in a university community. *American Journal of Community Psychology, 17*, 317-321.

D'Augelli, A. R. (1992). Teaching lesbian/gay development: From oppression to exceptionality. In K. M. Harbeck (Ed.), *Coming out of the classroom closet: Gay and lesbian students, teachers, and curricula* (pp. 213-227). New York: The Haworth Press, Inc.

D'Emilio, J. (1990). The campus environment for gay and lesbian life. *Academe, 76*(1), 16-19.

Duncan, D. F. (1990). Prevalence of sexual assault victimization among heterosexual and gay/lesbian university students. *Psychological Reports, 66*, 65-66.

Emert, T., & Milburn, L. (1997). Sensitive supervisors, prepared practicum, and "queer" clients: A training model for beginning counselors. In J. T. Sears & W. L. Williams (Eds.), *Overcoming heterosexism and homophobia* (pp. 272-286). New York: Columbia University Press.

Glaser, B. G. (1978). *Theoretical sensitivity.* Mill Valley, CA: Sociology Press.

Glaser, B. G., & Strauss, A. L. (1967). *The discovery of grounded theory.* New York: Aldine De Gruyter.

Harbeck, K. M. (Ed.). (1992). *Coming out of the classroom closet: Gay and lesbian students, teachers, and curricula.* New York: The Haworth Press, Inc.

Iasenza, S. (1997). Educating criminal justice college students about sexual orientation, homophobia, and heterosexism. In J. T. Sears & W. L. Williams (Eds.), *Overcoming heterosexism and homophobia* (pp. 311-325). New York: Columbia University Press.

Mager, D.N., & Sulek, R. (1997). Teaching about homophobia at a historically black university: A role play for undergraduate students. In J. T. Sears & W. L. Williams (Eds.), *Overcoming heterosexism and homophobia* (pp. 182-196). New York: Columbia University Press.

McNaron, T. A. H. (1997). *Poisoned ivy: Lesbian and gay academics confronting homophobia.* Philadelphia, PA: Temple University Press.

Myers, P., & Kardia, D. (1997). "But you seem so normal!": Multidimensional approaches to unlearning homophobia on a college campus. In J. T. Sears & W. L. Williams (Eds.), *Overcoming heterosexism and homophobia* (pp. 197-208). New York: Columbia University Press.

Norris, W. P. (1992). Liberal attitudes and homophobic acts: The paradoxes of homosexual experience in a liberal institution. In K. M. Harbeck (Ed.), *Coming out of the classroom closet: Gay and lesbian students, teachers and curricula* (pp. 81-120). New York: The Haworth Press, Inc.

Rey, A. M., & Reed Gibson, P. (1997). Beyond high school: Heterosexuals; self-reported anti-gay/lesbian behaviors and attitudes. *Journal of Gay & Lesbian Social Services, 7*(4), 65-84.

Serdahely, W. J., & Ziemba, G. J. (1985). Changing homophobic attitudes through college sexuality education. In J. P. De Cecco (Ed.), *Bashers, baiters, & bigots: Homophobia in American society.* New York: The Haworth Press, Inc.

Slater, B. R. (1993). Violence against lesbian and gay male college students. *Journal of College Student Psychotherapy, 8*(1/2), 177-202.

Strauss, A. L. (1987). *Qualitative analysis for social scientists.* Cambridge, England: Cambridge University Press.

Tierney, W. G. (1997). *Academic outlaws: Queer theory and cultural studies in the academy.* Thousand Oaks, CA: Sage.

Vaid, U. (1995). *Virtual equality: The mainstreaming of gay and lesbian liberation.* New York: Doubleday.

Wallick, M. M., & Townsend, M. H. (1997). Gay and lesbian issues in U.S. medical schools: Climate and curriculum. In J. T. Sears & W. L. Williams (Eds.), *Overcoming heterosexism and homophobia* (pp. 299-310). New York: Columbia University Press.

Walters, A. S., & Hayes, D. M. (1998). Homophobia within schools: Challenging the culturally sanctioned dismissal of gay students and colleagues. *Journal of Homosexuality, 35*(2), 1-23.

Social Justice Advocacy Readiness Questionnaire

Stuart F. Chen-Hayes

SUMMARY. Social service providers of consultation, counseling, and education can benefit from determining their social justice awareness, knowledge, and skills to ensure culturally competent practice and to challenge the multiple oppressions facing clients and staff on individual, cultural, and institutional/systemic levels. The Social Justice Advocacy Readiness Questionnaire (SJARQ) provides a means to advocate for social justice with persons of multiple cultural identities, including all sexual orientations and gender identities. The SJARQ instrument contains three areas of self-assessment for social services staff: individual social justice advocacy awareness, comfort, and values; cultural social justice advocacy knowledge; and institutional/systemic social justice advocacy skills. *[Article copies available for a fee from The Haworth Document Delivery Service: 1-800-342-9678. E-mail address: <getinfo@haworthpressinc. com> Website: <http://www.HaworthPress.com> © 2001 by The Haworth Press, Inc. All rights reserved.]*

KEYWORDS. Social justice advocacy, counseling, consultation, education

---

Stuart F. Chen-Hayes, PhD, is Assistant Professor and Coordinator, Counselor Education, Department of Specialized Services in Education at Lehman College of the City University of New York.

Address correspondence to: Stuart F. Chen-Hayes, Lehman College of CUNY, Dept. of Specialized Services Ed., Carman Hall B-20, 250 Bedford Park Boulevard West, Bronx, NY 10468 (E-mail: stuartc@lehman.cuny.edu or swagalu@earthlink.net)

[Haworth co-indexing entry note]: "Social Justice Advocacy Readiness Questionnaire." Chen-Hayes, Stuart F. Co-published simultaneously in *Journal of Gay & Lesbian Social Services* (Harrington Park Press, an imprint of The Haworth Press, Inc.) Vol. 13, No. 1/2, 2001, pp. 191-203; and: *From Hate Crimes to Human Rights: A Tribute to Matthew Shepard* (ed: Mary E. Swigonski, Robin S. Mama, and Kelly Ward) Harrington Park Press, an imprint of The Haworth Press, Inc., 2001, pp. 191-203. Single or multiple copies of this article are available for a fee from The Haworth Document Delivery Service [1-800-342-9678, 9:00 a.m. - 5:00 p.m. (EST). E-mail address: getinfo@haworthpressinc.com].

INTRODUCTION

Somewhere, on the edge of consciousness, there is what I call a mythical norm, which each one of us within our hearts knows "that is not me." In america (sic), this norm is usually defined as white, thin, male, young, heterosexual, christian (sic), and financially secure. It is within this mythical norm that the trappings of power reside within this society. Those of us who stand outside that power often identify one way in which we are different, and we assume that to be the primary course of all oppression, forgetting other distortions around difference, some of which we ourselves may be practicing. (Lorde, 1984, p. 116)

Issues of culturally competent service provision and inclusion of all cultural voices and identities are major issues for lesbian, bisexual, gay, transgendered, two-spirit, queer, and questioning (LBGT2QQ) service providers. Because organizations are staffed by persons from different backgrounds, professions, and educational herstories and histories, it is difficult to standardize training and education. When it comes to issues of social justice advocacy, however, providers and consumers of social work, consultation, counseling, and other educational services can all benefit from a questionnaire that helps to evaluate staff and clients' social justice advocacy awareness, knowledge, and skills. To be culturally competent and responsive to human rights and social justice issues, it is important to explore our individual, cultural and institutional/systemic issues of oppression in the provision of LBGT2QQ social services.

What is a "gay" or "transgender" issue? Who decides? How do our LBGT2QQ agencies provide for the multiple identities and social justice needs for a culturally diverse community? When services are provided for LBGT2QQ people of color, are issues of heterosexism addressed while racism is dismissed? When services are provided to persons of transgendered experience, are issues of transgenderism addressed while issues of classism and beautyism are ignored?

CULTURALLY COMPETENT LBGT2QQ COUNSELING, EDUCATION, AND ADVOCACY LITERATURE

Oppression can be defined as prejudice multiplied by power (Chen-Hayes, 2000). LGBT2QQ service providers are often most familiar with the challenges of oppressions such as heterosexism and trans-genderism. The daily lives of LGBT2QQ service providers and clients are steeped in ongoing struggles to appropriately service LGBT2QQ persons in a culture that keeps resources away from nondominant sexual orientations and gender identities. However, challenging these two oppressions is not enough. Social service providers also need to challenge the interlocking multiple oppressions (Reynolds & Pope, 1991), including racism, classism, sexism, ageism, ableism, linguicism, anti-Semitism, and beautyism, to fully empower clients, colleagues, and other community members.

One way to appropriately challenge multiple oppressions in social service agencies is to study the struggles of oppressed persons across multiple identities (Zinn, 1995). Critical theory readers are available that help persons to look at individual, cultural, and systemic issues of oppression that cross multiple identities; see, for example, Andrze-jewski (1996) and Rothenberg (1998). Like the rest of the population, most lesbian, bisexual, gay, and transgendered social service providers are products of the dominant culture's educational systems. We have not been given accurate and appropriate information about ourselves as LBGT2QQ, let alone about the multiple cultural identities that are found in our communities. Leadership in our communities has varied, and many of us hunger for ways to be more inclusive in our agencies, with our staffs, and, most of all, with our clients. LGBT2QQ persons can benefit from developing ally relationships (Chen-Hayes & Haley-Banez, in press; Gelberg & Chojnacki, 1996; Lewis & Arnold, 1998; Washington & Evans, 1991). Allies are persons who are members of a dominant cultural group who choose to take on the struggles of mem-bers of the nondominant group. As LBGT2QQ persons, we look to heterosexual and traditionally gendered allies to challenge heterosexism and transgenderism. Yet, as LBGT2QQ persons, we also need to enter into ally relationships related to age, gender, disability, appearance, social class, ethnicity/race, religion, and other cultural variables to chal-lenge all of the oppressions (Lorde, 1984; Reynolds & Pope, 1991).

CONNECTING THE OPPRESSIONS
THROUGH CRITICAL THINKING

Many LBGT2QQ persons come to an understanding of oppression through a starting point of heterosexism or transgenderism (Chen-

Hayes, 2000; Chen-Hayes, in press). For others, it is a first awareness of racism, ableism, or sexism that is the entry point into examining who is in power and who is disempowered. The challenge for all LBGT2QQ service providers, however, is to notice that the salience (Cross, 1996) of one's multiple cultural identities (Reynolds & Pope, 1991) varies based on membership in various groups and our perception of the importance of those group identities at any point in time.

Critical thinking is a tool to help one continually evaluate the norms, values, beliefs, and policies upheld in daily work and family environments and how daily work and family environments honor or dishonor multiple cultural identities. Educators, practitioners, administrators, and clients may reach similar goals for social justice by stimulating critical thinking as a tool of social justice advocacy and multicultural competency. The literature is replete with authors of various sexual orientations and gender identities who continue to assist us in developing critical thinking skills. hooks (1994) wrote about the importance of transgressing in educational practice, including looking at race, class, gender, and the intersections thereof. Sleeter and Grant (1994) discussed the concept of social reconstructionist and multicultural education to focus on multiple contexts. Pedersen (1994) created a list of ways to provide concrete strategies to providers and agencies interested in increasing multicultural competence. Trickett, Watts, and Birman (1994) addressed issues of multiple cultural identities, including age, disability, sexual orientation, and race. Dworkin and Gutierrez (1992), Comas-Diaz and Greene (1994), Firestein (1996), and Israel and Tarver (1997) provided culturally competent models of advocacy, counseling, consultation, and education with LBGT persons.

In addition, Lee and Walz (1998) and Lewis and Bradley (2000) addressed issues of advocacy in counseling and the need for a social justice perspective in all social services contexts. Ivey (1996) and D'Andrea and Daniels (1996) both provided models of liberatory counseling and consultation practice in challenging oppression and creating socially just practitioners, clients, and social systems. Arredondo (1999) drew upon earlier work on multicultural competencies and further refined the personal dimensions of identity model to challenge racism and other oppressions in a social services context.

THE SOCIAL JUSTICE ADVOCACY READINESS
QUESTIONNAIRE (SJARQ) INSTRUMENT

In light of the evolving literature on multiculturally competent practice and social justice advocacy, the Social Justice Advocacy Readiness Questionnaire (SJARQ) (included in Figure 1) was designed as a way for educators, practitioners, and clients to begin or to continue dialogue attempting to ensure that all members of our community are a part of the process of change in our organizations to promote competence, human rights, social justice advocacy, and challenge multiple oppressions. Lee and Walz (1998) encouraged counselors to use assessment instruments that evidence cultural competency and socially just measurement "to facilitate the psychosocial development of persons rather than hinder, stigmatize, or falsely categorize them" (p. 309).

The SJARQ is a 188-item awareness, knowledge, and skills self-report set of questions based on a sampling of social justice items. It is divided into three parts. Part I is based on an individual's perceptions of personal and institutional herstory and history, cultural comfort, and values and beliefs. The second part, knowledge of social justice advocacy, is based on a series of questions about prominent and not-so-prominent persons, dates, and events/items related to social justice struggles across multiple cultural identities. Most of the items from part two were derived from two main sources: the Syracuse Cultural Worker's 1999 Peace Calendar (Syracuse Cultural Workers, 1999) and from the work of historian Howard Zinn's history of the United States through the eyes of the oppressed (Zinn, 1995). Part III is a list of institutional and systemic social justice advocacy skill questions to develop abilities for persons who operate agencies as they may be perceived by their employees and clients. An answer key is available for the second part of the SJARQ; however, parts I and III are open-ended or Likert-scale questions designed to provide optimal discussions and qualitative data for LBGT2QQ agencies and social service providers. Most importantly, the SJARQ is designed for ongoing reflective practice for LBGT2QQ and other service providers, clients, and educators to continually monitor social justice advocacy issues. Practitioners, clients, administrators, and community members can all benefit from evaluating themselves and their organizations to promote greater cultural competency and social justice advocacy in LBGT2QQ social services.

FIGURE 1. The Social Justice Advocacy Readiness Questionnaire (SJARQ)

Part I: Individual Social Justice Advocacy Awareness, Comfort, & Values

Directions (items #1-10): Answer the following questions:

1. How have staff members/clients' cultural background(s) affected communication processes/ counseling/consultation/advocacy/leadership styles used by you/staff?
2. What cultural groups would you/staff/clients like to learn more about?
3. What multicultural, social justice, and advocacy experiences have you/staff/clients had with persons of differing cultural background(s)? Describe how these interactions have affected your perceptions of persons/groups who are different from you/your culture(s) and the changes you have made to affirm various staff and client cultural backgrounds.
4. How do you/staff/clients define the terms multicultural and social justice? Who is excluded? How might this change on individual, cultural, and systemic levels?
5. Discuss a cross-cultural experience/situation that has given you great discomfort and what you learned from it on individual/cultural/systemic levels. How can you make changes to ensure all persons are affirmed and welcomed in your organization?
6. In what ways have you made (or not made) adjustments for people who differ from you/your culture(s) at work, school, in your neighborhood, your community, your family/friends? How have your clients, colleagues, and staff made adjustments?
7. How have you/the organization/clients resisted heterosexism, biphobia, transphobia, racism, sexism, classism, linguicism, beautyism, and other oppressions over time? What oppressions have been the easiest to resist and what have been the hardest? Why? How will you continue to resist oppressions and advocate for social justice within your organization and communities and with your clients/staff?
8. What are the resources in your local and metropolitan communities for accessing multicultural and social justice advocacy awareness, knowledge, and skills for yourself, your significant others, and your clients/colleagues in your organization?
9. When people enter your organization's premises, what images are on the walls, in artwork, in magazines, in advertising, and in brochures? Who is missing? How could this challenge or reinforce cultural oppression?
10. When people view your organization's brochures, handouts, and intake and service provision forms, is the language inclusive of all people? Who is missing? How could this challenge or reinforce cultural oppression?

Directions: (Items #11-48) 1.) Picture yourself in a place where you are the only one of your culture(s) in the presence of the following persons. If you would feel very comfortable with persons of this cultural identity, circle SA/Strongly Agree, if you would feel comfortable, circle A/Agree, if you are unsure, circle U/Undecided, if you would feel uncomfortable, circle D/Disagree, and if you would feel very uncomfortable, circle SD/Strongly Disagree. 2.) Complete the list a second time considering any persons listed as your new client(s), consultees, colleagues, or supervisors/administrator(s). How do you feel? What changed, if anything? Why?

	Level of Comfort				
11. Lesbian, bisexual, gay, transgendered, two-spirit persons	SA	A	U	D	SD
12. Whites of European ethnicities	SA	A	U	D	SD
13. Alcoholics and addicts who are actively using	SA	A	U	D	SD
14. Asian persons	SA	A	U	D	SD
15. Union members	SA	A	U	D	SD
16. Catholics	SA	A	U	D	SD

17. Persons of African ethnicities and/or Black racial identity   SA   A   U   D   SD
18. Atheists   SA   A   U   D   SD
19. Black Muslims   SA   A   U   D   SD
20. Prostitutes   SA   A   U   D   SD
21. Unwed pregnant mothers   SA   A   U   D   SD
22. Persons who have an accent or don't speak standard English   SA   A   U   D   SD
23. Latinas and Latinos   SA   A   U   D   SD
24. Jews   SA   A   U   D   SD
25. Hindus   SA   A   U   D   SD
26. Feminists   SA   A   U   D   SD
27. Welfare recipients   SA   A   U   D   SD
28. Ku Klux Klan members   SA   A   U   D   SD
29. Rich or wealthy people   SA   A   U   D   SD
30. Heterosexuals   SA   A   U   D   SD
31. Native American Indians, Indigenous/First Nations peoples   SA   A   U   D   SD
32. Persons living with HIV/AIDS   SA   A   U   D   SD
33. Persons who are over the age of 65   SA   A   U   D   SD
34. Children and adolescents   SA   A   U   D   SD
35. Person with a facial disfiguration or other physical disability   SA   A   U   D   SD
36. Prisoners   SA   A   U   D   SD
37. Persons with very attractive bodies, hair, clothes, etc.   SA   A   U   D   SD
38. Pagans   SA   A   U   D   SD
39. Working class persons   SA   A   U   D   SD
40. Muslims   SA   A   U   D   SD
41. Persons with learning disabilities   SA   A   U   D   SD
42. Protestants   SA   A   U   D   SD
43. Fat persons   SA   A   U   D   SD
44. Divorced persons   SA   A   U   D   SD
45. Survivors of domestic violence   SA   A   U   D   SD
46. Immigrants   SA   A   U   D   SD
47. Arabs and other persons of Middle Eastern ethnicities   SA   A   U   D   SD
48. Homeless persons   SA   A   U   D   SD

Directions (Items #49-73): Circle the response that fits your beliefs: Strongly Agree (SA), Agree (A), Undecided (U), Disagree (D), Strongly Disagree (SD).

Beliefs

49. Social services workers should help clients adjust to society.   SA   A   U   D   SD
50. African American women are strong and don't need counseling.   SA   A   U   D   SD
51. Counseling and consulting benefit everyone.   SA   A   U   D   SD
52. Same-race/gender/sexuality counselors and clients are ideal.   SA   A   U   D   SD
53. Culturally diverse clients need specialized counseling/consulting.   SA   A   U   D   SD
54. It is easy for People of Color to achieve the American dream.   SA   A   U   D   SD
55. People of Color are better off now than 15 years ago.   SA   A   U   D   SD
56. An empathic counselor/consultant will be successful.   SA   A   U   D   SD

FIGURE 1 (continued)

57. Lesbian, bisexual and gay, and transgendered clients can be counseled like heterosexuals and the traditionally gendered– the only difference is whom they fall in love with.	SA	A	U	D	SD
58. Clients are clients, people are people, everyone is the same.	SA	A	U	D	SD
59. Native Americans are simple-minded and live on reservations	SA	A	U	D	SD
60. All white people are racist.	SA	A	U	D	SD
61. Asians are gifted in math and the sciences.	SA	A	U	D	SD
62. Most immigrants want equal opportunity.	SA	A	U	D	SD
63. Being lesbian, bisexual, or gay is a choice.	SA	A	U	D	SD
64. Jews are money-grubbing and snobbish.	SA	A	U	D	SD
65. Arabs and Muslims are self-destructive, women-hating tyrants.	SA	A	U	D	SD
66. Persons with HIV/AIDS deserve the consequences.	SA	A	U	D	SD
67. Whites are one of the smaller racial groups in the world, yet they control the majority of the world's wealth and assets.	SA	A	U	D	SD
68. Women and girls are survivors of misogyny.	SA	A	U	D	SD
69. Multiculturalism is a way for radical activists to force their politically correct ideology on everyone else.	SA	A	U	D	SD
70. The United States is a melting pot and always will be.	SA	A	U	D	SD
71. Before I can effectively counsel or consult with culturally diverse persons, I must be an expert on my own cultural identities, beliefs, value systems, and biases.	SA	A	U	D	SD
72. Indigenous or traditional healers with no professional counseling training are as effective as professionals.	SA	A	U	D	SD
73. Gender, sex, and gender identity and expression are the same.	SA	A	U	D	SD

Part II: Social Justice Advocacy Knowledge

Directions: (Items #74-149): Identify the following persons' multiple cultural identities, dates, and events and their importance in social justice struggles.

74. Daniel Inouye
75. W. E. B. DuBois
76. Rigoberta Menchu
77. James Dale
78. Daniel Patrick Moynihan
79. Sojourner Truth
80. Kate Bornstein
81. Maxine Hong Kingston
82. Carlos Fuentes
83. Audre Lorde
84. Rudy Galindo
85. Urvashi Vaid
86. Paula Rust
87. Sharon Kowalski

88. Ralph Ellison
89. Essex Hemphill
90. Haunani-Kay Trask
91. Tracy Baim
92. Cesar Chavez
93. Rosa Parks
94. Gloria Anzaldua
95. Noam Chomsky
96. Tom Ammiano
97. Leonard Peltier
98. Pauline Park
99. Harvey Milk
100. bell hooks
101. Benazir Bhutto

102. Graciela Sanchez
103. Greg Lougainis
104. Lani Kaahumanu
105. Ang San Suu Kyi
106. Ron Fox
107. Jeannette Rankin
108. Ben Knighthorse Campbell
109. Loretta Sanchez
110. Casey Kasem
111. Starhawk
112. Achy Obejas
113. Leslie Feinberg
114. Tiger Woods
115. Lev Raphael
116. Harry Hay
117. Melanie Kay-Kantrowitz
118. Riki Anne Wilchins
119. Mumia Abu-Jamal
120. Feb. 19, 1942
121. March 8
122. March 21, 1995
123. April 4, 1968
124. April 24
125. May 1

126. June 26, 1969
127. July 1, 1997
128. Aug. 6, 1945
129. September 20
130. Trail of tears
131. Seder
132. 1954 Supreme Court decision
133. Suffragette movement
134. Torah
135. Yellow Menace
136. Jim Crow laws
137. School of the Americas
138. Kwanzaa
139. Vedas
140. Shinto
141. African National Congress
142. Ramadan
143. Chiapas & the Zapatistas
144. Freedom Summer
145. SNCC
146. Infitada
147. Manifest Destiny
148. Sinn Fein
149. East Timor

Directions: (Items #150-180) Answer the following questions:

150. What is culture? What are your multiple cultural identities?

151. How do you define the terms multiculturalism and social justice? How do you implement them in your organization/communities?

152. What are benefits/problems with the phrase "culturally different"?

153. What is the definition of oppression and/or the "ISMS," i.e., racism, sexism, ageism, classism, beautyism/looksism, ableism, heterosexism, linguicism, transgenderism, anti-Semitism and other forms of nondominant religious bias?

154. What do the terms inner city, urban, ghetto, welfare mothers, disadvantaged, gangs, minority, bad family values, criminals/prisoners, illegal alien, undocumented immigrant, underclass, and naturalization have in common? What are they code words for, who uses them, and how?

155. What are "the dozens" (a.k.a., the "snaps" or "snapping")?

156. What does hegemony mean, and what dominant cultural groups have the power and control for cultural hegemony in the United States?

157. What makes the terms foreign, Eskimo, Oriental, Hispanic, homosexual, less fortunate, gypped, chink, handicapped, Indian-giver, Indian summer, AIDS victim, minority, disadvantaged, overly emotional, and hysterical, imprecise and/or offensive?

158. What happens to oppressed persons seen through a negative or romantic filter?

FIGURE 1 (continued)

159. What makes "reverse racism" a myth? What cultural group has had the greatest financial benefit from affirmative action policies in the U.S.?

160. What nation was provoked into war and eventually had large amounts of land forcibly annexed by the U.S. in the early 1800s?

161. What three sovereign nations were invaded and/or forcibly annexed by the United States in the late 1890s?

162. In what one state (USA) are the following communities: Akron, Alabama, Athens, Atlanta, Babylon, Belgium, Bombay, Cairo, Damascus, Cuba, Delhi, Dublin, Florida, German, Holland, Indian Village, Italy, Jordan, Little France, Madrid, Mexico, Monterey, North Boston, North Stockholm, Oakland, Phoenix, Portland, Russia, Salem, Savannah, Texas Valley, Urbana, & Wyoming?

163. What recent ballot initiatives have caused civil rights and human rights advocates to worry about the erasure of democratic freedoms in the U.S.?

164. What is the largest ethnic and or racial identity group of new immigrants in the U.S.? What racial media images are most often associated with current immigrant groups in the U.S.? Why are the answers to these two questions similar or different?

165. What are the names of mental health/counselors/traditional healers/social service persons in indigenous and traditional ethnic/racial cultures?

166. What country protects lesbian, bisexual, and gay citizens by name in its constitution?

167. What country receives the most financial aid, primarily military, from the U.S.?

168. What group of dispossessed persons lost their homeland and are still fighting for their land when the country of #166 was forcibly created by the U.S. and its allies?

169. Where is Aeotearoa and what is it known as in the colonizer's language?

170. What cultural groups are referred to in the term 500 Nations?

171. What cultural group did the city of Evanston, IL add to their human rights ordinance ensuring protection in housing, credit, public accommodations and employment, joining a few other cities and one state (Minnesota)?

172. What are nondominant culture publications? Name at least 5 in varying nondominant groups across ethnicity/race/gender/gender identity/religion/sexual orientation:

173. What cultural group did the United Nations declare 1993 as dedicated to? The Year of "_____ _____." Why was it delayed a year? Are members of this group members of the United Nations? Why/not?

174. What countries have suffered from and/or perpetrated genocide in the 1900s?

175. What are the strengths of multilingualism and bilingual education? What are the fears in the U.S. about bilingualism?

176. To what indigenous group did the early USA feminists and women's rights advocates owe much of their ideas about equality amongst the genders and women in positions of leadership and power and what state do their descendants continue to live in? Hint: the indigenous name is Haudenosaunee.

177. What do the names Matthew Shephard, Billy Jack Gaither, Brandon Teena, Abner Louima, Yusef Hawkins, and Amadou Diallo have in common? Why? What are their multiple cultural identities?

178. In 1998-99, what country was the largest arms purchaser from the United States (over $4 billion worth)?

179. In what country have an estimated over 500,000 children died directly due to lack of food and medical aid cut off by continuing U.S. sanctions?

180. Name the countries that the United States has bombed in the 20th century. Of those countries, how many that were previously nondemocratic have set up democracies?

Part III: Cultural/Institutional Social Justice Advocacy Skills

Directions: (Items #181-188) Answer the following questions to develop an action plan for change to promote greater social justice awareness, knowledge, and skills in your organization.

181. Who's excluded in your organization, including policies and procedures (clients, staff, administration) and who's not? How will this change in the future?

182. Who funds the organization? How much do funders influence the decision-making culture (i.e., the Board of Education, United Way, grantmakers, etc.)?

183. Whose ethnic/racial identities/world view/gender roles/sexual orientations/gender identities dominate your organization? How might this change in the future?

184. Who are your traditional healers/cultural consultants with clients/consultees whose cultural and language identities you don't have experience with? How do you find and collaborate with cultural consultants on their terms?

185. What issues of oppression are regularly addressed by those with power in your organization? Which ones are not? How could this change in the future?

186. How is good leadership defined/implemented in your organization? Are leadership and social justice/advocacy skills development offered? How are decisions made (collectively or hierarchically) in your organization?

187. Whom do you want as allies inside and outside the organization? What groups do you advocate for best in your family, community, or organization and what groups do you need to advocate for more openly?

188. What are the barriers and fears to cultural and systemic change in your organization? Who are the blockers? How can the blockers be neutralized or developed as allies?

CONCLUSION

LBGT2QQ social service providers, administrators, clients, and allies can benefit from reflecting on their social justice advocacy awareness, knowledge, and skills. The SJARQ provides a unique questionnaire to assist providers and recipients of services in developing their own critical thinking skills. It expands the definition of social justice beyond one cultural variable so that persons of all sexual orientations and gender identities can be affirmed and provided appropriate services in multiple identities and contexts.

Note: answers to Part II of the SJARQ instrument, social justice advocacy knowledge, are available on-line at: *www.lehman.cuny.edu/education/facpages/sch.htm*–the author's website.

REFERENCES

Andrzejewski, J. (Ed.). (1996). *Oppression and social justice: Critical frameworks* (5th ed.). Needham Heights, MA: Simon & Schuster.

Arredondo, P. (1999). Multicultural counseling competencies as tools to address oppression and racism. *Journal of Counseling & Development, 77*(1), 102-108.

Chen-Hayes, S. F. (2000). Advocacy with lesbian, bisexual, gay, and transgendered persons. In J. Lewis, & L. Bradley (Eds.), *Advocacy in counseling.* Greensboro, NC: ERIC/CASS.

Chen-Hayes, S. F. (2001). Counseling and advocacy with transgendered and gender-variant persons in counseling and advocacy. *Journal of Humanistic Counseling, Education, and Development, 40*(1), 34-48.

Chen-Hayes, S. F., & Haley-Banez, L. (In press). The case of Janine. In J. Goodman, S. Niles, & M. Pope (Eds.), *Career counseling casebook.* Alexandria, VA: National Career Development Association.

Comas-Diaz, L., & Greene, B. (Eds.). (1994). *Women of color: Integrating ethnic and gender identities in psychotherapy.* New York: Guilford.

Cross, W. E. (1996). The psychology of nigrescence: Revising the Cross model. In J. G. Ponterotto, J. M. Casas, L. A. Suzuki, & C. M. Alexander (Eds.), *Handbook of multicultural counseling.* Thousand Oaks, CA: Sage.

D'Andrea, M., & Daniels, J. (1996). Promoting multiculturalism and organizational change in the counseling profession: A case study. In J. G. Ponterotto, J. M. Casas, L. A. Suzuki, & C. M. Alexander (Eds.), *Handbook of multicultural counseling.* Thousand Oaks, CA: Sage.

Dworkin, S. H., & Gutierrez, F. J. (1992). *Counseling gay men & lesbians: Journey to the end of the rainbow.* Alexandria, VA: American Counseling Association.

Firestein, B. A. (Ed.). (1996). *Bisexuality: The psychology and politics of an invisible minority.* Thousand Oaks, CA: Sage.

Gelberg, S., & Chojnacki, J. T. (1996). *Career and life planning with gay, lesbian, and bisexual persons.* Alexandria, VA: American Counseling Association.

hooks, b. (1994). *Teaching to transgress: Education as the practice of freedom.* New York: Routledge.

Israel, G. E., & Tarver, D. E. (1997). *Transgender care: Recommended guidelines, practical information, & personal accounts.* Philadelphia, PA: Temple University Press.

Ivey, A. E. (1996). Psychotherapy as liberation: Toward specific skills and strategies in multicultural counseling and therapy. In J. G. Ponterotto, J. M. Casas, L. A. Suzuki, & C. M. Alexander (Eds.), *Handbook of multicultural counseling.* Thousand Oaks, CA: Sage.

Lee, C. C., & Walz, G. R. (Eds.). (1998). *Social action: A mandate for counselors.* Alexandria, VA: American Counseling Association and ERIC/CASS.

Lewis, J., & Arnold, M. S. (1998). From multiculturalism to social action. In C. C. Lee & G. R. Walz (Eds.), *Social action: A mandate for counselors.* Alexandria, VA: American Counseling Association and ERIC/CASS.

Lewis, J., & Bradley, L. (Eds.). (2000). *Advocacy in counseling.* Greensboro, NC: ERIC/CASS.

Lorde, A. (1984). *Sister outsider.* Freedom, CA: The Crossing Press.

Pedersen, P. (2000). *A handbook for developing multicultural awareness* (3rd ed.). Alexandria, VA: American Counseling Association.

Reynolds, A. L., & Pope, R. L. (1991). The complexities of diversity: Exploring multiple oppressions. *Journal of Counseling & Development, 70*(1), 174-180.

Rothenberg, P. (Ed.). (2000). *Race, class, and gender in the United States: An integrated study* (5th ed.). New York: St. Martin's.

Sleeter, C. E., & Grant, C. A. (1994). *Making choices for multicultural education: Five approaches to race, class, and gender* (2nd ed). New York: Merrill.

Syracuse Cultural Workers. (1999). *1999 peace calendar.* Syracuse, NY: Syracuse Cultural Workers.

Trickett, E. J., Watts. R. J., & Birman, D. (Eds.). (1994). *Human diversity: Perspectives on people in context.* San Francisco: Jossey-Bass.

Washington, J., & Evans, N. J. (1991). Becoming an ally. In N. J. Evans & V. A. Wall (Eds.), *Beyond tolerance: Gays, lesbians, and bisexuals on campus.* Alexandria, VA: American College Personnel Association.

Zinn, H. (1999). *A people's history of the United States 1492-present* (rev. ed.). New York: Harper Collins.

Competencies at the Intersection of Difference, Tolerance, and Prevention of Hate Crimes

Irene R. Bush
Anthony Sainz

SUMMARY. This article develops competencies for social workers to enable them to counter harassment and hate crimes by examining the intersection of "self" and "other" when the "other" is either a gay man or a lesbian or when the "other" is the perpetrator of hate crimes. The authors contend that there is a cultural foundation to hate crimes and that it involves oppression like that experienced by other minority groups, that this oppression is supported by the dominant culture, and that oppressive behaviors can be changed. A typology of five competency areas is presented to develop culturally relevant knowledge, attitudes, and skills that strengthen understanding and tolerance for gay men and lesbians and to work with those who oppress them. *[Article copies available for a fee from The Haworth Document Delivery Service: 1-800-342-9678. E-mail address: <getinfo@haworthpressinc.com> Website: <http://www.HaworthPress.com> © 2001 by The Haworth Press, Inc. All rights reserved.]*

KEYWORDS. Hate crimes, sexual harassment, oppression, marginalization, homophobia, heterosexism, cultural competency, human rights

Irene R. Bush, DSW, is Associate Professor, Monmouth University Department of Social Work. Anthony Sainz, DSW, is Associate Professor, Hunter College School of Social Work.

Address correspondence to: Irene R. Bush, DSW, Social Work Dept., Monmouth University, West Long Branch, NV 07764 (E-mail: ibush@monmouth.edu).

[Haworth co-indexing entry note]: "Competencies at the Intersection of Difference, Tolerance, and Prevention of Hate Crimes." Bush, Irene R., and Anthony Sainz. Co-published simultaneously in *Journal of Gay & Lesbian Social Services* (Harrington Park Press, an imprint of The Haworth Press, Inc.) Vol. 13, No. 1/2, 2001, pp. 205-224; and: *From Hate Crimes to Human Rights: A Tribute to Matthew Shepard* (ed: Mary E. Swigonski, Robin S. Mama, and Kelly Ward) Harrington Park Press, an imprint of The Haworth Press, Inc., 2001, pp. 205-224. Single or multiple copies of this article are available for a fee from The Haworth Document Delivery Service [1-800-342-9678, 9:00 a.m. - 5:00 p.m. (EST). E-mail address: getinfo@haworthpressinc.com].

A supervisor of young adult workers announced that a series of three mandatory sexual harassment workshops would be held for staff at three different times. She stated that all employees were expected to attend. One young man called out, "What if we already know how to do it?" Without missing a beat, the supervisor said, "That is not funny." Quiet ensued, broken by an apology from the would-be joker.

Social work practitioners are confronted by clients' and colleagues' bigoted remarks, jokes, comments, and behaviors that smack of intolerance and prejudice. They are also confronted with clients capable of committing hate crimes against lesbian, gay, bisexual, transgendered, or two-spirited persons (LGBT^2). How can social workers attain the knowledge, attitudes, and skills necessary to deal with verbal insensitivity of others and, more critically, to prevent hate crimes? What are the competencies social workers need so that they can contribute services that will move society to embrace human rights and social justice?

We need to ask how educators and trainers conceptualize and develop the knowledge, skills, and attitudes needed to counter harassment and hate crimes. The authors of this article contend that cultural competence and work with difference provide the conceptual framework for developing competencies vital to countering hate crimes. The supervisor in the vignette responded instantaneously and accurately while respecting self-determination, intrinsic worth, and esteem: Her response demonstrated her understanding of oppression and marginalization, and her ability to hold the oppressor and the oppressed in empathic regard. We suggest that the basis for this ability is cultural sensitivity, which involves a personal commitment by social workers to identify their own attitudes that marginalize others by undertaking a personal "coming out process" with respect to their own homophobic feelings.

The authors examine the intersection of "self" and "other" when the "other" is either a LGBT^2 person or when "other" is the perpetrator of hate crimes against LGBT^2 persons. We propose that there is a cultural foundation to hate crimes, that it involves oppression, that oppression is supported by the dominant culture, and that oppressive behaviors can be changed. We present arguments to these points and a typology of five competency areas for culturally relevant knowledge, attitudes, and skills to strengthen understanding and tolerance for

LGBT[2] persons and to prepare for work with their oppressors as required by social work codes of ethics.

A CULTURE THAT COUNTENANCES HATE CRIMES

That anti-gay violence pervasive in American society today is an outgrowth of cultural oppression and is evident in the definition of heterosexism–"an ideological system that denies, denigrates, and stigmatizes any non-heterosexual form of behavior, identity, relationship, or community" (Herek, 1992b, p. 89). Herek (p. 89) states that, "Like racism, sexism, and other ideologies of oppression, heterosexism is manifested both in societal customs and institutions, such as religion and the legal system (referred to as *cultural heterosexism*), and in individual attitudes and behaviors (referred to here as *psychological heterosexism*)." He adds (p. 98) that there is an emerging paradigm defining LGBT[2] persons as members of a minority community similar to those of ethnic groups and similarly struggling for civil rights.

Discrimination and hate crimes arise, in part, from unquestioning acceptance of pejorative definitions of the other. In effect, permission is given to discount the humanity of another by defining that "other" as beyond the pale of one's own humanity, community, its values and beliefs. Socially sanctioned notions of sexuality and gender and their transmission through cultural institutions underpin heterosexism, which defines gay men and lesbians as deviant, sick, or evil, and, thus, lead to anti-gay violence. At some level, society sanctions the belief that discrimination or crimes are justified and, therefore, permissible.

The Cultural Meaning of Hate Crimes

Hate crimes can be understood as similar to the terrorism that the Ku Klux Klan perpetrated against African Americans (Herek & Berrill, 1992). Hate crimes against LGBT[2] persons often involve interplay with racial, gender, and ethnic violence (Hunter, 1992). Anti-LGBT[2] murders are often marked by extreme brutality (Berrill, 1992). Anti-lesbian violence is closely connected to violence against women and intensifies the sense of intimidation already experienced daily by women (Von Shulthess, 1992). LGBT[2] youths may experience violence from their parents, their peers, and their schools.

As more LGBT[2] persons refuse to remain hidden, violence against them increases. As a result, in an increasingly vicious cycle, LGBT[2] persons fear for their safety, modify behavior to reduce risk of attack, take self-defense classes, avoid certain locations, and avoid contact with lovers in public places to name only a few general ways their lives are unfairly constricted (Berrill, 1992). Despite caution taken, hate crimes continue to make headlines and will continue as long as LGBT[2] persons are seen as a devalued and dangerous group.

Goals of Cultural Competence

It is difficult to define the antithesis of racial, gender, and ethnic violence. Is it *acceptance* (the absence of bias and reactivity)? Or is it *tolerance* (bias without reactivity)? Or might it be *indifference* (suspension of judgement, action/reactivity)? How might this be achieved in those whose prejudices lead to hate crimes?

A growing number of organizations provide counseling and advocacy for victims, work with police and prosecutors to sensitize them, and educate the public about the causes and consequences of anti-gay violence. Increased community intolerance for hate crimes works against "cultural codes of silence and invisibility" (Herek & Berrill, 1992, p. 3). Yet to truly change oppression, it is necessary to change norms–about institutional and individual power and control, economic power and dependence, and violence (Pharr, 1997). To do this, Pharr (1997) states that we must bring the "other" into the norm rather than continuing to permit LGBT[2] persons to be seen as deviant or marginal. We need to decrease invisibility, false information, distortion of events by selective presentation or re-writing of history, stereotyping, blaming the victim, isolation of individuals or marginalized groups, tokenism, and assimilation.

EDUCATION AND TRAINING OF SOCIAL WORKERS

Research on homophobia, that is, fear, disgust, hatred, anger, and/or aversion toward LGBT[2] persons, in social work students and professionals reveals that a range of 30% to 90% are homophobic (Cramer, 1998). Reasons proposed for this (and that underscore the need for the model described in this article) are lack of awareness or concern about the LGBT[2] population; paucity of literature concerning social work practice with LGBT[2] persons; anxieties about personal sexual identity; societal, cultural, and religious values and beliefs; and a dearth of openly LGBT[2] social workers. She concludes that, "Attitude change toward oppressed groups is most likely to be achieved when information about the subject is broad (dispelling myths) and when there is a positive exposure to members of the population" (Cramer, 1998, p. 463).

We do know that social work education can influence behavior. A study by Van Soest (1996) of the impact of coursework on societal oppression on MSW students indicated that acceptance of the "just world ideology" and "self-reported advocacy behaviors increased somewhat, particularly in first year students immediately after completing the oppression course, particularly on behalf of African Americans and gay men and lesbians" (p. 198). Although results were uneven and inconsistent across the populations studied, Van Soest (1996) affirms that social work students can be socialized to be advocates for social justice and that education is an ideal vehicle for addressing attitudes and beliefs that impede effective social change.

The impact of oppression and the infusion of material on vulnerable groups is increasingly woven through social work education. However, the knowledge, attitudes, and skills to be imparted are not well-defined, particularly for performing competently in work with LGBT[2] clients or with those who victimize them. The authors believe that the following diagram captures a structure of cultural competency to begin to define this content. Figure 1 presents visually the type of educational process Van Soest recommends, depicting how an individual appreciates uniqueness, compatibility with those who are most similar, and shared humanity.

As can be seen in Figure 1, there is a central shared area where the three spheres, and, the three concerns of "self," the "culture of" group (whether LGBT[2] or hate mongers) and "all" others intersect. A competent worker must be knowledgeable not only about each of the three areas of concern but also about their tripartite interface (Bush & Sainz, 1997). Norman and Wheeler (1996) recommend a similar model as a way to integrate new information into existing models. They further state, "Practitioners must keep in mind that each individual is unique, with unique experiences, perceptions, feelings, and behaviors,

FIGURE 1. World View Framework

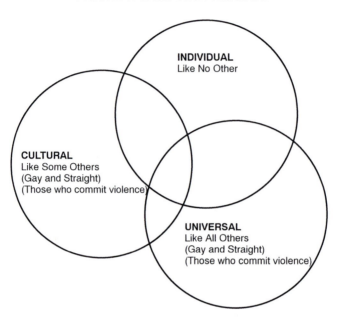

INDIVIDUAL
Like No Other

CULTURAL
Like Some Others
(Gay and Straight)
(Those who commit violence)

UNIVERSAL
Like All Others
(Gay and Straight)
(Those who commit violence)

**EVERY PERSON IS LIKE ALL PERSONS,
LIKE SOME PERSONS, AND
LIKE NO OTHER PERSON**

and yet has much in common with other human beings. It is that shared humanity that must be accessed" (p. 209).

Thus, an effective schema for teaching and practicing psychosocial assessment and intervention must incorporate the concept that a given individual is: (a) *like no other human being*; (b) *like some others*–females or males, gay or straight, that is, belonging to subgroups or categories); and (c) *like all others* in the human community–females and males, gays and straight, all with common human rights and needs (Norman & Wheeler, 1996).

In teaching about oppression of LGBT[2] persons, it is necessary to help students examine their knowledge and notions (attitudes) to either reinforce empathy or to create cognitive dissonance to motivate development of appropriate skills. The remainder of this article develops specific competencies through which this can be accomplished in social work education, specifically for the prevention of hate crimes and advancement of human rights.

THE COMPETENCIES

Awareness and acceptance of differences in communication, lifestyle, patterns of behavior, worldview, definitions of family, and health and illness are critical to protecting human rights and to reducing the discrimination experienced by LGBT[2] persons.

Several models of cultural competence have been developed in mental health and human services to improve access and services to members of minority groups. These models have been variously labeled as "ethnic sensitive practice," "cross cultural awareness practice," and "cultural competence." The goal of these models is for agencies and professionals to provide individualized, culturally appropriate services to persons who are different. Competencies for work with LGBT[2] persons have received less attention in social work literature; competencies for working with those who commit hate crimes have received even less attention.

Dimensions of Cultural Competence

Five dimensions of cultural competence adapted from Woody (1991) locate information, knowledge, attitudes, and behaviors on LGBT[2] culture and reactions to it, so that avenues are opened for understanding and work both with LGBT[2] persons and those who threaten them because of their membership in this group. The dimensions are described in Table 1.

Table 1 provides descriptions for each of the five competency areas. As can be seen in the table, when a worker achieves this "Competency" because she or he holds and understands the "Value" that underlies it, the "Result" will be culturally competent work. To master these competencies, workers need to enlarge their perspective through a systematic process of self-questioning and learning about others through information gathering.

Table 2 presents specific areas within each dimension around which this process can occur. Table 2 also provides sample descriptions for each of the five competency areas. Social workers need to examine each competency area shown in Table 2 in relation to their practice with LGBT[2] persons and those who threaten them just as they would with other client groups with whom they work. Discussion and examples that follow will describe the competencies further.

TABLE 1. Providing Services in the Appropriate Context for Gay and Lesbian Clients or Those That Victimize Them*

COMPETENCY	+	VALUE	=	RESULT
Informational competency which illustrates the worker's competency with community functions of the particular cultures of gay men and lesbians and of those who victimize them		the cultural value which demonstrates that the provider knows the dignity of the individual is not guaranteed unless the dignity of his/her specific group is preserved		the worker is familiar with the history and worldview which is portrayed in community values and behavior of the particular group being served
Intellectual competency which demonstrates the worker's ability to do problem identification within the context of the specific gay culture or the victimizer		the cultural value which recognizes that minority people must be at least bicultural, which presents its own set of mental health issues such as identity conflicts resulting from accommodation or assimilation		the worker has the ability to anticipate role conflict resulting from attempting to balance two cultures and can plan with the client the best method for approaching such situations
Interpersonal competency which allows the worker to communicate with genuineness and warmth		the cultural value which acknowledges that behaviors exist that are adjustments to being different from the majority culture		the worker is familiar with and capable of responding to a set of communication patterns that include slang, gestures, and processes that are unique to the particular community being served
Intrapersonal competency in which the worker holds a genuine affinity for the community in which he/she is working		the cultural value which evidences the awareness on the part of the worker that the dignity of the person is not guaranteed unless the dignity of his/her group is preserved		internal value sets which reflect stereotypes, prejudices, and preferences which are not in conflict with the community being served
Interventional competency which evidences the worker's capacity to bring a number of different skills to bear in a needed situation		the cultural value which views natural systems (family, community, church, healers, etc.) as a primary mechanism of support for minority populations		the worker can assist the client in balancing the role of each of the helping systems

* Adapted from Woody (1991).

TABLE 2. Competencies for Gay and Lesbian Human Rights*

INFORMATIONAL	INTELLECTUAL	INTRAPERSONAL	INTERPERSONAL	INTERVENTION
Familiarity with history and worldview portrayed in community values and behaviors toward Gays and Lesbians	Understanding and empathy that enhances problem identification in the context of Gay and Lesbian identity, and non-traditional family forms and life style choices, with their ethnic, cultural and other variations	Awareness of own worldview and internal value sets which reflect stereotypes, prejudices, and orientations that may be in conflict with those of the group being served	Ability to communicate, with genuineness and warmth, with awareness of different patterns of interaction congruent with the individuals and groups being served	Ability to bring knowledge, appropriate attitudes and skills to assist individuals, couples, and families to balance the role of each of the helping systems in the formal and informal support networks in the group ecology
Informed about cultural beliefs and values toward Gays and Lesbians as they are embodied in language, religions, cultural views toward family, traditional family roles, and the preservation of family traditions and about cultural patterns of response to a Gay or Lesbian child	Able to assimilate cultural facts, myths, and attitudes to reframe Gay and Lesbian orientation to help others understand issues and problems in terms of their own values and cultural frameworks	Able to identify differences and similarities of own worldview, including beliefs and values toward Gays and Lesbians who may have a different or similar worldview	Able to engage clients without violation of norms with reference to family roles and respect for customary salutation, manner, and deference to issues such as sexual orientation and partner choice while confronting inappropriate talk or action	Able to organize an intervention plan which acknowledges and respects the client's culture and values by incorporating these into the intervention
Informed of sources of emotional support, child rearing arrangements, gender roles, and families response to Gay or Lesbian family units	Able to identify the cultural premise embedded in practice approaches traditionally followed in work with Gays and Lesbians	Able to distinguish the role of own cultural values, biases, and preferences in the perception, diagnosis, and assessment of problems that occur for Gays and Lesbians, particularly in relation to prejudice and hate crimes	Able to understand the concerns and use appropriate language for the group being served	Able to engage appropriate networks and helping systems, such as community, welcoming churches, associations, and so forth, as mechanisms of support for problems, including discrimination, hate crimes, AIDS, and other social problems that disproportionately affect Gays and Lesbians
Informed of reliable Gay and Lesbian literature, research and practice wisdom and implications of this in relation to those who victimize	Able to identify conflict or clashes between social work approaches and interventions and client beliefs and values	Able to distinguish personal judgements about Gays and Lesbians from the perspective of the client's worldview	Able to understand and respond to communication patterns that include slang and other verbal and nonverbal behaviors	Able to engage appropriate networks and helping systems as mechanisms to reinforce appropriate values in relation to differences in those who would victimize Gays and Lesbians
Informed of groups, affiliations, and points of view that promote victimization of Gays and Lesbians	Able to identify and sort out diversity within the Gay and Lesbian cultures and its impact vulnerabilities to hate crimes			Devise and implement a monitoring, feedback, and evaluation plan that is congruent with goals and expectations of the group being served
	Able to understand the role of oppression and disempowerment and their relationship to Gay and Lesbian orientation issues for both victims and victimizers			

* Adapted from Woody (1991).

213

Informational competence (Table 2, column 1). Informational competence requires that workers become aware of traditional and nontraditional areas of knowledge that include information about theory, treatment, rehabilitation, empowerment, and community helping resources as related to those who are victimized and those who commit hate crimes.

To gain competence as it is described in column 1 of the table, it is necessary to gather information not only from clients, but from related literature. Berk, Boyd, and Hamner (1992) review the literature and state that "criminology literature is almost silent on the topic of hate-motivated crimes" (p. 127). Knowledge of perpetrators of anti-gay violence–"gay bashers"–is limited; anecdotal information, surveys of victims, and reports by victims to community-based assistance organizations supply the only profile. This profile depicts a "young male, often acting together with other young males, all of whom are strangers to the victim(s)" (Berrill, 1992, p. 29).

Harry (1992) outlines three subtypes of gay bashers: those who commit serious physical assaults and homicides against adult lesbians and gay males and the more common, random beatings; those who commit assaults and related harassment of lesbian and gay adolescents by their peers; and, what he believes are the most common, those who commit "sissy bashing" (p. 117), beatings of effeminate boys who do not conform to rigid rules of male gender roles, both future homosexuals and heterosexuals.

The majority of hate crimes do not appear to be committed by individuals affiliated with organized hate groups that exist to promote hostility and violence toward others because of racial, religious, sexual identity, or political ideology. Rather, such groups fan and support abuse. In the absence of a body of literature on hate crimes, knowledge about what fuels them may come from a variety of sources: work with batterers, those who are incarcerated for violent crimes, advances in anger management, and so on.

It is essential that workers become informed about the history of oppression, victimization, and violence against LGBT[2] persons, including facts about stereotypes, myths, and misinformation. Class, ethnicity, race, culture, and intracultural diversity within the larger category of LGBT[2] culture will need to emerge as significant considerations for understanding and intervention since hate crimes against lesbians and gay men of color, for example, may require additional refinement. As previously stated, attitudes toward oppressed groups will be changed when information about the subject is broad, when myths are dispelled, and when there is a positive exposure to members of the oppressed population (Cramer, 1998).

A basic knowledge of oppression and the challenges of the coming out process are necessary, but not sufficient for problem recognition. Workers also need to understand the history and contributions, spiritual traditions, symbols, customs, social roles, social statuses, and the economic, social, and political organizations of the LGBT[2] communities. Information is also needed about community resources and the characteristics of agencies in relation to the values and characteristics of clients. The understanding of family functioning and behavior in relation to the availability of resources (treatment adequacy, helping networks, in-home services, etc.) is essential, as is understanding of isolation, invisibility, lack of safety for the victim of a hate crime. That HIV/AIDS is used to rationalize prejudice, discrimination, and violence against LGBT[2] persons means that educating oneself and others about transmission may be an essential element in this work. Similarly, information is needed about ways to maximize impact by using multiple systems such as the court, child welfare, and substance abuse treatment services.

Homophobia is a human rights issue. It is essential to reject information based on "sick" and "sinful" theories (Pharr, 1997). It is also a civil rights issue, and it is extremely important to know the law (Herek & Berrill, 1992). Appropriate information is critical to understanding both human and civil rights issues.

Intellectual Competence (Table 2, Column 2). Intellectual competency requires that workers adopt novel patterns of thinking and synthesizing information. Effective workers must develop appropriate cognitive and behavioral responses–the skills of assessment, intervention, and evaluation–distinctively adapted to those situations where characteristics of LGBT[2] culture become motivators for hate crimes. Workers develop competence in handling new concepts and applying new rules for problem-solving as they apply new knowledge (and their reactions to it) to enhance the specialization and appropriateness of treatment. Intellectual competence transforms informational competence to judgments in specific situations presented by clients.

The dimensions in column 2 require workers to use multilayered knowledge about cultural worldview, strengths and deficits, treatment models, and resources as applied to particular clients. If "Information-al Competency" provides a picture of the gay basher as a young man with an external locus of control, "Intellectual Competency" trans-lates this knowledge into hypotheses about leverage for change: the implications drawn from this piece of information that can be used therapeutically. In effect, the worker asks questions such as: "How do I confront the patterns of behavior described to me? Do I provide services that provide an alternate reference group for this young man? How do I adapt services to promote compliance with more positive values?" Pharr (1997) presents an analysis that puts economics as the root cause of sexism that, with racism, keeps oppressive systems in place. LGBT[2] people become targets because they have "stepped out of line from sexual/economic dependence" and are threats to male dominance and control (p. 18). If she is correct, how is this informa-tion to be used to intervene?

"Intellectual Competence" must also include understanding and attention to policies and laws under which operations take place that continue to reflect cultural biases and stereotypes. Complex under-standings about the role of oppression in relation to gay men and lesbians and those who harm them will lead a knowledgeable worker also to question the appropriateness of a disempowering treatment model that stresses safety over visibility and freedoms.

Intrapersonal Competence (Table 2, Column 3). Intrapersonal com-petence suggests development of empathy through in-depth knowl-edge of one's own standpoint and the ability to take the other person's standpoint (Swigonski, 1993). It includes self-assessment skills that promote awareness about personal attitudes and practices in relation to LGBT[2] cultures and to work to mitigate violence against LGBT[2] people. Workers, themselves cultural vessels, need to understand the schema they carry with them that are derived from their own cultural experience. They need to understand, anticipate, and cope effectively with their own emotional and behavioral reactions to other lifestyles or cultures and to modify their own culturally determined behavior in order to practice effectively with marginalized clients or those who intimidate them. Social workers must become more aware of, and engaged with, their attitudes toward clients, as well as their beliefs about clients, and must learn to identify and work with affective, cognitive, and behavioral consequences of such attitudes.

Three essential areas of self-assessment are worker beliefs, attitudes, and practices about homosexuality; their understanding of the impact of violence on gay men and lesbians; and their beliefs about working with clients who are gay and lesbian or those who abuse them. If social workers are limited in experience, they must commit to broadening their knowledge.

Most heterosexual adults think of themselves as husbands or wives, fathers or mothers, parents and members of a family rather than as heterosexuals. The institution of marriage publicly legitimizes heterosexual partnerships (through weddings, rituals, tax and inheritance laws, employee benefit programs, and immigration and naturalization policies). LGBT[2] people, like other minorities, are defined in terms of the characteristic that sets them apart (sexual orientation). This relegates them to unequal status with respect to the dominant group (Herek, 1992). If social workers believe that heterosexual roles are the only acceptable identities or that they are preferable identities, the experiences of LGBT[2] people are largely negated. Moreover, workers must realize that LGBT[2] people do not have corresponding public sanctioning of their relationships. Many LGBT[2] relationships remain invisible, because, for example, those who are parents are in danger of being judged unfit and, therefore, they keep their sexual orientation hidden. Moreover, explicit expression of any non-heterosexual sexuality receives accusations of inappropriate flaunting and becomes a rationale for retribution through verbal or physical assault.

There are many ways for workers to conscientiously get in touch with their beliefs and reactions. One way to broaden understanding is to read biographies or fiction by those who describe experiences related to sexual orientation (Brenner, 1992; Feinberg, 1993; Gravel, 1992; Hassel, 1992; Sarris, 1992). Another way is to engage in a mental exercise, for example, an exercise in which social workers imagine their reactions to a photograph on a colleague's desk of the colleague and his or her opposite sex spouse in an embrace, smiling for the camera; then, they are asked to imagine the person with a same-sex partner and to analyze their reaction. Both photos convey persons in a relationship. Yet, the intimacy of the relationship of the LGBT[2] couple may be more problematic to the social workers who are subjects of this "thought experiment," because LGBT[2] intimacy is not as mundane and implicit as heterosexual intimacy, and it can be experienced as a violation of the private-public barrier in ways that expressions of heterosexual sexuality are not. Whatever reactions occur are important to explore.

Workers also must be aware of and careful to avoid notions about "good" LGBT[2] persons (who may be most like "straights") and "bad" LGBT[2] persons (who may conform more closely to stereotypical views that are less comfortable) and thus, continue the mythology about what is acceptable and what is not. The question that Pharr (1997, p. 49) raises, "What is it we put forward about ourselves in order to prove we are acceptable, that is the ways we assert that we are heterosexual?" is relevant to intrapersonal competency. Perhaps ultimately, the goal of intrapersonal examination is as Pharr (1997) advocates in relation to lesbian women:

- becoming openly supportive of lesbian identity, both in personal and public life;
- learning to honor and affirm choices, celebrations, sorrows;
- appreciating lesbian culture and making it visible in our organizations, and making a public commitment to work for a world where sexual identity and sexual roles are not coerced and restricted, where there isn't socially condoned power to dominate and control because of gender and identity.

This commitment is an affirmation of the most fundamental human rights that are all too often denied lesbians, gay men, bisexual, transgendered and two-spirited people.

Interpersonal Competence (Table 2, Column 4). Interpersonal competence suggests the ability to take the other person's standpoint despite our own strongly held values and beliefs. It also requires that workers identify and learn appropriate ways for communicating with and engaging clients in their efforts to combat violence without tolerating it. They must be prepared to understand, anticipate, and cope effectively with reactions of gay bashers to a different value system and to consequences that a worker can bring to bear. By using knowledge and the perspective of cultural conflict, workers must learn to effectively exercise qualities of sincerity, empathy, warmth, respect, and ability to deal with clients who may, because of their violence and stereotypical attitudes, be unappealing and even frightening.

While Ehrlich (1992) states that more research is needed, he identifies a number of factors he believes are the basis of anti-gay prejudice and violence. He notes that violence and prejudice are woven into the fabric of society. Among these, traditional sex role attitudes (of male superiority) and other less explicit teachings transmitted by parents that make LGBT[2] persons "ideological renegades" who have "rejected the appropriate hierarchy of beliefs, attitudes and behavior" (p. 106). The resulting prejudices are then legitimated by larger social forces that pinpoint certain groups as appropriate targets for the expression of prejudice. In essence, it is individual psychology met by the structure of society that makes patterns of prejudice normative, maintained by major social institutions: school, church, mass media, and family.

The resulting closed belief systems and self image deficits may combine as prejudice–generalized to religious, ethnic, racial groups– and in homophobic violence. The group's visibility, distinctiveness, and salience of stereotypes contribute to making it a target of hate. Ehrlich (1992) explains that "the more negative one's self-attitudes, the greater the number of unacceptable others one will find and the more negative one's attitudes toward them will be" (p. 106). He posits that, if one is unable to meet his or her own idealized sex role expectations, homosexuality may provoke anxiety and the response to anxiety is increased closed-mindedness and greater rejection of those who are different.

Berk et al. (1992) suggest that what looks like homophobia may stem from a young heterosexual male's lack of information about what to expect, for example, from a gay teammate in the locker room. Developing guidelines to avoid affronting clients' sensibilities is one form of interpersonal competence that enhances client retention in treatment. Just as presenting a genogram with circles for females and squares for males to designate spousal roles may be off-putting to an adult in a same-sex relationship, it would be off-putting to belittle someone who uses offensive or pejorative language to refer to LGBT[2] people. Interpersonal competence implies finding appropriate ways to confront inappropriate words and actions.

Interventional Competence (Table 2, Column 5). Interventional competence is what social workers do with the information gathered in the first four competencies. It includes skills that bridge knowledge of LGBT[2] culture and homophobic responses to it and that connect clients to treatment resources, particularly those that provide an acceptable view of LGBT[2] people, including religious, legal, psychological, economic, and media institutions. The kinds of strategies for eliminating homophobia may include Pharr's (1997) notions of disarming language–

using the word "lesbian" positively, often and powerfully. Social workers can be truly inclusive of all by such fearless use of language. By using social work principles of non-judgmental exploration, he or she can confront reactive homophobic baiting with appropriate variations on questions posed by Pharr (1997, p. 48): Why are different sexual identities difficult for you? What is it in you that reacts to LGBT[2] persons? Why do you think what LGBT[2] persons are doing is harmful? What experiences led you to develop these thoughts and feelings?

Ehrlich (1992) suggests that, for any given actor, there are elements of power, affiliation, and conformity and/or a "recreational" or expressive components to violence. Social workers have the tools to help clients meet these needs in constructive ways through alternate affiliations and alternate activities. Further, informational competence tells social workers about the peak years of delinquency/criminality: Violence is perpetrated by males in their late teens to early twenties in groups. Perpetrators are generally strangers to the victims and random in their motives rather than committing violence for profit (Berk, 1997; Harry, 1997). This knowledge suggests a preventive, group approach that addresses the status needs of immature males. Thus, knowledge from the risk and resilience and the delinquency and substance abuse literature can be used to determine strategies and to plan intervention programs.

Herek (1992a, p. 151) recommends taking a functional approach to attitudes in work with perpetrators: assume that "people hold and express particular attitudes because they get some sort of psychological benefit from doing so." This suggests a strategy of making those attitudes "dysfunctional" by "preventing the individual's anti-gay attitudes or actions from fulfilling those psychological need or helping her or him to meet the same need in another, less destructive way" (p. 165). He gives an example of helping reduce prejudice by disentangling the role played by religious dogma through the presentation of alternative, non-condemnatory theological perspectives from respected religious leaders or by juxtaposing religious values against equally important but contradictory values like justice and liberty. Another means of disarming homophobia is to underscore the realization that someone one is fond of or admires is gay to create conflict between moral condemnation and feelings for a particular individual. Societal sanctions also may need to be used. Just as an impending threat to an abusive parent of removal of a child can shape more appropriate behavior, intervention against hate crimes may require sanctions supplied by the legal or other systems to reinforce interventions.

The five dimensions in column 5 can help workers originate interventions that include a client-centered view of the problem; identify culturally relevant and appropriate interventions within interviewing, counseling, teaching, consulting, behavior management, and group and community organizing; and emphasize the use of and the importance of formal and informal support systems. The first four competency domains–informational, intellectual, intrapersonal, and interpersonal, provide creativity and resources to develop effective interventions *despite* the realities of a society that reinforces the heterosexism and homophobia at the root of human rights violations. Intervention competency not only requires that social workers effectively address individual cases of oppression, but that they undertake the critical issue of advocacy through media, legislative initiatives, and affirmative action in the larger political arena as well.

IMPLICATIONS FOR SOCIAL WORK: NEXT STEPS

The authors find it easy to present a model for work with those who perpetrate hate crimes. It is less easy to supply information about LGBT[2] cultures or about those who commit hate crimes. This requires the development and systemization of knowledge in social work from other disciplines and from clients themselves. This will involve a practice development and research agenda that includes developing a literature that reflects the tripartite intersection of social workers, LGBT[2] cultures, and the extremes of heterosexist, dominant cultural attitudes and behaviors; qualitative tracking of practice wisdom resulting from expanding interventional competency; and evaluation of outcomes based on culturally sensitive risk-assessment tools and attention to intervention effectiveness, as well as targets for intervention (such as schools) where preventive work might be accomplished.

Moreover, the cultural lens from which sexual orientation is viewed needs expansion. The dominant culture conveys a deficit perspective and a problem view of LGBT[2] relationships. Other cultures, Native American for example, see differences in sexual orientation and gender identity as a gift. The language of difference between cultures and in relation to LGBT^2 cultures requires attention. Within this larger context, we can enrich exploration of violence, cross-cultural manifestations of tolerance and of violence, and methods for increasing tolerance and decreasing violence.

Ultimately, what is needed is cultural change so that LGBT^2 persons no longer have "symbolic status" that targets them as victims of hate-motivated violence because of membership in this social category (Berk, Boyd, & Hamner, 1992). To do this, attention may need to be paid to the societal context of disadvantage, threats to religious values, and oppression which may mediate hate crimes. At the same time, the safety and well-being of LGBT^2 individuals remains a critical concern and attention must also be given to current state and federal regulations which leave ambiguous the supports against hate crimes.

This suggests that advocacy and prevention with young families and in grade schools is a primary intervention target. Other targets include those who are reluctant to condone homophobia, but who are unready to take a public stand against violence toward LGBT^2 individuals. Herek (1992a) recommends reaching out to this group by the LGBT^2 communities to become known to them as individuals and part of the human family. He states:

> coming out, which can be fraught with danger . . . is the most powerful strategy for overcoming heterosexism and anti-gay violence since it is intergroup contact that reduces prejudice as it makes shared goals salient, when cooperation is encouraged, and contact is ongoing and intimate rather than brief and superficial, when status in each group is equal, and there are shared important values. (Herek, 1992a, p. 166)

Social workers might help mediate such a process.

CONCLUSIONS

Social workers must do this important work, working with individuals by advocating for their fullest participation in society, encouraging their growth and development, and empowering them to advocate for themselves. Also essential is a social work presence in education and in the larger arena–attending vigils, writing letters to the editor, as well as in research and writing for journals–to help professionals broaden their understanding and their intellectual and intrapersonal skill.

In her review of Herek and Berrill's book *Hate Crimes: Confronting Violence Against Lesbians and Gay Men* and Martin Duberman's *Cures: A Gay Man's Odyssey*, Ann Pollinger Hass (1994, p. 121) says, "Although in *Hate Crimes* lesbians and gay men will certainly find sufficient reasons for hiding, *Cures* leaves the reader with a larger truth: that the surest weapon against fear is to be fully and bravely who we are." Perhaps it is more true that those who hate must enlarge their humanity and become who they are not. Human service professionals must have the competencies for both of these crucial tasks.

The responsibility to work with individuals and large entities for human rights, then, promises workers personal liberation from debilitating, unexplored homophobic reactions. If this can occur, transformational change hopefully must follow.

REFERENCES

Berk, R.A., Boyd, E.A., & Hamner, K.M. (1992). Thinking more clearly about hate-motivated crimes. In G.M. Herek & K.T. Berrill (Eds.), *Hate crimes: Confronting violence against lesbians and gay men*. Newbury Park, CA: Sage.

Berrill, K.T. (1992). Anti-gay violence and victimization in the United States: An overview. In G.M. Herek & K.T. Berrill (Eds.), *Hate crimes: Confronting violence against lesbians and gay men*. Newbury Park, CA: Sage.

Brenner, C. (1992). Survivor's story: Eight bullets. In G.M. Herek & K.T. Berrill (Eds.), *Hate crimes: Confronting violence against lesbians and gay men*. Newbury Park, CA: Sage.

Bush, I.R., & Sainz, A. (1997). Preventing substance abuse from undermining permanency planning: Competencies at the intersection of culture, chemical dependency and child welfare. *Journal of Multicultural Social Work, 5*(1/2), 79-97.

Cramer, E. (1998). Effects of an educational unit about lesbian identity development and disclosure in a social work methods course. *Journal of Social Work Education, 33*(3), 461-472.

Ehrlich, H.J. (1992). In G.M. Herek & K.T. Berrill (Eds.), *Hate crimes: Confronting violence against lesbians and gay men*. Newbury Park, CA: Sage.

Feinberg, L. (1993). *Stone butch blues*. Ithaca, NY: Firebrand Books.

Gravel, B. (1992). Survivor's story. In G.M. Herek & K.T. Berrill (Eds.), *Hate crimes: Confronting violence against lesbians and gay men*. Newbury Park, CA: Sage.

Harry, J. (1992). Conceptualizing anti-gay violence. In G.M. Herek & K.T. Berrill (Eds.), *Hate crimes: Confronting violence against lesbians and gay men*. Newbury Park, CA: Sage.

Hass, A.P. (1994). Book review: Hate crimes and cure. *Journal of Gay & Lesbian Social Services, 1*(1), 119-121.

Hassel, W.E. (1992). Survivor's story. In G.M. Herek & K.T. Berrill (Eds.), *Hate crimes: Confronting violence against lesbians and gay men*. Newbury Park, CA: Sage.

Herek, G.M. (1992a). The social context of hate crimes: Notes on cultural heterosexism. In G.M. Herek & K.T. Berrill (Eds.), *Hate crimes: Confronting violence against lesbians and gay men*. Newbury Park, CA: Sage.

Herek, G.M. (1992b). Psychological heterosexism and anti-gay violence: The social psychology of bigotry and bashing. In G.M. Herek & K.T. Berrill (Eds.), *Hate crimes: Confronting violence against lesbians and gay men*. Newbury Park, CA: Sage.

Herek, G.M., & Berrill, K.T. (Eds.). (1992). *Hate crimes: Confronting violence against lesbians and gay men*. Newbury Park, CA: Sage.

Hunter, J. (1992). Violence against lesbian and gay male youths. In G.M. Herek & K.T. Berrill (Eds.), *Hate crimes: Confronting violence against lesbians and gay men*. Newbury Park, CA: Sage.

Norman, J., &. Wheeler, B. (1996). Gender-sensitive social work practice: A model for education. *Journal of Social Work Education, 32*(2), 191-202.

Pharr, S. (1997). *Homophobia: A weapon of sexism*. Berkeley, CA: Chardon Press.

Sarris, K. (1992). Survivor's story. In G.M. Herek & K.T. Berrill (Eds.), *Hate crimes: Confronting violence against lesbians and gay men*. Newbury Park, CA: Sage.

Swigonski, M.E. (1993). Feminist standpoint theory and the questions of social work research. *Affilia, 8*(2), 171-183.

Van Soest, D. (1996). Impact of social work education on student attitudes and behavior concerning oppression. *Journal of Social Work Education, 32*(2), 191-202.

Von Schulthess, B. (1992). Violence in the streets: Anti-lesbian assault and harassment in San Francisco. In G.M. Herek & K.T. Berrill (Eds.), *Hate crimes: Confronting violence against lesbians and gay men*. Newbury Park, CA: Sage.

Woody, D.L. (1991). *Recruitment and retention of minority workers in mental health programs*. Washington, DC: National Institute of Mental Health, Human Resource Development Program.

Index

TO ORDER: CALL: 1-800-429-6784 / FAX: 1-800-895-0582 (Outside US/Canada: + 607-771-0012) / **E-MAIL: getinfo@haworthpressinc.com**

Please complete the information below or tape your business card in this area.

☐ **YES, please send me Gay and Lesbian Parenting**

___ in hard at $49.95 ISBN: 0-7890-1349-5.
___ in soft at $19.95 ISBN: 0-7890-1350-9.

- Individual orders outside US, Canada, and Mexico must be prepaid by check or credit card.
- Discounts are not available on 5+ text prices and not available in conjunction with any other discount. • Discount not applicable on books priced under $15.00.
- 5+ text prices are not available for jobbers and wholesalers.
- Postage & handling: in US: $4.00 for first book; $1.50 for each additional book.
  Outside US: $5.00 for first book; $2.00 for each additional book.
- NY, MN, and OH residents: please add appropriate sales tax after postage & handling.
  Canadian residents: please add 7% GST after postage & handling. Canadian residents of Newfoundland, Nova Scotia, and New Brunswick, also add 8% for province tax. • Payment in UNESCO coupons welcome.
- If paying in Canadian dollars, use current exchange rate to convert to US dollars.
- Please allow 3-4 weeks for delivery after publication.
- Prices and discounts subject to change without notice.

Signature _____

☐ **BILL ME LATER($5 service charge will be added).**
(Not available for individuals outside US/Canada/Mexico. Service charge is waived for jobbers/wholesalers/booksellers.)
☐ Check here if billing address is different from shipping address and attach purchase order and billing address information.

☐ **PAYMENT ENCLOSED $** _____
(Payment must be in US or Canadian dollars by check or money order drawn on a US or Canadian bank.)

☐ **PLEASE BILL MY CREDIT CARD:**

☐ AmEx ☐ Diners Club ☐ Discover ☐ Eurocard ☐ JCB ☐ Master Card ☐ Visa

Account Number _____

Expiration Date _____

Signature _____

THE HAWORTH PRESS, INC., 10 Alice Street, Binghamton, NY 13904-1580 USA

NAME _____

INSTITUTION _____

ADDRESS _____

CITY _____

STATE _____ ZIP _____

COUNTRY _____

COUNTY (NY residents only) _____

E-MAIL _____
(type or print clearly)

May we use your e-mail address for confirmations and other types of information?
( ) Yes ( ) No We appreciate receiving your e-mail address and fax number. Haworth would like to e-mail or fax special discount offers to you, as a preferred customer. We will never share, rent, or exchange your e-mail address or fax number. We regard such actions as an invasion of your privacy.

☐ **YES,** please send me **Gay and Lesbian Parenting (ISBN: 0-7890-1350-9)** to consider on a 60-day no risk examination basis. I understand that I will receive an invoice payable within 60 days, or that if I decide to adopt the book, my invoice will be cancelled. I understand that I will be billed at the lowest price. (60-day offer available only to teaching faculty in US, Canada, and Mexico / Outside US/Canada, a proforma invoice will be sent upon receipt of your request and must be paid in advance of shipping. A full refund will be issued with proof of adoption.)

Signature _____

Course Title(s) _____

Current Text(s) _____

Enrollment _____

Semester _____ Decision Date _____

Office Tel _____ Hours _____

This information is needed to process your examination copy order.

(24) (26) 04/01 BIC01